AUTOMOTIVE DYNAMICS AND DESIGN

THE EVOLUTION OF AUTOMOTIVE ECOSYSTEM

KARTIK S. KAMEPALLI

For everyone with a redline under their name in Microsoft Word.

Contents

Preface

Automobile dynamics should be a branch of Dynamics, but, in my opinion, too often it does not look like that. Dynamics is based on rigorous reasoning and terse concepts, whereas the typical approach to automobile dynamics is much more intuitive. Qualitative reasoning and intuition are certainly very valuable, but they should be supported and confirmed by scientific and quantitative results.

I understand that automobile dynamics is, perhaps, the most popular branch of Dynamics. Almost everybody has been involved in discussions about some aspects of the dynamical behaviour of a motor vehicle (how to brake, how to negotiate a bend at high speed, which tires give best performance, etc.). At this level, we cannot expect a deep knowledge of the dynamical behaviour of a vehicle.

But there are people who could greatly benefit from mastering vehicle dynamics. From having clear concepts in mind. From having a deep understanding of the main phenomena. This book is intended for those people who want to build their knowledge on sound explanations, who believe equations are the best way to formulate and, hopefully, solve problems. Of course, along with physical reasoning and intuition. The main focus of this book is on the fundamentals of 'Automobile Dynamics & Design" and the designing of motor vehicles. As the complexity of automotive vehicles increases this book encompasses complex technology of modern motor vehicles and increasing functions need a reliable source of information to understand the components or systems. Motor vehicles are complex machines and are likely to become more and more complex in the future. The requirements their designers must satisfy are increasingly demanding and it is possible to state that designing a motor car is one of the most difficult tasks engineers must face. It is true that there are machines that are more complex, must operate in a more hostile environment or must satisfy more demanding requirements (just to mention two examples, a nuclear submarine or a space shuttle, but the list could be much longer), but what makes the design of a modern car so difficult is the conflicting nature of the design requirements and the complex nature of its development and production processes.

The automotive industry proved to be able to innovate and to adapt itself to new needs and requirements in an ever-changing scenario and the motor car of the first decade of the twenty-first century is deeply different from the motor car of the 1960s and 1970s. The automotive industry is based on large-scale production, and as such it has an inertia that prevents changes to be sudden and swift, but this has not prevented changes to be pursued and implemented, sometimes even at an unpredictable rate.
These are the reasons why I feel that a book about basics of automobile design and production, as well as the evolution of automobile ecosystem, would still be interesting reading and a useful source of information for students and for the general public.

Self-propelled ground vehicles represented a fairly recent achievement in the history of technology; except for a few precursors that had little effect on technology or found practical applications, they did not really appear until quite late in the industrial revolution. It was only in the nineteenth century that working models of self-propelled vehicles could be built and they became truly practical only at the end of the century.

As usual with any technological development, the development of motor vehicles, particularly in its early phases, can be seen from two conflicting viewpoints: one that recognizes discontinuities and one that emphasizes the slow evolution of ideas and designs. In the first case a number of heroic figures of inventors and their revolutionary contributions to the technology are described. This book series will focus especially on the state of knowledge in the various fields in the automotive industry, starting from the basics and describing the necessary background information. In particular, the new elements of future propulsion systems, battery management system and their mutual influence and system considerations will be addressed. In addition to the technical content, introduction to hybrid electric vehicle and energy source battery are presented. The different types of standard driving cycles and their respective requirements will be set out in concepts.

This book provides a comprehensive insight into both students at universities and colleges as well as practitioners in the industry with a guidebook from which they can acquire the accumulated experience of my research and knowledge.

Kartik S. Kamepalli

CHAPTER I

Design of Principle Engine Components

Mankind has been building cars for over a century, and nearly everyone has an internal combustion engine under the hood. For the past 100 years, the principle has not changed. Air and fuel flow in, an explosion occurs in the cylinder, and the power propels it forward. But every year, engineers develop internal combustion engines to make them faster, farther, and more efficient and produce the kind of power previously noticed only in supercars.

The first to experiment with internal combustion engines was the Dutch physicist Christian Huygens around 1680. J. Etienne Lenoir built a double-acting gasoline engine capable of continuous operation. In 1862, French scientist Alphonse Baudrochat patented his four-stroke engine, but it never made it to production. Sixteen years later, when Nikolaus A. Otto built his successful four-stroke engine, it is widely known as the Otto cycle. His first successful two-stroke engine was completed in the same year by Sir Dougald Clerk and is still in use today. American engineer George Brayton developed a two-stroke kerosene engine in 1873, but it was too enormous and too slow to be commercially successful. Starting in the early 17th century, several scientists approached the development of the internal combustion engine. However, Jean-Joseph Etienne Lenoir patented the first ever commercial internal combustion engine in the year 1860. At that time, the engine was prone to overheating as it had only one cylinder. However, it was able to power a tricycle at about 2 miles per hour. This was a major milestone for the internal combustion engine as Lenor proved that this type of continuous operation is possible. In the future, other inventors have developed more efficient internal combustion engines.

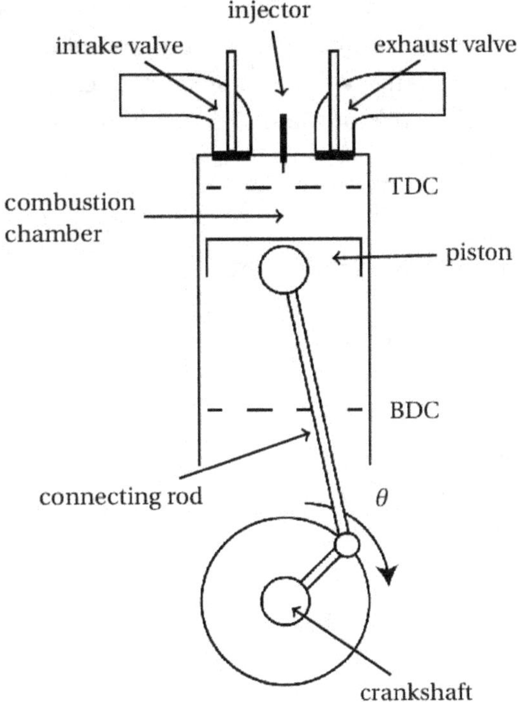

Figure 1.1: Design of Engine Components

The main parts of the internal combustion engine shown in the diagram below are the piston, piston ring, combustion chamber, gudgeon pin, connecting rod, crankshafts, crankpins, and valve gear mechanism. The design of the above-mentioned components is further explained in brief.

Design of Piston

A piston is a disc that moves back and forth in a cylinder. It either moves the fluid or is moved by the fluid which enters the cylinder The principal function of the piston in an IC engine is to receive the momentum of expanding gases and transfer the energy to the crankshaft through a connecting rod. The piston also has to disperse an ample amount of heat from the combustion chamber to the cylinder wall. Pistons in Internal Combustion engines are generally of the barrel type as shown in Fig. pistons are usually open at one end and consist of:

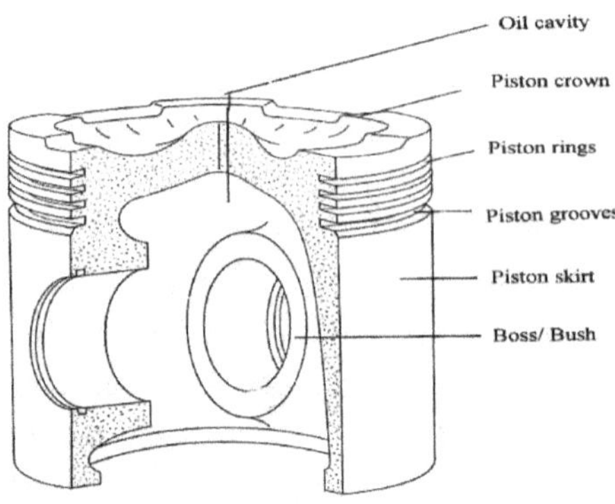

Figure 1.2: Design of Piston

- **Piston head:** The piston head or crown can be flat, convex, or concave depending on the combustion chamber design. Thus, withstanding the pressure of gas in the combustion chamber.
- **Piston Rings:** Piston rings are used to seal the cylinder to prevent gases from bypassing the piston.
- **Piston skirt:** The piston skirt acts as a bearing for the side thrust of the connecting rod in the wall of the cylinder.
- **Piston pin:** It is also known as the gudgeon pin which is used to connect the connecting rod to the piston.

Considerations for the design of Piston:

When designing the piston of the I.C. engine, please note down the following points:

1. Mass should be minimized to minimize inertial forces.
2. It must form an effective gas and oil seal for the cylinder.
3. High-speed reciprocating motion without noise is required.
4. Combustion heat must be released quickly to the cylinder walls.
5. An adequate bearing surface must be provided to avoid excessive wear.
6. Requires tremendous strength to withstand high gas pressure and inertial forces.

1. Piston Head:

The piston head or crown is designed with two main considerations:

1. Combustion heat must be dissipated to the cylinder wall as quickly as possible.
2. Must be strong enough to withstand the straining action of the detonation pressure within the engine cylinder.

Based on the first consideration of the straining effect, the thickness of the piston head was determined by treating it as a flat circular plate of uniform thickness, mounted on the outer edge and evenly distributed by gas pressure across the cross-section. The piston head thickness (t_h) is given by Grashoff's equation:

$$``t_h = \sqrt{(3.p.D^2)/16.\sigma_t} \,(in\ mm)"$$

where p = maximum gas pressure in N/mm²,
   D = cylinder bore or outside diameter of the piston in mm,
   σ_t = Permissible bending stress for the material of piston in N/mm².
   The amount of heat (H) flowing through the piston head can be calculated by the following equation i.e.;

$$``H = C \times HCV \times m \times B.P.\ (kilowatts)"$$

where C = constant represents the fraction of heat input to the engine that is absorbed by the piston. Its value is usually assumed to be 0.05.
   HCV = higher heating value of fuel (kJ/kg).
   We can assume 45 × 103 kJ/kg for diesel and 47 × 103 kJ/kg for petrol.
   m = mass of fuel consumed per brake power per second (kg),
   B.P. = Brake Power

2. Piston Ring:

Piston rings are used to apply the radial pressure required to maintain a seal between the piston and cylinder bore. Due to their excellent wear properties, these are usually made of gray cast iron or alloy cast iron and retain their spring properties even at high temperatures. These are classified into two types:

1. Compression ring or thrust ring
2. Oil scraper ring or scraper.

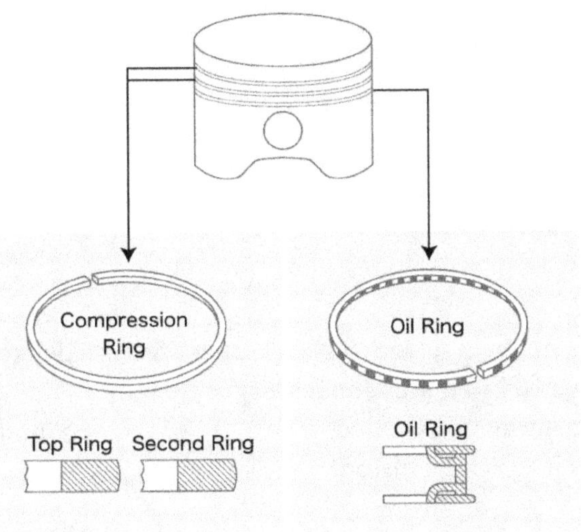

Figure 1.3: Design of Piston ring

Compression rings or thrust rings fit into grooves in the top of the piston and can have 3-7 rings. These rings also transfer heat from the piston to the cylinder liner and absorb the side thrust fluctuations of the piston. The oil control ring or oil wiper is located under the compression ring. These rings ensure proper lubrication of the liner by directing the lubricant from the surface of the liner to the oil in the combustion chamber while allowing enough oil to move up during the upstroke.

Compression rings are usually made of rectangular crosses to minimize flow area, and the ring diameter is slightly larger than the cylinder bore. A portion of the ring has been cut away so that it can be inserted into the cylinder against the wall of the liner. When the ring is cold, the gap between the ends should be large enough so that the ends do not touch each other when the ring expands. Otherwise, the ring might buckle.

The radial thickness of the ring (t_1) can be obtained by considering the radial pressure between the ring and the cylinder wall. The radial thickness is given by:

$$``t_1 = D\sqrt{(3.p_w)/\sigma_t}\,"$$

where, D = cylinder bore (mm),

p_w = gas pressure at the cylinder wall in N/mm2 which is limited from 0.025 N/mm2 to 0.042 N/mm2,

σ_t = Allowable bending stress (tensile stress) in MPa. For cast iron rings the value can be from 85 MPa to 110 MPa.

The axial thickness (t_2) of the ring can be assumed to be between 0.7 t_1 and t_1. The minimum axial thickness (t_2) can also be obtained from the following empirical relationship:

$$``t_2 = D/10.n_R\,"$$

where n_R = number of rings.

The width of the top land (that is, the distance from the first ring groove to the top of the piston) is larger than the other ring lands to protect the top ring from the high-temperature conditions experienced at the top of the piston.

$$``\therefore Top\ land\ width\ b_1 = t_h \sim 1.2t_h\,"$$

The width of the other ring lands of the piston (the distance between the ring grooves) can be the same as or slightly less than the axial thickness of the ring (t_2).

$$``\therefore Other\ ring\ land\ width\ b_2 = 0.75t_2 \sim t_2\,"$$

The groove depth of the ring should be greater than the depth of the ring so that the ring does not receive pressure from the piston side. The gap between the free ends of the rings is given by 3.5t_1 to 4t_1. If the ring is inside the cylinder, the gap should be between 0.002D and 0.004.

3. Piston Skirt:

The piston skirt length should be maintained such that the bearing pressure due to the side thrust on the piston barrel does not exceed 0.5 N/mm2 of the projected area for high-speed engines and 0.25 N/mm2 for low-speed engines. The cylinder liner side thrust (R) is normally assumed to be 1/10 of the maximum gas load on the piston.

We know that the maximum gas load on the piston,

$$``P = p\ x\ (\pi.D^2)/4\,"$$

$\therefore$ Maximum side thrust on the cylinder,

$$``R = P/10 = 0.1p\ x\ (\pi.D^2)/4\ \text{------- (i)}\,"$$

where P = Maximum gas pressure (N/mm2)
  D = Cylinder bore (mm)
  The side thrust (R) is given by,

"R = Bearing pressure x projected bearing area (piston skirt) = Pb x D x l"

Where, l = Length of Piston skirt (mm)
  The piston skirt length (l) is determined from equation (i) and Pb × D × l. In numerical, the length of the piston skirt is assumed to be 0.65 to 0.8 times the cylinder bore. The total piston length (l) is given by

"L = skirt length + ring section length + top land"

The piston length typically varies between D and 1.5D. Note that longer pistons provide a better bearing surface for the engine to run smoother, but pistons should not exceed the desired length, as this will increase length, mass, and thus inertial force.

4. Piston Pin:

Piston pins (also called gudgeon pins) are used to connect the piston and connecting rod. The interior is typically hollow and conical, with the smallest inner diameter at the center of the bolt, as shown. The piston pin passes through a boss on the inside of the piston skirt and a bushing on the small end of the connecting rod. The center of the piston pin should be 0.02D to 0.04D higher than the center of the skirt to balance the torsional effects of friction and even pressure distribution between the piston and cylinder liner. The materials used for piston pins are typically case-hardening steel alloys containing nickel, chromium, molybdenum, or vanadium with tensile strengths between 710 MPa and 910 MPa.

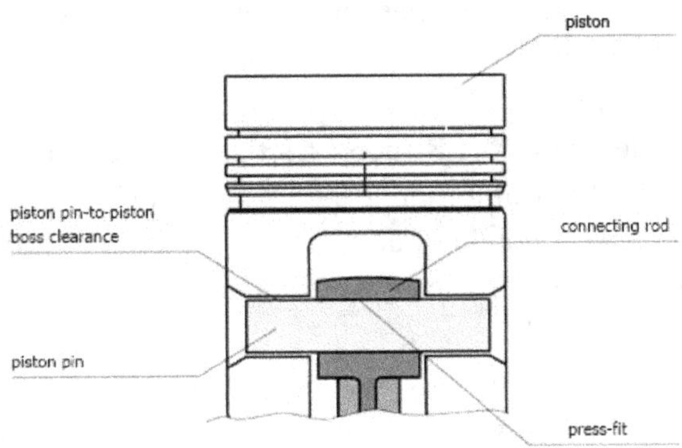

Figure 1.4: Design of Piston pin

"Z = $\pi/32 \times [((d_o)^4-(d_i)^4)/ d_o]$"

We know that the maximum bending moment,

"M = Z × σ_b = $\pi/32 \times [((d_o)^4-(d_i)^4)/ d_o] \times \sigma_b$"

where σ_b = Allowable bending stress of piston pin.
  Usually, considered 84 MPa for case hardened carbon steel and 140 MPa for heat-treated alloy steel. Assuming d_i= 0.6d_o, we can see the bending stress induced in the piston pin.

Design of Connecting Rod

A connecting rod is a link between the piston and the crankshaft. Its main function is to transfer compression and tension from the wrist pin to the crank pin, converting the reciprocating motion of the piston into the rotary motion of the crank. A typical shape of a connecting rod for an internal combustion engine is shown in the figure below. It consists of a long shaft, a small end, and a big end. The shank cross-section or H-section may be circular, rectangular, and I-section. Circular sections are generally used for low-speed engines and I-sections are preferred for high-speed engines.

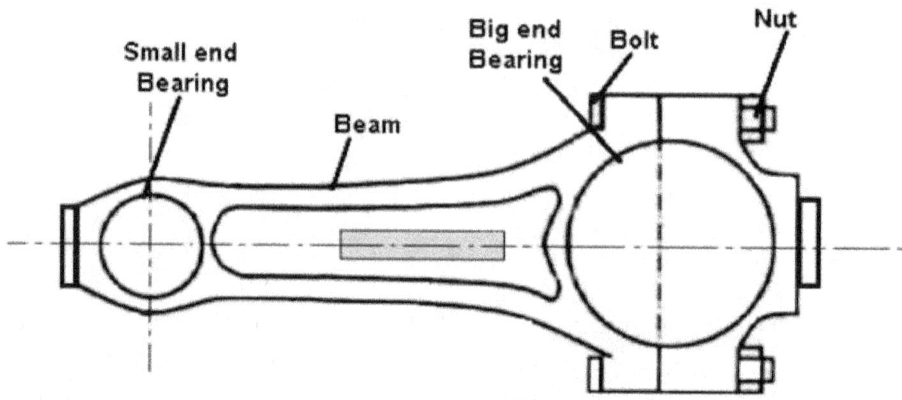

Figure 1.5: Design of Connecting Rod

Connecting rod length (l) is determined by the ratio l/r. where r is the radius of the crank. It can be seen that the l/r ratio decreases as the length decreases. This increases the angle of the connecting rod, increasing the side thrust of the piston against the cylinder liner and increasing liner wear. The longer the connecting rod, the greater the l/r ratio. This reduces the connecting rod angle, reduces side thrust, and thus reduces cylinder wear. However, the longer the connecting rod length, the higher the overall height of the engine. Therefore, a compromise is made and the ratio l/r is usually kept between 4 and 5.

The smaller end of the connecting rod is usually lug-shaped and has a phosphor bronze bushing. It is connected to the piston via a gudgeon pin. The large end of the connecting rod is usually split (into two halves) for easy attachment to the crankpin cup. The split cap is attached to the large end with two cap screws. Big end cups are made of steel, brass, or bronze with a thin coating (approx. 0.75 mm) of Babbit metal or white metal. The wear of the connecting rod bearing is adjusted by inserting a thin piece of metal (called a shim) about 0.04 mm thick between the cap and the fixed half of the connecting rod. As wear occurs, one or more strips are removed to realign the bearing.

The different forces acting on the connecting rod are:

1. Forces on piston due to inertia of reciprocating parts and gas pressure.
2. Force due to friction between the piston ring and piston.
3. Connecting rod inertial or inertial bending forces,
4. Friction force between piston pin bearing and crank pin bearing.
Derive the equations for the forces acting on the vertical motor as described below.

Considerations for the design of Connecting rod:

When designing connecting rods, the following dimensions should be determined:
1. The dimensions of the cross-section of the connecting rod,
2. The dimensions of the big end crank pin and the small end piston pin;
3. Large end cap and screw size to attach the end cap
4. Thick end cap.
The procedure for determining the above dimensions is described below.

1. Dimensions of the cross-section of the connecting rod

A connecting rod is a mechanical element that is subjected to alternating direct compression and tension forces. Compressive forces are much greater than tensile forces, so the connecting rod cross section is designed as a strut, and Rankine's formula is used.

As shown in the figure, a connecting rod subjected to an axial load W can buckle with the X axis as the neutral axis (i.e., in the plane of movement of the connecting rod) or the Y axis as the neutral axis (i.e., in the plane of movement). in the plane perpendicular to the plane). A connecting rod is considered pivoted at both ends to buckle about the X axis and fixed at both ends to buckle about the Y axis. The connecting rod should buckle evenly about both axes.

A = cross-sectional area of connecting rod,

l = connecting rod length,

σc = compressive yield stress,

WB = buckling load,

I_{xx} and I_{yy} = moment of inertia of section about X and Y axis respectively and k_{xx} and k_{yy} = radius of gyration of the section about X and Y axis respectively.

According to Rankine's formula,

$$\text{``}W_B \text{ about X-axis} = \sigma_c.A \,/\, (1 + a.(L \,/\, k_{xx})^2) = \sigma_c.A \,/\, (1 + a.(l \,/\, k_{xx})^2)\text{''}$$

Since, for both ends hinged, L = l

$$\text{``}W_B \text{ about Y-axis} = \sigma_c.A \,/\, (1 + a.(L \,/\, k_{yy})^2) = \sigma_c.A \,/\, (1 + a.(l \,/2.k_{yy})^2)\text{''}$$

Since, for both ends hinged, L = l/2

where L = equivalent length of connecting rod and rod

a = constant = 1/7500 for mild steel

= 1/9000 for wrought iron

= 1/1600 for cast iron

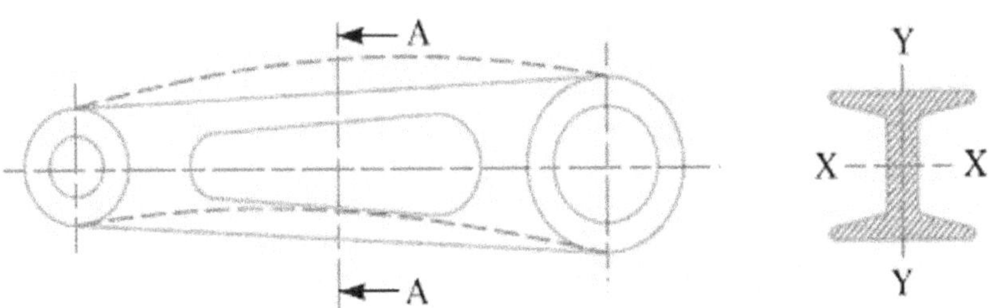

Figure 1.6: Connecting rod I-section

In order for the connecting rod to buckle equally about both axes, the buckling loads must be the same.

"$\sigma_c.A / (1 + a.(l / k_{xx})^2) = \sigma_c.A / (1 + a.(l /2.k_{yy})^2)$ or
$(l / k_{xx})^2 = (l /2.k_{yy})^2$ or
$k_{xx}^2 = 4.k_{yy}^2$ or
$I_{xx} = 4.I_{yy}$"

This indicates that the connecting rod buckles four times more about its Y-axis than the X-axis. If $I_{xx} > 4\,I_{yy}$, buckling occurs about the Y axis, and if $I_{xx} < 4I_{yy}$, buckling occurs. $4I_{yy}$, buckling occurs around the X axis. In practice, I_{xx} is kept slightly less than $4I_{yy}$. Typically, between 3 and 3.5, the connecting rod is designed to bend around the X axis. Buckling about the Y axis is always a satisfactory design. The best cross-section for a connecting rod is the I cross-section with the proportions shown in the figure.

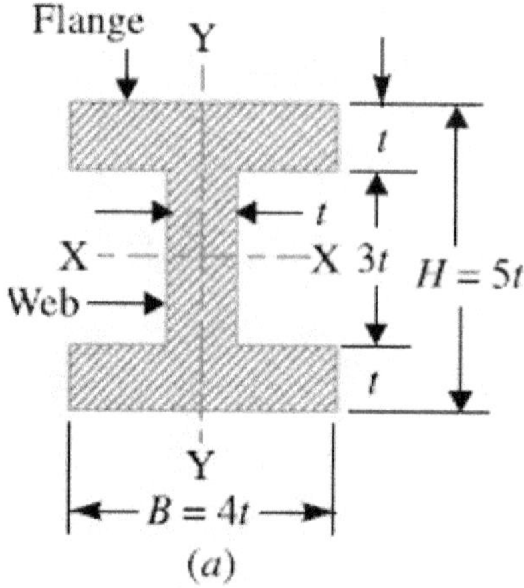

The flange and web thickness of the section is = t
section width, B = 4t, and section depth or height, H=5t
From Figure (a), find this area of the section.

"$A = 2(4t \times t) + 3t \times t = 11t^2$"

the moment of inertia of the cross-section about the X axis,

"$I_{xx} = 1/12 [4.t.(5t)^3 - 3.t.(3t)^3] = (419/12).t^4$"

And the moment of inertia of the cross-section about the Y-axis,

"$I_{yy} = [2.(1/12)t.(4t)^3 + (1/12).(3t).t^3] = (131/12).t^4$
$I_{xx}/I_{yy} = 419/12 \times 12/131 = 3.2$"

After the connecting rod I-section proportions are established, its dimensions are determined by considering the buckling of the rod about the X axis (assuming both ends are articulated) and applying Rankine's equation will be This buckling load is known,

"$W_B = \sigma_c.A / (1 + a.(L / k_{xx})^2)$"

Buckling load (W_B) can be calculated using the relationship: i.e.

$$“W_B = maximum\ gas\ power \times safety\ factor”$$

The safety factor can be assumed to be about 5-6.

Dimensions B = 4 t and H = 5 t are in the middle of the connecting rod, as obtained by applying the Rankine equation above. The width of section (B) remains constant over the length of the connecting rod, but the depth or height varies. The depth near the small end (or piston end) is H_1 = 0.75H to 0.9H, and the depth near the big end (or crank end)

$$“H2 = 1.1H\ to\ 1.25H”$$

where H is the sectional depth or height

2. Dimensions of the big end crank pin and the small end piston pin

The dimensions of the big-end crankpin and the small-end piston pin (also known as the gudgeon pin) are limited, so the bearings on these two pins must allow for fairly high bearing pressures.

Big-end crankpin made of removable precision brass, bronze, or steel with a thin lining (1 mm or less) of bearing metal (tin, lead, Babbitt copper, lead, etc.) inside the shell of the bearing surface. Allowable crankpin bearing pressure depends on many factors, including the material of the bearing. Bearing pressures can be assumed between 7 N/mm2 and 12.5 N/mm2, depending on the material used and the lubrication method. Gudgeon pin bearings are usually phosphor bronze bushings about 3mm thick, and the allowable bearing pressure is estimated to be 10.5N/mm2 to 15N/mm2.

The maximum load that the crankpin and gudgeon pin bearings can support is the maximum force of the connecting rod (F_C), so the dimensions of these two pins are determined by the maximum force of the connecting rod (F_C). Neglecting inertial forces equals the maximum force on the piston due to gas pressure (F_L).

We know this maximum gas force,

$$“F_L = ((\pi.D^2) / 4) \times p”$$

where D = cylinder bore or piston diameter (mm) and

p = maximum gas pressure in N/mm2

The crankpin and gudgeon pin dimensions are now determined as follows:

d_c = crank pin diameter (mm),

l_c = crankpin length (mm),

p_{bc} = permissible bearing pressure in N/mm2 and

d_p, l_p, and p_{bp} = corresponding values for piston pin,

We know that load on the crankpin,

$$“= projected\ area\ x\ bearing\ pressure$$
$$= d_c.l_c.p_{bc} ... (ii)”$$

Similarly, load on the piston pin,

$$“= d_p.\ l_p.p_{bp} ...(iii)”$$

Equating equations (i) and (ii) yields

$$``F_l = d_c.l_c.p_{bc}\text{''}$$

Assuming l_c = 1.25 d_c to 1.5 d_c, the above equation determines the values of d_c and l_c. Equating equations (i) and (iii) again, we get

$$``F_L = d_p.l_p.p_{bp}\text{''}$$

where F_L is the maximum force on the piston due to gas pressure.

Design of Crankshaft

A crankshaft (that is, a shaft with a crank) is responsible for converting the reciprocating motion of the pistons into rotary motion and vice versa. A crankshaft consists of a shaft section that rotates in the main bearing, a crank pin to which the big end of a connecting rod is connected, and crank arms that connect the crank pin and the shaft section. Crankshafts are divided into the following two types according to the position of the crank.

    1. Lateral crankshaft or overhang crankshaft

    2. Center crankshaft

    Crankshafts can also be classified as single-stroke or multi-stroke, depending on the number of cranks in the shaft. Crankshafts with only one side or center crank are called single-stroke crankshafts, while crankshafts with two side cranks (one at each end) or more than one center crank are called multi-stroke crankshafts.

Crankshaft bearing pressure and stress:

Bearing pressure is very important in crankshaft design. Maximum allowable bearing pressure depends on maximum gas pressure, journal speed, amount and type of lubrication, and changes in direction of bearing pressure. Crankshafts experience two types of stress: 1. bending stress; and

    2. Shear stress due to torsional moment of shaft

    Most crankshaft failures are caused by progressive fractures due to repeated bending stress or reverse torsional stress. Therefore, the crankshaft is under fatigue loading and its design should be based on fatigue strength. A high safety factor of 3-4 is used for the endurance limit because a crankshaft failure can lead to severe engine damage and it is not possible to accurately measure all the forces and stresses acting on the crankshaft.

Considerations for the design of the Crankshaft:

The following steps can be used to design the crankshaft:

    1. Firstly, determine the magnitude of the various loads on the crankshaft.

    2. Determine the distance between supports and their position relative to the load.

    3. For simplicity and safety, assume the shaft is supported at the center of the bearings and all forces and reactions act at these points. The distance between the supports depends on the bearing length, which in turn depends on the shaft diameter due to the permissible bearing pressure.

    4. Web thickness is assumed to be 0.4ds to 0.6ds. where ds is the shaft diameter. It can also be considered as 0.22D to 0.32D. where D means the diameter of the cylinder(mm).

    5. Calculate the distance between the supports.

    6. Determine the major dimensions of the crankshaft, assuming the allowable bending and shear stresses.

    We further discuss the design of the center crankshaft for two particular positions namely: when the crankshaft experiences the maximum bending moment and when the crank is at the angle where the torque is maximum. These two cases are explained in detail below.

1. *When the crank is at the dead center*

At this position, maximum gas pressure on the piston will transmit maximum force to the crankpin in the plane of the crank, causing only the bending of the shaft. The crankpin and crankshaft ends are subjected only to bending moments. Therefore, when the crank is at dead center, the bending moment of the shaft is maximum and the torsional moment is zero.

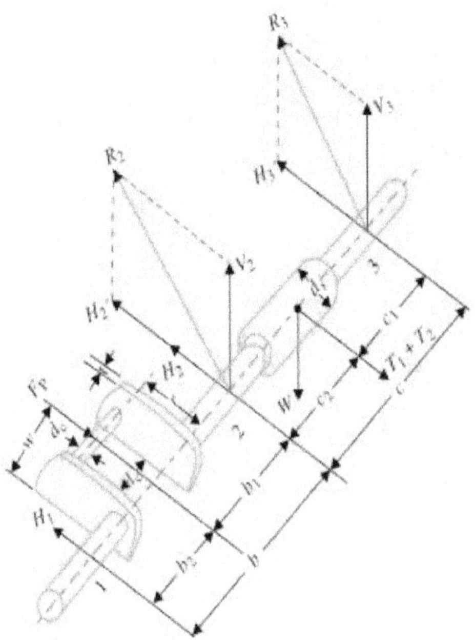

Figure 1.7: When the crank is at dead center

    D = piston diameter or cylinder bore (mm),
    p = maximum pressure strength of the piston (N/mm²),
    W = weight of flywheel acting downwards at N and $T_1 + T_2$ = resulting belt tension or horizontal pulling force at N. The connecting rod thrust equals the gas load on the piston (F_P). The gas load on the piston is

"$F_P = (\pi/4) \times D^2 \times p$"

Cielo

2. *When the crank is at an angle of a maximum twisting moment*

When the crank tangential force (F_T) is at its maximum, the crankshaft torque is at its maximum. The maximum value of the tangential force is at a crank angle of 25° to 30° from the dead center for a constant volume internal combustion engine (such as a gasoline engine) and at a crank angle of 30° to 40° for a constant pressure internal combustion engine (such as a diesel engine). Consider the position of the crank at the maximum torque angle as shown. If p' is the amount of pressure in the piston at that point, then the gas load on the piston is at that position in the crank.

The connecting rod (F_Q) thrust can be subdivided into two components, one perpendicular to the crank and one along the crank. The component of F_Q perpendicular to the crank is the tangential force (F_T), and the component of F_Q along the crank is the radial force (F_R), producing thrust in the crankshaft bearings. From the figure,

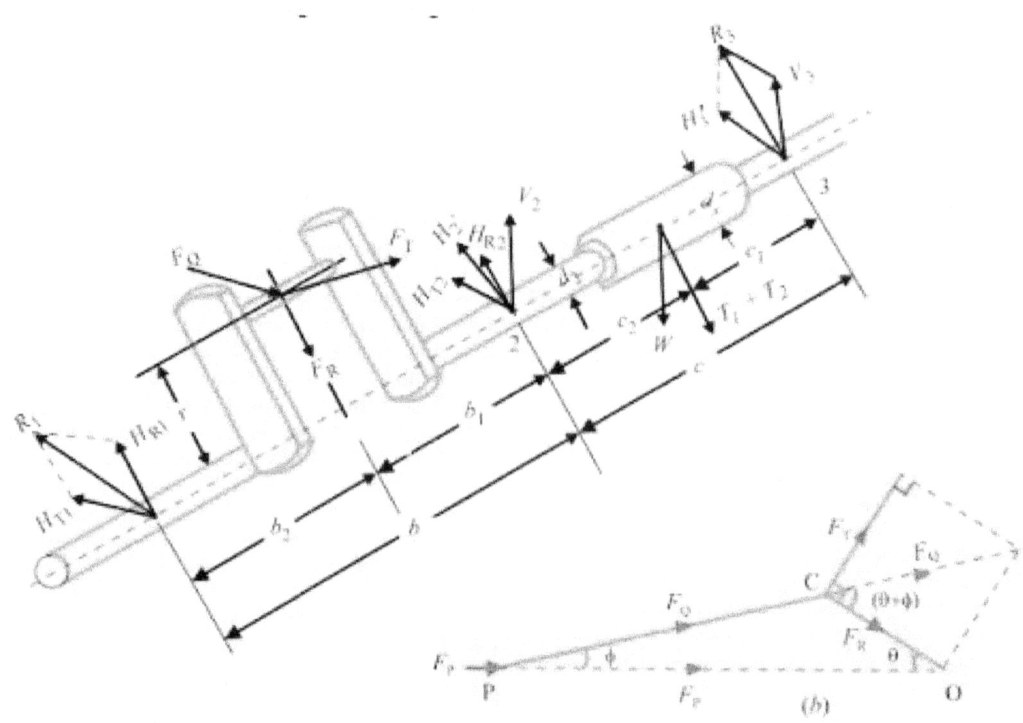

Figure 1.8: When the crank is at an angle of a maximum twisting moment

$$\text{“}F_T = F_Q.sin(\,\Theta + \emptyset\,)\ and$$
$$F_R = F_Q.cos(\,\Theta - \emptyset\,)\text{”}$$

It may be noted that the tangential force will cause twisting of the shaft and the crankpin while the radial force will cause bending of the shaft.

Design of Flywheel

A flywheel acts as a reservoir that stores the energy during the period when the supply is greater than the requirement and vis-e-versa release the energy during the period when the requirement is more than the energy supply. In the case of IC Engines, steam engines, pumps, and reciprocating compressors, the engine is run based on the energy generated during one stroke. For instance, in IC Engines, the energy produced during one single stroke is greater than the energy load, and no energy is produced during compression, suction, and exhaust strokes. The excess energy generated during a power stroke is stored by the flywheel and released to the crankshaft during other strokes in which no energy is developed. In Fact, when the flywheel releases energy, speed decreases, and when it absorbs, speed increases.

Instead of maintaining a constant speed, the flywheel produces speed variations. In machines i.e. shears, punch presses, crushers, riveters flywheels stores energy from the source and release energy only for a short period of the cycle. Thus, energy from the power source is supplied to the machine virtually constantly during all operations.

Coefficient of Fluctuation of Speed

The difference between the maximum and minimum speed during the cycle is called maximum speed variation. The ratio of the maximum speed variation to the average speed is called the speed variation coefficient.

Let N_1 = maximum speed (rpm). during the cycle,

N_2 = minimum speed in rpm. during the cycle and

N = mean speed in r.p.m. = $(N_1 + N_2)/2$

∴ Coefficient of fluctuation of speed,

$$C_S = (N_1 - N_2)/N = 2 \times (N_1 - N_2)/(N_1 + N_2)$$
$$= (v_1 - v_2)/v = 2 \times (v_1 - v_2)/(v_1 + v_2)$$

The coefficient of variation of speed is the limiting factor in flywheel design. It depends on the type of service the flywheel is used for.

Maximum Fluctuation of Energy

A turning moment diagram for a multi-cylinder engine is shown in a wavy curve. Horizontal line AG represents the average torque line. Let a1, a3, and a5 be the areas above the average torque line, and let a2, a4, and a6 be the areas below the average torque line. These ranges represent the amount of energy added or subtracted from the energy of the moving parts of the engine.

The flywheel energy is A = E and from the figure

"Energy at B = E + a1

    Energy at C = E + a1 – a2

    Energy at D = E + a1 - a2 + a3

    Energy at E = E + a1 - a2 + a3 - a4

    Energy at F = E + a1 - a2 + a3 - a4 + a5

    Energy at G = E + a1 – a2 + a3 – a4 + a5 – a6 = Energy at A"

Now suppose that the maximum of these energies is in B and the minimum in E.

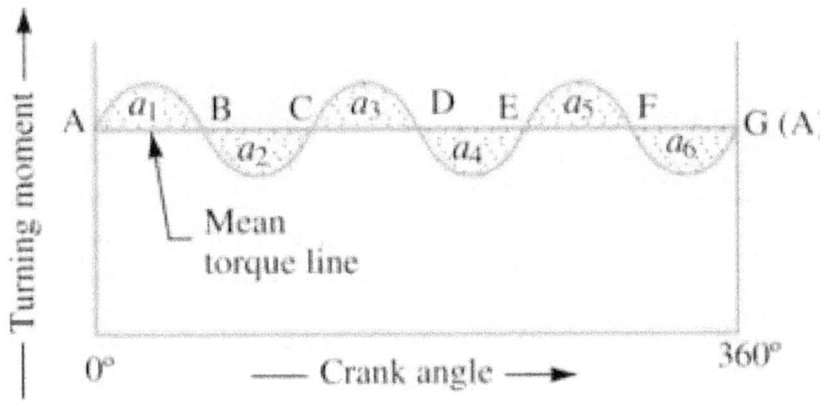

Figure 1.9: Maximum fluctuation of energy

∴ Maximum flywheel energy

" = E + a1 and minimum flywheel energy
    = E + a1 − a2 + a3 − a4 "

∴ maximum energy variation,

"ΔE = maximum energy - minimum energy
    = (E + a1) - (E + a1 - a2 + a3 - a4) = a2 - a3 + a4 "

Design of Cooling System

Power is generated by burning fuel in the cylinders of an internal combustion engine. The temperatures that occur during the engine power cycle can reach 1600°C, higher than the melting point of engine parts. Cooling an internal combustion engine is very important as the optimum operating temperature for an internal combustion engine is between 140- and 200 degrees Fahrenheit. It is estimated that about 40% of the total heat generated is lost to the atmosphere via exhaust gases, 30% is removed by cooling, and about 30% is used to generate electricity.

Purpose of cooling:

1. Maintain the engine at the optimum temperature and operate efficiently in all conditions.
2. Dissipate excess heat to protect engine components such as cylinders, cylinder heads, pistons, piston rings, and valves
3. To maintain the lubricating properties of the oil in the engine

Types of Cooling Methods:

1. Air-cooled
2. Water cooling

Air cooling system:

An air-cooled engine is one in which heat from the working parts of the engine is conducted directly to the atmosphere. Air-cooled engine cylinders have fins to increase the air contact area for rapid cooling. The cylinder is usually housed in a sheet metal case called a cowl. The flywheel has blades that protrude from the front and act like a fan, drawing air through holes in the hood and directing it around the finned cylinder. To maintain the air-cooling system, remove grass and other debris with a stiff airbrush to keep the airways clear.

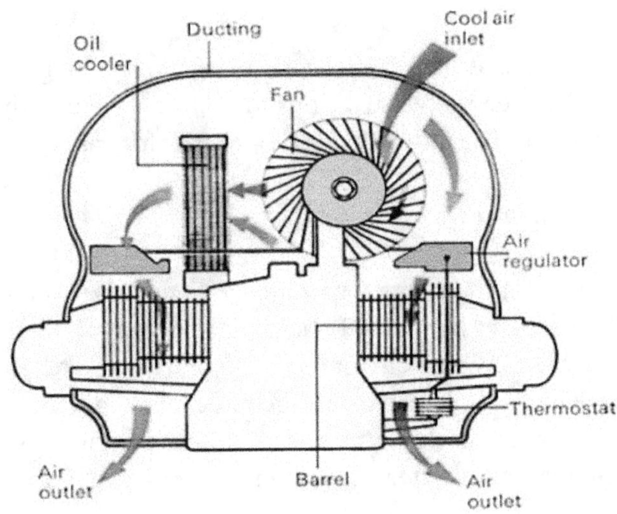

Figure 1.10: Air Cooling System

Advantages of air-cooled engines:

1. Simple design and construction
2. No water jacket, radiator, water pump, thermostat, pipes, or hoses are required
3. More compact
4. Light Weight

Disadvantages of air-cooled engines:

1. Uneven cooling of engine parts
2. Engine temperatures are generally high during the working period

Water cooling system:

An engine that uses water as a coolant is called a water-cooled engine. Water circulates in the cylinder and absorbs heat from the cylinder wall. The heated water passes through a radiator to dissipate heat and cool the water.

Types of water-cooling methods:

1. Open jacket or hopper process
2. Thermosiphon method
3. Forced circulation method

1. Open jacket method

Around the engine, the cylinder is a funnel or jacket that contains water. As long as there is water in the funnel, the motor will continue to run normally. When the water begins to boil, replace it with cold water. The hopper is large enough to run for hours without refilling. The drain plug is located low for easy access to drain water as needed.

2. Thermosiphon manufacturing method

Consists of the radiator, water jacket, fan, thermometer, and hose connector. The system is based on the principle that heated water around a cylinder becomes lighter and rises into a column of liquid. Hot water reaches the radiator and flows through tubes surrounded by air. Water circulation is done with a water jacket and radiators on both sides. i.e., top and bottom are connected. The fan is driven by a V-belt and draws air from the tubes of the radiator unit to cool the water in the radiator. The drawback of this system is that the accumulation of deposits and foreign matter in the ducts will greatly reduce the circulation of water, resulting in overheating of the engine.

3. Forced circulation system

This method uses a water pump to push water from the radiator into the engine's water jacket. After circulating through the water jacket, the water returns to the radiator and loses heat through radiative processes. A thermostatic valve is located at the outer end of the cylinder head to maintain the correct engine temperature. Coolant is channeled through the engine's water jacket until the engine reaches the desired temperature. The thermostatic valve opens and the bypass is closed so that water flows to the radiator.

Design of fuel system for C.I. Engine

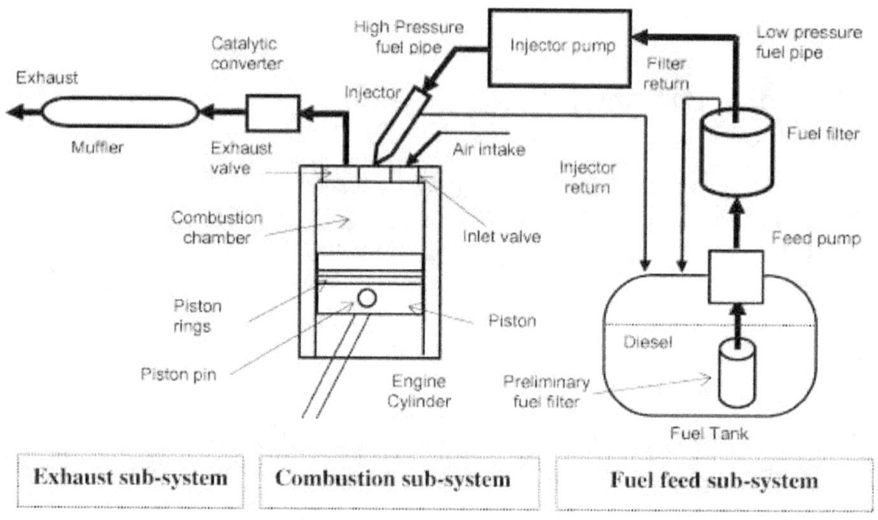

Figure 1.11: Layout of the fuel system, in diesel engine

The diesel engine fuel supply system consists of the following components:

- Fuel tank
- Fuel Transfer Pump
- Fuel filter

- Fuel injection pump
- High-pressure line
- Overflow valve
- Fuel injection system

Fuel is drawn from the fuel tank by the fuel supply pump and sent through the fuel filter to the injection pump. The injection pump supplies high-pressure fuel to the injectors through a supply valve and high-pressure line. Fuel is injected into the combustion chamber from injectors. However, fuel exiting the injectors exits through the leaking pipe and returns to the fuel tank through the overflow pipe. An overflow valve mounted on top of the filter keeps the supply pressure below a set limit. When the supply pressure exceeds a specified limit, the overflow valve opens and excess fuel flows back through the overflow pipe to the fuel tank.

Fuel tank: A storage tank for diesel. There is a wire gauge strainer under the lid to prevent foreign objects from entering the tank

Fuel supply pump: Carries fuel from the fuel tank to the intake of the fuel injection pump

Pre-filter (sediment shell structure): This filter is usually installed on the fuel supply pump. Prevents foreign objects from entering the fuel line. Consists of a glass cap with a seal.

Fuel filter: Diesel engines typically use a two-stage filter.

1. Primary filter
2. Secondary filter

The main filter removes large particles, water, and dust. A secondary filter removes fine dust.

Injection pump: This is a high-pressure pump that delivers fuel to the injectors in the firing order of the engine. Used to generate pressure from 120kg/cm2 to 300kg/cm2. Delivers the required amount of fuel to each cylinder at the right time.

Bleed the fuel system: If air gets into the fuel line or the intake chamber of the injection pump, it must be properly vented. Air is expelled from the priming pump through the injection pump bleed hole.

Injector: This is the component that delivers fuel under high pressure in a finely atomized form to the engine's combustion chamber. Modern tractor engines use multi-hole fuel injectors. The main parts of the injector are the nozzle body and the needle valve. A spring presses the needle valve against a cone seat in the nozzle body. The injection pressure is set by adjusting the screw. During operation, fuel from the injection pump enters the nozzle body through the high-pressure pipe. When the fuel pressure builds up and exceeds the set spring pressure, the needle valve lifts off its seat. Fuel is pushed into the combustion chamber through nozzles and injection holes.

Design of Governor

The governor is attached to the engine and maintains constant speed even when speed fluctuations are observed at full load and idle. In normal operation, a good governor will show a deviation of about 100 rpm between full load and idle. So by changing the spring tension, you can adjust the governor to speed it up or down. The amount of adjustment performed is expressed in percent and is called the percentage regulation. This is also called speed drop. This is the change in engine speed between full load and idle conditions. Usually expressed as a percentage of rated speed. This is given by,

$$\text{``}R = [(N_1 - N_2) / ((N_1 + N_2)/2)] \times 100\text{''}$$

where, R – % regulation,

N_1 - idle speed, RPM

N_2 – the speed at full load, rpm

Governor hunting

Governor hunting is when the governor's speed changes erratically when overcompensating for speed changes. If the governor has a cyclical effect on engine speed (too fast, then too slow, then too fast, etc.), this is a sign of governor chase. In such cases, when the engine accelerates sharply, it is observed that the governor suddenly responds, the speed drops rapidly, the governor responds again, and the process repeats. Governor hunting can be caused by improper fuel pump or carburetor adjustment, improper idle screw adjustment, and excessive friction. Vibration can be caused by the governor being too stiff or restricting the free movement of the governor components.

Design of Carburettor

Some petrol engines have the fuel tank above the level of the carburetor. Fuel flows from the fuel tank to the carburetor by gravity. There are one or two filters between the fuel tank and the carburetor. A clear sediment tray is also provided to collect dust and dirt from the fuel. When the tank is below the level of the carburetor, a lift pump is provided between the tank and the carburetor to force fuel from the tank to the engine's carburetor. Fuel is channeled from the fuel tank to the sediment container and then to the lift pump. From there, the fuel travels through appropriate lines to reach the carburetor. From the carburetor, fuel travels through the engine's intake manifold to the engine cylinders.

Definition:

The process of preparing the air-fuel mixture outside the engine cylinder is called carburetion. The device in which this process takes place is called a carburetor. The function of the carburetor is to:

1. Thoroughly mix air and fuel
2. Atomize the fuel
3. Adjust the air/fuel ratio at different engine speeds and loads.
4. Provides the right amount of mix at various speeds and loads

Design of Intake and Exhaust system

The intake manifold's job is to direct the air to the cylinder head. On fuel-injected vehicles, a throttle plate or throttle body is attached to one end and used to control the airflow entering the manifold. Many racing engines use separate throttle bodies for each cylinder, as opposed to road-going cars which typically use one.

Intake parts to be manifold:

Plenum: A plenum is a large, usually circular section of a manifold. All runners are fed from the plenum. The plenum size should be 50-70% of the actual engine displacement.

Runner: A runner exits the plenum and connects to the cylinder head. They have a tapered shape, becoming larger in the plenum and gradually smaller near the cylinder head. Variable runner length affects the car's powerband. Shorter, wider runners are best for higher motor power, while longer, narrower runners are best for low to medium-speed operation.

Throttle body: Controls airflow to the intake plenum. Throttle body size affects how fast air enters. Airspeed should be maintained at approximately 300 ft/sec to ensure consistent throttle response. V = (air flow rate/cross-sectional area)

Position of the fuel injector:

Two main guidelines to follow:

1. Aim directly at the center of the port on each runner.
2. Unload at maximum speed and at an angle of fewer than 20 degrees to the impeller.

High speed helps atomize the fuel along with the air. It also reduces the chance of fuel pooling in the manifold. A secondary injector can be added to the exhaust upstream, but the airflow must be high. This also helps with atomization.

Exhaust manifold:

Exhaust manifolds collect exhaust gases from the engine cylinders and release them into the atmosphere through the exhaust system. Engine efficiency and combustion characteristics depend on how exhaust gases are removed from the cylinders. Below are some of the key aspects associated with the design of an exhaust manifold for an internal combustion engine. The design of the exhaust manifold keeps a high temperature inside the exhaust pipes. This is necessary because catalytic converters placed closer to the end of the exhaust pipe absorb more pollutants under hot conditions. In addition, the design must ensure that the natural frequency of the exhaust manifold is not within the excitation frequency.

Selection of Lubricants

Lubricants are derived from animal fats, vegetables, and minerals. Vegetable lubricants are derived from seeds, fruits, and plants. Cottonseed, olive, linseed, and castor oils are used as lubricants. Mineral lubricants are most popular for engines and machinery. It is derived from naturally occurring crude oil. Petroleum-based lubricants are inexpensive and suitable for internal combustion engines.

Lubricant selection depends on the following key points:

Function: Lubricants have a wide range of functions including control of:

* Friction (lubricants reduce energy consumption and heat generation)
* Wear (lubricants can reduce corrosive and mechanical wear)
* Corrosion (high-quality lubricants protect surfaces from corrosive agents)
* Contamination (lubricants carry particles and other contaminants to separators and filters)
* Temperature (lubricants can transfer and absorb heat)

Viscosity: It describes the viscosity or fluidity of the lubricant. High viscosity means high flow resistance.

Material: Lubricating oils have many components, but base oils actually contain various additives. These ingredients are carefully selected according to the intended use of the lubricant. Many people don't realize that grease is actually oil to which a thickener has been added. Thickeners are usually made up of fibrous particles that act like sponges, It holds the oil in place and provides a more viscous quality. Each type of thickener has different strengths and weaknesses, especially with respect to shear stability, heat, and water resistance.

Durability: Lubricants have an optimal lifespan and should be replaced when their lifespan expires. Otherwise, problems such as runout, metal-to-metal contact, and blown bearings can occur, leading to downtime and higher costs. The problem is that it's not always obvious when this happens. An important way to track lubricant life is to monitor equipment operating temperature. Excessive heat will destroy the lubricant. For every 10°C (18°F) increase in temperature above 65°C (150°F), lubricant life is halved. This means that a lubricant that typically lasts 1 month at 150 degrees F will only last 2 weeks at 168 degrees F, 1 week at 186 degrees F, and 3-4 days at 204 degrees F.

Cost: Inferior-quality lubricants may lead to downtime, workplace accidents, and mechanical wear of bearings.

Lubricant system

Internal combustion engines consist of moving parts. The continuous motion of two metal surfaces over each other might cause wear of moving parts, heat generation, and loss of power in the engine. Lubrication of moving parts is essential to prevent all these detrimental effects.

Purpose of lubrication:

1. Reduce the effects of friction
2. cooling effect
3. Seal effect
4. Cleansing effect

An engine's lubrication system is the arrangement of mechanisms that maintains the lubricating oil supply to the engine's friction surfaces at the correct pressure and temperature.

Parts that require lubrication are:

- Cylinder wall and piston
- Gudgeon pin
- Crankshaft and connecting rod bearings
- Camshaft bearing
- Valve mechanism
- Fan
- Water pump and
- Launch Mechanism

Type of lubrication system:

Splash system:

Splash lubrication is commonly used in early motorcycle engines. This technology is used on lawn mowers and engines or outboards that should have enough oil in the sump to fully lubricate the machine.

Working of Splash lubrication system:

First, inject oil into the crankcase. The oil strainer removes impurities contained in the oil, and the oil pump supplies all parts including the oil in the trough.

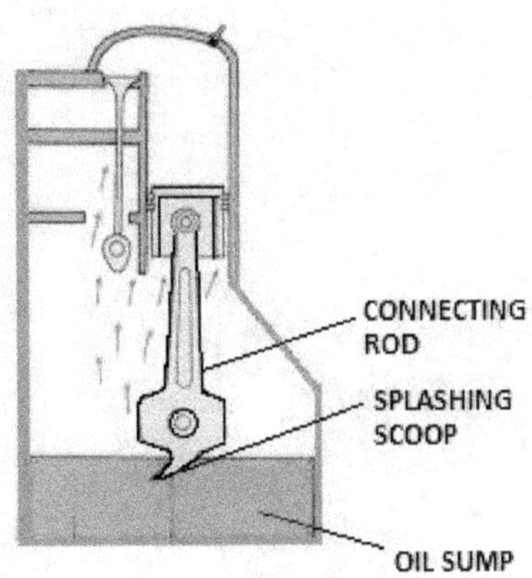

Figure 1.12: Splash System Lubrication

In the splash lubrication system, oil splashes up from the trough at the bottom of the crankcase each time the crankshaft rotates, generating an oil splash. The oil is thrown upwards as fine mist or droplets, providing proper lubrication to piston pins, piston rings, cylinder walls, valve mechanisms, etc. Oil flows through holes drilled in the crankshaft and main bearings to lubricate them. This system is too unsafe for automotive applications. A full oil in the bottom, of the trough, will consume more oil and result in excessive lubrication, and a slightly low oil level will result in insufficient lubrication and engine failure.

Advantages of the splash lubrication system:

Splash lubrication systems are also used in some automobiles where the machine can provide little power compared to the internal combustion engine.

Disadvantages of splash lubrication systems:

Due to the presence of vanes at the ends of the pistons, they do not help to properly lubricate the entire engine cylinder. Only lubricant spills on the piston area, thus resulting in wear and tear of the components.

Pressure lubrication system:

Since the splash lubrication system has no forced lubrication, it is not suitable for automobile engines, so the pressure lubrication system has appeared.

Working of Pressure lubrication system:

In this system, oil is pumped out of the wet sump through a strainer and sent to the main oil gallery at a pressure of 200-400 kPa. Hydraulic pressure is maintained by a pressure relief valve located in the filter unit/pump housing. A hydraulic regulator maintains the hydraulic level.

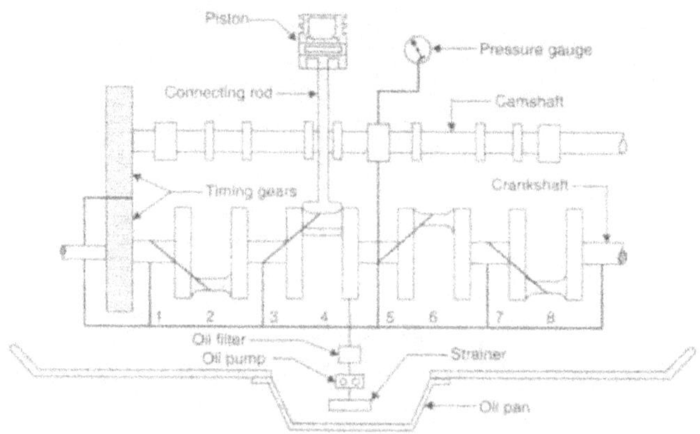

Figure 1.13: Pressure feed lubrication system

In-line engines use one main duct, and V-type engines use one or two main ducts. The oil filter removes all dust particles present in the oil and supplies clean oil to all oil lines. Pressurized oil flows through oil lines and galleries to lubricate moving engine parts. Oil from the main gallery flows through holes drilled in the crankshaft and main bearings to lubricate them. An oil outlet connected to the gallery pushes oil up, lubricating the piston and all its parts from the inside.

Oil flows through the oil ring, lubricates it, and forms a thin film around the cylinder wall. After all the parts in the first gallery have been lubricated, the oil can be pumped into her second gallery to lubricate all the parts associated with the camshaft. The rungs connected to the galleries help lubricate the camshafts, valves, and valve springs. After lubricating the engine parts, the oil begins to flow to the oil pan through another channel. Oil pressure in the system is calculated by a pressure gauge and then displays it on the dial.

Advantages of pressure lubrication systems:

Due to the presence of oil passages, oil reaches all components of the engine cylinder through them, so there is no wear between mating parts.

Disadvantages of pressure lubrication systems:

Even with this system, if the oil isn't getting properly into the engine, parts will wear out with each service, albeit a pressure system.

Pump and Filters

A fuel supply pump also called a lift pump, is responsible for drawing fuel from the tank and delivering it to the high-pressure pump. Modern fuel pumps can be driven electrically or mechanically by the engine. By using an electric fuel pump, the pump can be placed anywhere in the fuel system, including the fuel tank. A pump driven by the engine is attached to the engine. Some fuel pumps may be built into units that serve other functions.

For example, a so-called tandem pump is a unit that includes a fuel pump and a vacuum pump for the brake booster. Some fuel systems such as distributed pumps contain a mechanically driven feed pump and a high-pressure pump in one unit. Fuel pumps are usually sized to deliver more fuel than the engine consumes on a given operating system.

This additional fuel flow serves several important functions, such as providing additional fuel to cool injectors, pumps, and other engine components, and maintaining a more consistent fuel temperature throughout the fuel system. Additionally, excess fuel heated by contact with hot engine parts can be returned to the tank or fuel filter to improve vehicle handling in cold temperatures.

Fuel Filters:

Trouble-free operation of diesel injection systems is possible only with filtered fuel. Filters help reduce pollution damage and premature wear by retaining very fine particles and water to prevent them from entering the fuel injection system. Fuel systems can include one or more stages of filtration, as shown in Figure. Often the fuel intake in the fuel tank also has a course strainer.

A two-stage filter system typically uses a primary filter on the inlet side of the fuel lift pump and a secondary filter on the outlet side. The main filter is required to remove large particles. A secondary filter must be able to withstand high pressures and remove small particles that can damage engine components. A single-stage system removes large and small particles with a single filter.

Filters can be box-type or exchange-element type, as shown.

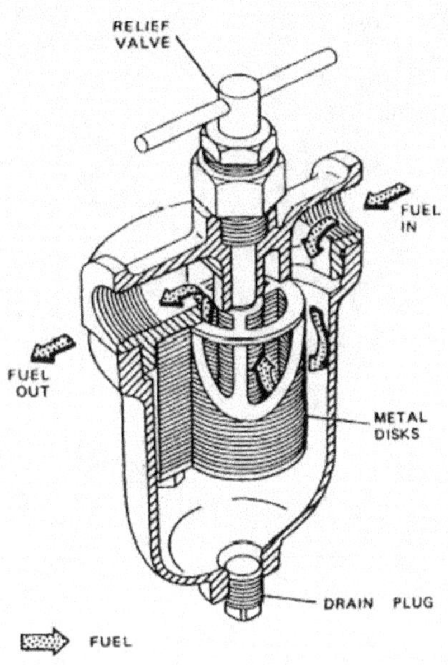

Figure 1.14: Design of fuel filter

The box filter can be completely replaced if needed, no cleaning required. Filters with replaceable elements must be thoroughly cleaned when the element is replaced, and care must be taken to keep debris out of the complex parts of the fuel injection system.

Common materials for modern fuel filter elements are synthetic fibers and/or cellulose. Microfiber glass can also be used but is avoided in some applications due to the risk of small pieces of glass fiber breaking off the main element and migrating to critical fuel system components. Pleated paper, wrap cotton yarn, wood scraping, blends of wrap cotton yarn and wood fibers, and wrap cotton have also been used in the past. The level of filtration required will depend on the specific application. When two filters are used in series, the primary filter typically retains particles up to about 10-30 μm in size and the secondary filter can retain particles greater than 2-10 μm. As fuel systems evolve, margins and loads on high-pressure components increase, making the need for clean fuel even more important. There was a need to further develop both the fuel filter's ability to meet the demand for clean fuel and methods to quantify acceptable fuel contamination levels.

Not only should the particular matter be kept out of the fuel supply and injectors, but water in the fuel should also be prevented from entering critical components of the fuel injection system. Free water can damage fuel lubrication components in the fuel injection system. Also, water can freeze at low temperatures, and ice can block small passages in the fuel injection system, cutting off fuel flow to the rest of the fuel injection system. Fuel filters can also include additional features such as fuel heaters, thermal switching valves, breathers, fuel moisture sensors, and filter change indicators.

• • •

CHAPTER II

Design of Drive Train, Axle and Steering

In a vehicle, the engine is in front and drives the front wheels of the vehicle. Some vehicles have an engine in the rear that is driven by the rear wheels. Each wheel is driven by a small Cardan shaft. With the help of flexible brackets or bearings, the engine and transmission units are attached to the vehicle frame. The rear axle, including the differential and wheels, is attached to the body frame via suspension springs. Looking at the arrangement below, the transmission's output and input shafts are on different levels within the rear axle housing. This leaves the propeller shaft connecting the two shafts tilted. When the rear wheels hit a bump in the road, the rear axle moves up and down, compressing and stretching the suspension springs. This changes the angle between the gearbox output shaft and the Cardan shaft. Also, the length occupied by the propeller or drive shaft changes. This variation occurs because the Cardan shaft and rear axle rotate on an arc with their pivot points.

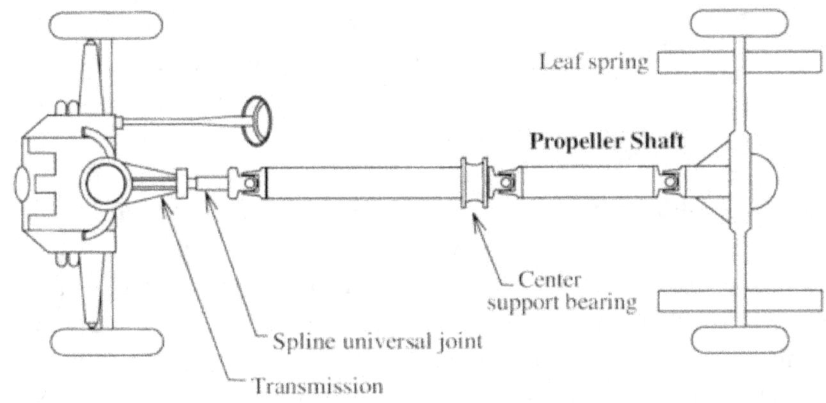

Figure 2.1: Design of Drive Train

A propeller shaft is a component used to transmit mechanical power, torque, and rotation. These shafts are also called drive shafts, stern shafts, and Cardan shafts. Driveshafts are used to transmit torque between components that cannot be directly connected due to the need to allow spacing or relative motion. As torque is transmitted by the drive shaft, it experiences torsional or shear stress. Therefore, it should be strong enough to withstand the strain while not adding too much extra weight due to the increased inertia. Driveshafts are used differently in different vehicles in different configurations of front-wheel drive, four-wheel drive, and front-engine rear-wheel drive in automobiles. Driveshafts are also used in vehicles such as motorcycles, locomotives, and ships.

Propeller shafts are solid or tubular and require little or no maintenance. Solid shafts are typically used where high shaft speeds are not required. It is often used to power auxiliary equipment such as winches and hydraulic pumps. Hollow shafts are used almost exclusively to transmit power to vehicle axles. Hollow shafts rotate at high speed and must be balanced to prevent transmission and differential assembly vibration and premature bearing failure. A slip joint at one end of the propeller shaft provides endplay. The spring-mounted drive axle is free to move up and down while the gearbox is mounted to the frame and does not move. Moving the axle up or down bends the suspension springs. This action shortens or lengthens the distance between the axle assembly and the transmission. Slip joints compensate for this varying vertical distance. The type of slip joint commonly used consists of a splined stub shaft welded to the propeller shaft and fitted into the splined sleeve of the universal joint as shown.

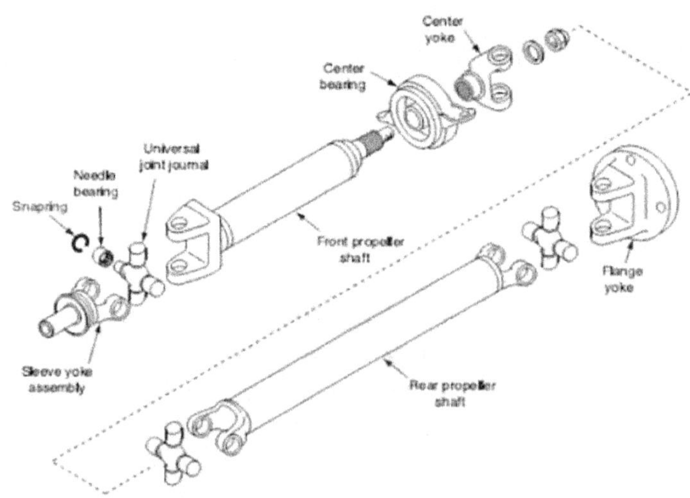

Figure 2.2: Components of Propellor shaft

The main components of the propeller shaft are explained in brief below:

- *U-joints:* Universal joints (U-joints) are mechanical joints used to connect axes of rotation. Today, driveshafts and Cardan joints are mainly found on rear-wheel drive vehicles and four-wheel drive vehicles.
- *Tube:* The tube is part of the drive shaft. It is widely used in front-engine and rear-wheel-drive vehicles. The purpose of using the hose is to hold the rear end in place during acceleration and braking.
- *Center Bearing:* The center bearing is used to connect the two sections of the drive shaft. These bearings are designed to stabilize both parts of the driveshaft and reduce harmonic vibrations as the vehicle accelerates.
- *Center shaft:* The center shaft is the basic component of the clutch shaft and part of the drive shaft that is attached to the frame via a center bearing.
- *End yoke:* End yoke is adopted for accuracy and durability. The advantage of using end yokes is that they reduce noise and vibration to keep the drivetrain running smoothly.
- *Sliding yoke and tubular yoke:* The sliding yoke is attached to the driveshaft itself with a universal joint. The slip yoke transfers power by sliding it in and out of the transfer case. A tube yoke is also required to allow the U-joint to rotate properly with the driveshaft.
- *Flanges:* Flanges are used in automotive applications to connect drive shafts to gearboxes, transfer cases, and differentials. Flanges are also used to connect drive shafts to power take-offs, hydraulic pumps, and various accessories.

Design of Propeller Shaft

The drive shaft is made of tabular-formed hardened steel. A center bearing is installed between the two propeller shafts. The shaft is made up of alloy steel. Spring steel materials are also available. To achieve efficient functioning, Cardan shafts require:

High torsional strength: To achieve high torsional strength during work, the cross-section must be a solid or hollow sphere.

Toughened and Hardening: Normally you need a hard, hard material to make these. They are therefore made of high-quality steel and induction hardened.

Efficiently combined: Must be firmly connected during operation. Therefore, they are usually welded using the carbon dioxide submerged arc welding process.

Dynamic balance: Cardan shafts are checked with an electronic balance machine as the rotational coefficient can be important at high speeds.

Low thrust load: This is because the shaft life is poor due to resonance. To avoid this phenomenon, excessive dynamic forces are transmitted to the end supports of the shaft.

When designing the propeller shaft following considerations can be derived:

Mass of the propeller shaft:

The mass m of the hollow shaft is given by

$$\text{``}m = \rho \times A \times L$$
$$m = \rho \times \pi 4 (D_{o2} - D_{i2}) \times L\text{''}$$

where L is the length of the hollow shaft.

Shaft torque transmission capacity:

The torque transmission capacity of a steel drive shaft, T_{cr}, is given by the following formula:

$$\text{``}T = S_s \pi (D_{o4} - D_{i4}) / 16 D_o\text{''}$$

where S_s is the shear strength,

D_o and D_i represent the outer and inner diameters of the steel shaft.

Axial torsional buckling capacity:

If $(1 * L^2 t) / (\surd(1 - \mu^2) \times (2r)^3) > 5.5$ then long shanks, otherwise short medium shank. For long waves, the critical stress τ_{cr} is given by

$$\text{``}\tau_{cr} = (E(t/r)^\wedge(3/2)) / (3\surd 2 (1 - \mu^2)^\wedge(3/4))\text{''}$$

where E and μ represent the properties of steel.

The relationship between the buckling torsional capacity τ_{cr} and the critical stress is given by the following equation:

$$\text{``}T_{cr} = \tau_{cr} . 2\pi r . 2t\text{''}$$

L, t, and r are the shaft length, thickness, and mean radius, respectively.

Fundamental natural frequency:

The formula for the lowest natural frequency "f_n" is as follows.

$$\text{``}f_n = (\pi/2)\surd(gEI / wL4)\text{''}$$

where *g, E, I, w,* and *L* are gravitational acceleration, elastic modulus, polar moment of inertia, weight, and length, respectively.

Torsional deflection of the shaft:

The formula for the torsional deflection of the shaft "Θ" is:

$$``\Theta = (L \times T)/(G \times J)$$
$$\Theta = (32 \times L \times T)/(G\pi(D_{o4} - D_{i4}))\text{''}$$

where T and G are the transmitted torque and shear stiffness coefficient, respectively.

Theory of Failures:

Theories of failure help us to determine the safe dimensions of the machine components when subjected to combined stresses due to different loads acting on the components during their functionality. Theories of failures are also used in the design of machine parts due to the unavailability of failure stresses under all loading conditions when combined. This also plays a significant role in establishing the relationship between stresses induced under combined loading conditions and functionalities obtained from ultimate tensile strength (S_{ut}) and yield strength (S_{yt}).

Maximum shear stress theory:

The maximum shear stress is

$$``\tau_{max} = \sqrt{(\sigma_b/2)^2 + (\tau)^2}$$
$$= \sqrt{(16M/\pi d^3)^2 + (16T/\pi d^3)^2}$$
$$= 16/\pi d^3 \times \sqrt{M^2 + T^2} \leq [\tau]\text{''}$$

where $\sqrt{M^2 + T^2}$ is called the equivalent torque T_e, so

$$``\tau_{max} = T_e.r/J \leq [\tau]\text{''}$$

where r is the radius

Maximum principal stress theory:

The maximum principal stress is

$$``\sigma = \sigma_b/2 + \sqrt{(\sigma_b/2)^2 + (\tau)^2}$$
$$= 16M/\pi d^3 + \sqrt{(16M/\pi d^3)^2 + (16T/\pi d^3)^2}$$
$$= 16/\pi d^3 \times (M + \sqrt{M^2 + T^2}) \leq [\sigma_t]\text{''}$$

where $M + \sqrt{M^2 + T^2}$ is called the equivalent bending moment M_e, so

$$``\sigma = M_e.y / l \leq [\sigma_t]\text{''}$$

Causes of failures:

Proper sizing of a rotating system requires the identification of possible causes or types of failure. Most failures are due to unpredictable factors. Solving these mistakes requires developing robust designs that can cope with the unknown. Predictable failure or lifetime can be calculated, but many parameters are variable and statistical considerations must be taken into account.

The shaft is designed for unlimited service life. This is true as long as the shaft is not overloaded or damaged.

1. *Fatigue Cracks:* Shaft failure is usually caused by fatigue. Cracks can be caused by stress concentrations in keyways or sharp radii, or rarely by material contamination. Shaft surface imperfections such as scratches, notches, and corrosion can also initiate fatigue cracks. The crack-initiating loads are usually torsional loads from the direct online start or bending loads from the hydraulic side.
2. *Plastic Deformation:* Plastic deformation occurs only in extreme loads where debris is pushed into radial gaps and causes large deformations.
3. *Shaft Defects:* Shaft defects that go unnoticed during factory imbalance checks and tests are extremely rare. However, in the field, proper handling is important to prevent damage such as corrosion and notching.

Design of U Joints

A universal joint is a connection between two objects (usually shafts) that allows relative rotation about two axes. It consists of two pivots with vertical and cross axes. A universal joint (universal joint, U joint, Cardan joint, Spicer or Hardy Spicer joint, or Hooke joint) is a joint or coupling that connects rigid rods whose axes are inclined to each other, commonly used for shafts. rotational transfer motion. It consists of a pair of hinges arranged at a 90° angle to each other and connected by a cross shaft. Cardan joints are not constant velocity joints. When shafts are connected by universal joints, each shaft ends in a rotary joint whose axis is perpendicular to the axis of rotation of the shaft. This allows rotational motion to be transmitted between the shafts while allowing misalignment of both remaining rotational degrees of freedom. One rotational degree of freedom (shaft rotation) and all relative motion is constrained, giving the universal joint two degrees of freedom (2-DOF).

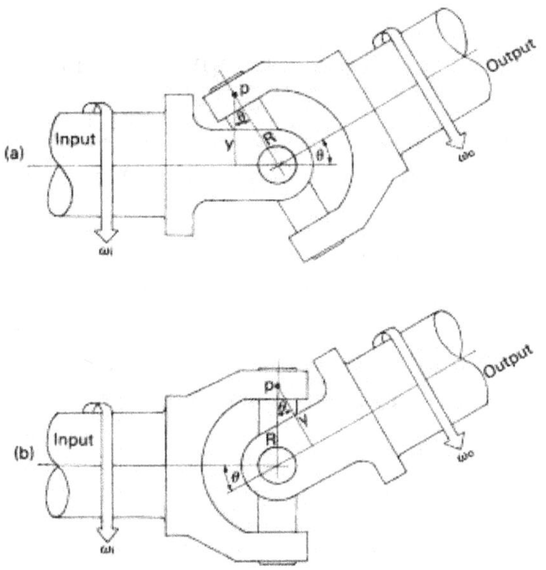

Figure 2.3: Design of U Joint

Universal joints are not constant velocity joints. When the input shaft rotates at a constant speed, the speed of the output shaft oscillates. The average speed is the same, but the output shaft speed at any point in time is slightly higher or lower than this average. The amount of vibration of the output shaft depends on the amount of misalignment between the shafts. If the shaft is coaxial, the output shaft will actually have a constant velocity. A constant velocity joint can be created by combining multiple universal joints. A double hook's joint is two universal joints arranged with a short connecting shaft, 90° out of phase with each other. If any bend angle is shared equally between two universal joints, the two joints will cancel the velocity oscillations and the final output shaft velocity will be constant. However, swinging of the intermediate shaft causes vibration and requires support to maintain equal angles.

Structure of universal joint

The Hook's joint consists of a spider (cross) and four grease-filled roller bearings. Large torque can be transmitted with low friction. Stars with journals and bearing housings as the outer ring is hot forged or cold formed and machined. They are later carburized in the furnace, which increases their robustness and wear resistance.

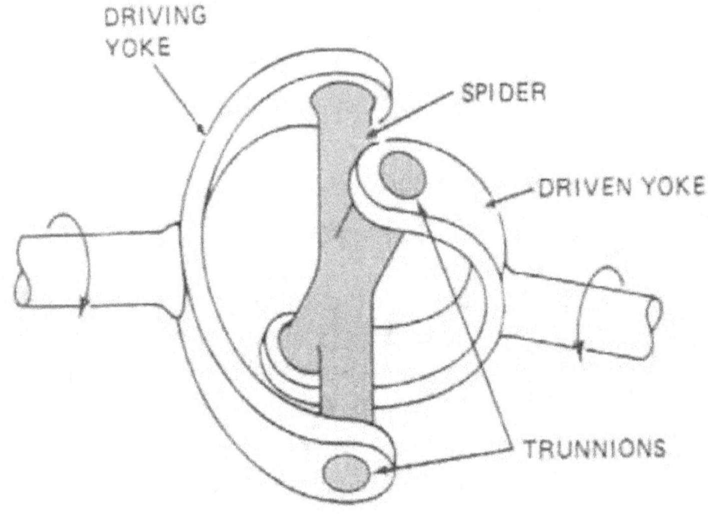

Figure 2.4: Parts of Universal Joint

Parts are finally ground to the desired size under tight tolerances. Oil seals or dust cover is also used to protect the internal journal area from foreign material intrusion. Different qualities and materials have been selected for extreme conditions such as very hot/very cold temperatures.

There are two types of universal joints defined by the number of flexures.

Single Joint: Only one bending surface and can be manipulated at angles up to 45 degrees.

Double Joints: Using two flex joints, the double U joints can move at angles of up to 90 degrees. In addition, a parallel offset between the two axes with working angles from 0 to 45 degrees at the center is possible.

Three types of commonly used universal joints are explained below.

Cross-type universal joint:

It consists of a crosspiece (spider) and two Y-shaped yokes. One yoke is connected to the input shaft and the other to the output shaft. The crosspiece has four arms called trunnions attached to the ends of the yoke. There are four needle bearings, one for each arm of the crosspiece. These bearings allow the yoke to swing about the trunnion when driven and remove the driven shaft obliquely along with it. This is a variable joint. That is, the driving and driven shafts do not rotate at the same speed during one revolution of her. However, the speed is the same. This happens because both waves are not in line. Ring and trunnion type and cross ball type designs also fall into this universal joint category.

Ball and Trunnion joint:

This type of joint consists of a ball head attached to one end of the propeller shaft. A pin is also pressed into this end of the shaft. The tip of this pin has two steel balls. Joints facilitate rotational movement via balls and pins. The ball can also move axially. Ball and socket joints are also variable speed joints.

The constant velocity universal joint:

This type of joint allows both the driving and driven shafts to move at a constant speed. In this case, the two joints move at the same angle. These joints are commonly used when the car has front-wheel (last) drive. This is because speed fluctuations between the input and output shafts make steering difficult and cause excessive tire wear.

Hook's joints are now widely used in many machines with long rotating shafts. Most notably, such joints are found between the gearbox and the rear driveshaft of rear-wheel drive vehicles, and in old-fashioned tower clocks. Common hook's joint applications include aircraft, appliances, controls, electronics, instruments, medical and optical equipment, munitions, radios, sewing machines, textile machinery, and tool drives. Universal joints are available for steel or thermoplastic body parts. Hook's joints made of steel have the maximum load capacity for a given size. Hook's joints with thermoplastic body members are used in light industrial applications where self-lubricating properties, light weight, negligible backlash, corrosion resistance, and the ability to operate at high speeds are major advantages.

Advantages Of Universal Joint

1. Universal coupling is extra flexible than knuckle joints.
2. It allows torque transmission among shafts that have an angular misalignment.
3. It is easy to be assembled and dismantled.
4. Torque transmission performance is high.
5. The joint allows angular displacements.

Disadvantages Of Universal Joint

1. Wear can also additionally arise if the joint isn't always well lubricated.
2. Maintenance is frequently vital to keep away from wear.
3. Universal joint produces fluctuating movement
4. No support for axial misalignment.

Design of final drive and differential

The terms differential and final drive are sometimes used imprecisely. Moreover, these mechanisms are often integrated into the same subsystem in various combinations. A differential is a mechanism that divides the torque from the input shaft into two predetermined parts and transmits it to the two output shafts. The torque ratio is independent of the speed ratio for the same shaft. This mechanism divides the torque from the final drive into equal parts acting on the drive wheels on the same axle or can be used to split the torque coming from the gearbox into two pre-determined working parts on different axles of the same vehicle. This second application of his is sometimes called transfer case differential or center differential. A final drive is a gear train that further reduces the speed of the gearbox output shaft adapted to drive wheels. This gear train is usually built into the differential mechanism. This name sometimes includes a reducer placed in the transmission line after the differential is integrated into the final drive and wheel hub.

Final Drive:

The final drive is the final stage of transmission of power from the propeller shaft to the rear axle (front axle for front-wheel drive vehicles) to the wheels. It rotates the motion of the propeller shaft at right angles and drives the rear axle. A final drive consists of bevel gear (or pinion) and ring gear. A leveling pinion is connected to the propeller shaft. The pinion meshes with the ring gear. The crown gear is part of the differential. A final drive provides constant deceleration. This is because the ring gear has more teeth and is connected to the rear axle, while the flat pinion has fewer teeth. A schematic diagram of the final drive is shown below.

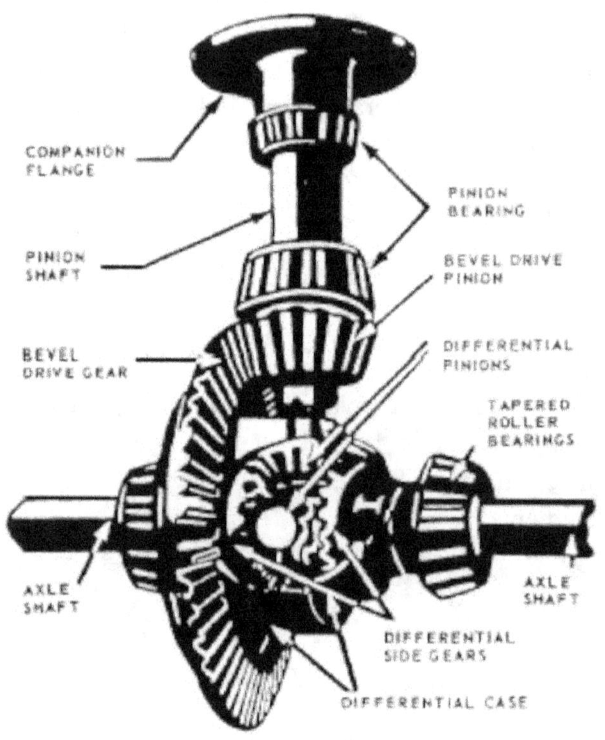

Figure 2.5: Design of Final Drive

Two types of gears are available for final deceleration. One of them is the use of level gears and the other is the use of worms and worm wheels. Worm and worm gear combinations allow large gear reductions without the use of large gears. It's also strong.

Slip joint:

The rear axle housing with wheels and differential is attached to the vehicle frame by springs. As the vehicle moves over uneven road surfaces, the springs expand and contract to move the assembly up and down. This changes the length of the universal shaft connected to the differential and gearbox. A slip joint allows the length of the propeller shaft to be varied. When the spring is compressed the pivot shaft shortens and when the spring is extended the pivot shaft returns to its original length.

Types of Gears in Final drive:

Helical gears:

Due to the tooth interaction, helical gears operate softer and quieter than spur gears. Worm gear teeth are cut at an angle to the face of the gear. As the two teeth begin to mesh, contact is gradually initiated from one end of the tooth and maintained until the gear is fully engaged and rotated. The pitch angle range is approximately 15 to 30 degrees.

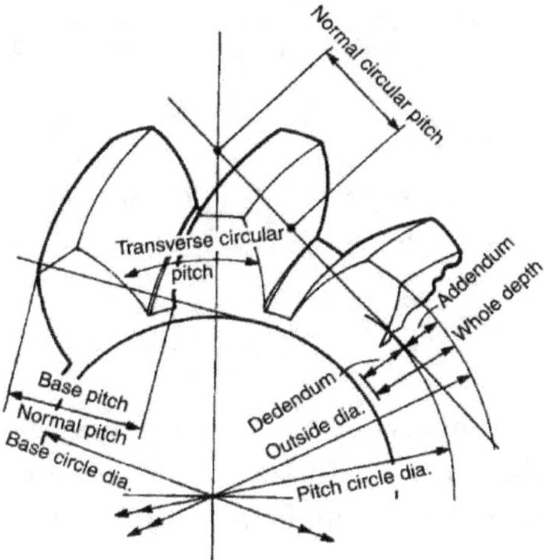

Figure 2.6: Design of Helical gear

Shear stress varies directly with the magnitude of the tangent of the torsional angle. Helical gears are the most common gear in gearboxes. They also generate a large amount of thrust and use bearings to carry the thrust load. A helical gear can be used to adjust the rotation angle by 90 degrees. When mounted on a vertical shaft, the average gear ratio range is 3:2 to 10:1.

Bevel gears:

Bevel gears are used to change the direction of the rotation of a shaft. Bevel gears have straight helical teeth. Spur gears have similar characteristics to spur gears and wobble when meshed. Similar to spur gears, the normal ratio range for spur bevel gears is 3:2 to 5:1.

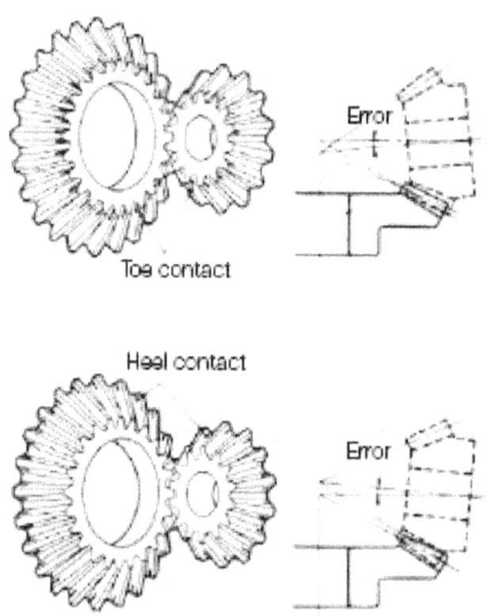

Figure 2.7: Design of Bevel gear

Worm gears:

Worm gears are used for large reducers. Common conversions are between 5:1 and 300:1. The adjustment is designed such that the worm can rotate the gear, but the gear cannot rotate the worm. The angle of the worm is flat and as a result, the gear is held in place by the friction between the two. Gears are found, for example, in transport systems where locking functions act as brakes.

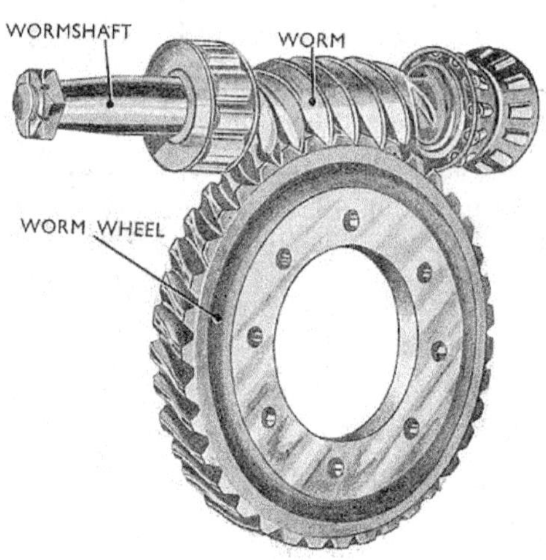

Figure 2.8: Design of Worm gear

Differential:

When a four-wheeled vehicle (car) turns, the outer wheels turn faster than the inner wheels. Therefore, there is relative motion between the inner and outer wheels. The function of the differential is that when the vehicle turns is to allow relative motion between the inner and outer wheels to turn (go). In this case, the torque transmitted to each rear wheel is the same, but the speed is different. The differential consists of a gear system connecting the Cardan shaft and the rear axle. This is part of the inner axle housing assembly. The assembly consists of differentials, rear axles, wheels, and bearings.

Working of Differential:

The diagram shows the structure of a simple differential. It consists of sun gear, planet pinion, cage, ring gear, and bevel pinion. A sun gear is attached to the inner end of each rear axle (half shaft). A cage is attached to the left axle. A face gear is attached to the cage, and the cage rotates together with the face gear. The ring gear is rotated by a bevel pinion. The crown wheel and cage remain free on the left rear axle. Two planetary gears are on a shaft supported by a cage. The planetary gear meshes with the sun gear.

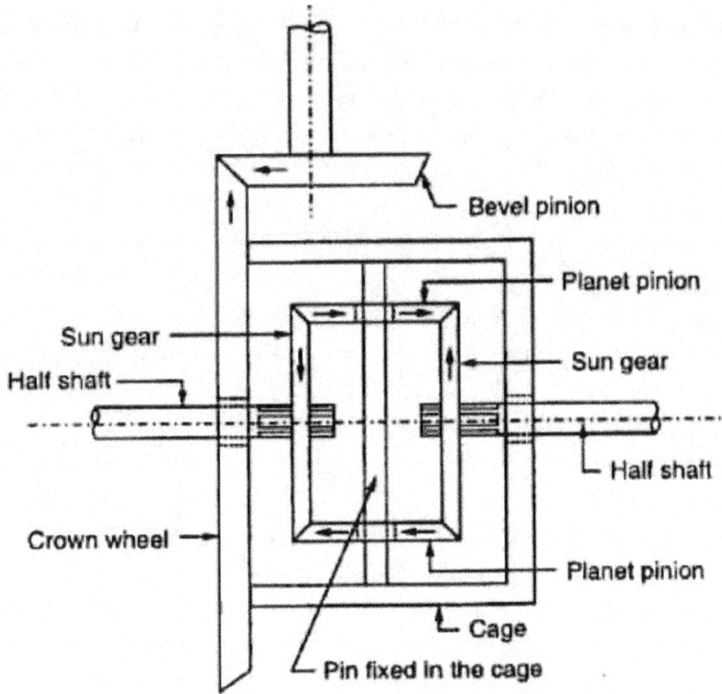

Figure 2.9: Working of differential

The rear wheels are mounted on the outside ends of the two rear axles. As the cage rotates, the sun gear rotates the wheels turn. When the vehicle is cornering, if one inside wheel is rotating slower than the other wheel, the planetary gear rotates on its shaft and transfers more rotary motion to the outside wheel. When traveling straight, the ring gear, cage, planetary gear, and sun gear rotate together. Therefore, there is no relative motion.

There are three types of differentials:

Conventional:

A traditional differential delivers equal torque to each rear wheel. If for some reason one of the wheels slips, the wheels won't turn and the vehicle won't move.

Non-slip or self-locking type:

A non-slip or self-locking differential overcomes this shortcoming. The structure is the same as the conventional differential type. However, two pairs of clutch discs are also available. Also, the ends of the planetary shafts are loose in notches in the differential cage.

Types of Double shrinkage:

A double-reduction differential slows you down even more by adding gears. This type of differential is used on heavy vehicles that require greater gear reduction between the engine and the wheels.

Design of Axle and Steering

The term shaft usually refers to a circular cross-section part that rotates and receives power from a drive such as a motor, an engine, or a machine transmitted by a machine. Shafts carry gears, pulleys, and sprockets and transmit rotation and power through meshing gears, belts, and chains. Alternatively, a shaft can simply be connected to another shaft via a coupling. A shaft is stationary and may support a rotating element such as a short shaft that supports the non-driven wheels of a vehicle, often called a spindle. Some common shaft arrangements are shown below:

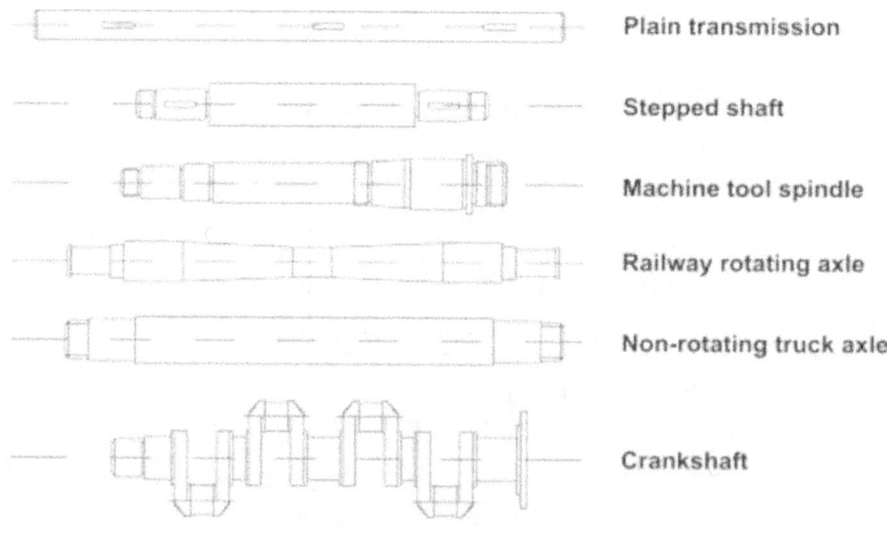

Figure 2.10: Types of Axle

Shaft design:

Shafts are designed for strength or stiffness, or both. The strength-based design aims to ensure that the stress does not exceed the yield strength of the material at any point on the shaft. The rigidity-based design aims to ensure that the maximum shaft deflection (due to bending) and maximum torsion (due to torsion) are within acceptable limits. In some cases, stiffness considerations are also very important. For instance, the position of a gear attached to a shaft changes as the shaft flexes. If this value exceeds the permissible limit, noises in the gears and high dynamic load can occur.

Shaft design considerations include:

Component size and spacing (as in the overview), tolerances,

- Material selection, material processing,
- Deflection and stiffness of,

1. bending deflection,
2. torsional deformation,
3. Slope at bearings,
4. shear deflection

- Stress and strength of,

1. static strength,
2. fatigue,
3. reliability,

- Frequency response,
- Manufacturing limits.

When designing shafts based on strength, the following cases are possible:

Shaft subjected to torque:

The maximum shear stress that occurs in a torqued shaft is given by:

$$\text{``}\tau = T.r \mathbin{/} J \le [\tau]\text{''}$$

where T = torque (or torque) acting on the shaft,
    J = polar moment of inertia of the shaft about the axis of rotation

$$\text{``} = (\pi.d^4)/32 \text{ for a solid shaft of diameter } d$$
$$= (\pi.[d_o{}^4 - d_i{}^4])/32 \text{ for hollow shafts with outer and inner diameters } d_o \text{ and } d_i.\text{''}$$

r = distance from the neutral axis to outermost fiber = d/2 (or $d_o/2$)
    Therefore, the dimensions of the torqued shaft can be determined from the above relationship for the known value of the allowable shear stress $[\tau]$.

Shaft subjected to bending moment:

The maximum bending stress that occurs in the shaft is given by the following formula.

$$\text{``}\sigma_b = (M.y) \mathbin{/} I \le [\sigma_t]\text{''}$$

where M = bending moment acting on the shaft,
    I = Moment of inertia of the shaft cross-sectional area about the axis of rotation

$$\text{``} = (\pi.d^4)/64 \text{ for a solid shaft of diameter } d$$
$$= (\pi.[d_o{}^4 - d_i{}^4])/64 \text{ for hollow shafts with outer and inner diameters } d_o \text{ and } d_i.\text{''}$$

y = distance from the neutral axis to outermost fiber = $d/2$ (or $d_o/2$)

Therefore, the dimensions of the shaft subjected to the bending moment can be determined from the above relationship for the known values of the allowable tensile stress $[\sigma_t]$.

Shaft subjected to combined torque and bending moment:

When a shaft is subjected to a combination of torques and bending moments, principal stresses are calculated and various failure theories are used.

$$\text{``}\tau = (T.r)/J = T.(d/2) / (\pi/32).\, d^4 = 16.T / \pi.d^3$$
$$\sigma_b = (M.y)/I = M.(d/2) / (\pi/64).\, d^4 = 32.M / \pi.d^3\text{''}$$

Bending and torsional shear stresses can be calculated using the above relationships.

Shaft subjected to axial loads in addition to combined torque and bending moment:

Tensile Stress due to axial load is given by,

$$\text{``}\sigma_t = P / A\text{''}$$

where P = axial load acting on the shaft

A = cross-sectional area of the shaft

Since the bending stress and this axial stress are of the same nature, they can be vectorially added at any point on the shaft to get the resulting tensile/compressive stress. This can be used to find the principal stress in the shaft.

Shaft subjected to Rigidity:

For shafts subjected to torsional moments, the torsion angle is given by the formula:

$$\text{``}\Theta = (T.L) / (G.J) \leq [\theta]\text{''}$$

where T = applied torque

Design of Axle

Axle shafts are heavy-duty, load-bearing components used in automobiles. Also known as CV axles or half-shafts, these components transmit rotational power from the vehicle's transmission system to the wheels attached to the axle. Axle shafts, by design, must support heavy loads including cargo, driver, and vehicle dead weight. Although designed to support heavy weights, components can be overloaded and the stress can cause them to warp or break. Similarly, physical impact from collisions, potholes, and rough roads can also cause damage. A drive axle is a key powertrain component that connects the vehicle's transmission to the vehicle's wheels. Axle shafts are primarily responsible for transmitting torque and power from the transmission to move the vehicle. When the transmission power turns the axle shaft, the wheels connected to it also turn. Each axle shaft has a differential between two semi-axles and two universal joints (UV). Ultimately, the axle shaft allows the vehicle to roll and the wheels to move in a controlled manner. Without a reliable drive shaft, a vehicle's wheels would either move incorrectly or not at all.

Two main functions of the axle are:

- to transmit power from the differential to the wheels
- to support the weight of the vehicle;

Different types can be compared considering the load that the shaft must withstand. The image above shows a line sketch of a simple stem with the following treatments:

- Torsional stress is caused by driving and braking torques.
- Shear stress due to vehicle weight.
- Bending stress due to vehicle weight.
- Tensile and compressive stresses due to cornering forces.

Axle shaft types vary according to vehicle type requirements and each axle shaft withstands different loads. This factor depends on the length of the axle relative to the location of the vehicle's hub and bearings and how the vehicle is designed to be mounted on the axle. These are the three most common axle shaft types.

Calculations of Axle Shaft:

The following forces act on a moving wheel:

- The torque is due to the traction or braking force (T_w and T_b)
- The traction or braking force (F_w and F_b)
- The lateral force (F_y) when the vehicle makes a turn or skid
- The normal reaction, R_w

The simultaneous appearance of maximum transverse and longitudinal forces at the wheel contact is not possible which is restricted by adhesion force for the joint action.

$$"R_w.\emptyset = \sqrt{(F_w^2 + F_y^{2)}}"$$

The loading condition of beams and axle shafts considers the following three cases:

A. Rectilinear motion

The longitudinal force (F_w or F_b) attains its maximum value equal to $R_w\emptyset$, Maximum torque is

$$"T_w = (1/2).T_{emax}.i_g.i_f.k_d(1 + k_l)$$
$$R_w = (1/2)/m_a.g \pm w_t"$$

Where T_w = wheel torque
T_{emax} = maximum engine torque
i_g = gearbox ratio (1st gear)
i_f = final drive ratio
k_d = dynamic factor
k_l = the coefficient of differential locking
m_a = automobile mass accounted for the driving axle
$g = 9.81$ m/s2
w_t = transferred weight

B. Skidding of automobile

In this case, a normal reaction and a lateral force are acting on the wheel.

Assuming that the longitudinal force $F_w = 0$

The largest centrifugal force whose value is limited to wheel-road grips equals to

$$``F_y = F_{yi} + F_{yo} = (m_a.v^2) \, / \, R \times (3.6)^2 = (R_{wi} + R_{wo}).\varnothing"$$

where v = vehicle speed (km/hr)

R = radius of turn of the road

$\varnothing$ = coefficient of adhesion on road during sidewise skidding = 1.0

- = negative sign is used for the axle shaft of the wheel which is outer relative to the skidding direction, and the positive sign, the inner wheel.

C. Driving wheels overcome irregularities

Here, only the vertical force is accounted for

$$``Rw = (m_a.g).k_{dr} \, / \, 2"$$

Where, k_{dr} = is the dynamic factor of road;

for cars, k_{dr} = 1.75; for trucks, k_{dr} = 2.50

The axle shaft dimensions are determined for the most dangerous case of loading. For s half-floating axle, the cress section lies in the bearing installation zone.

For the first condition, the equivalent stress due to torsion and bending is

$$``\sigma_b = \sqrt{(R_w^2.b^2 + F_w^2.b^2 + T_w^2)} \, / \, 0.1d^3"$$

Where, d = the axle shaft diameter

b = the overhanging length

The floating axle for torsion at the maximum traction force is

$$``\tau = T_w \, / \, 0.2d^3"$$

The axle shaft for the maximum twist angle is

$$``\theta^n = (T_w.L/G.J)(180^n/\pi)"$$

Where, L = the length of the axle shaft

G = the shear modulus

J = the moment of inertia of the cross-section of the axle shaft

sb = 55 MPa for shafts without keyway

40 MPa for shafts with keyway

***Note:**

The permissible twist angle, θ = 8o for 1 m length of the shaft.

The number of splines of the axle shaft is from 10 (for cars) to 18 (for trucks)

The shaft factor of safety = 2.0- 2.5

Type of Axles:

A. *Full floating axle:*

It is typically installed in commercial vehicles with high torque and axle loads. The design shown in the diagram consists of an independently mounted hub that rotates on two widely spaced bearings on the axle housing. This arrangement relieves all non-torsional stresses from the shaft, making the structure very strong. The bolt that connects the shaft and hub is used to transmit driving force, and by removing the nut on this bolt, you can pull out the shaft without jacking up the vehicle. The shaft should only transmit drive torque to the rear wheels.

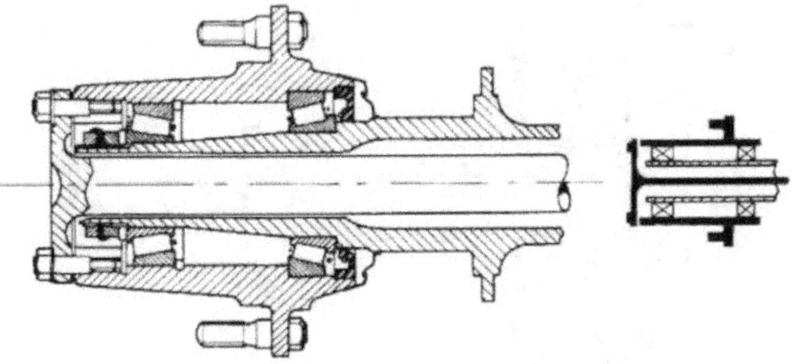

Figure 2.11: Representation of Full Floating Axle

B. *Half floating axle:*

The illustration shows a typical axle shaft installation suitable for light vehicles. A single hub-side bearing is installed between the shaft and housing, so the shaft must withstand all the aforementioned loads. The shaft diameter is increased to reduce the risk of breakage at the hub end (causing the wheel to fall off). Rapid changes in cross-sectional area cause increased stresses, increasing the risk of failure due to fatigue, so the increase should be gradual. (Fatigue can be defined as rupture due to a constant change in stress in a material).

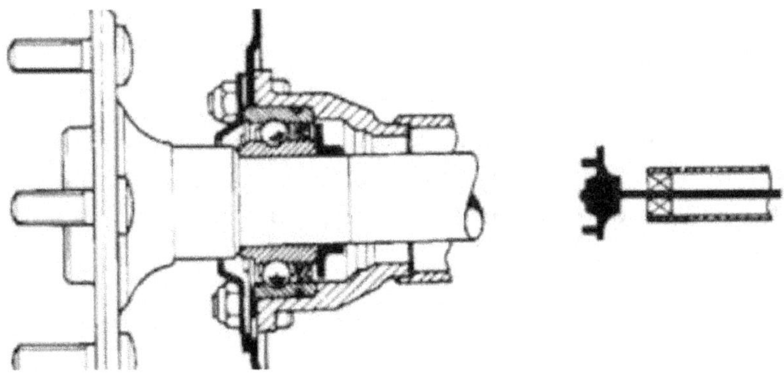

Figure 2.12: Representation of Half Floating Axle

The final drive oil level will be significantly lower than the axle shaft, but the large amount of "splash" will cause the lubricant to work along the shaft and penetrate into the brake drum. The seal assembly usually consists of an oil holder mounted on the hub end (the lip of the seal faces towards the final drive). The half shafts of this assembly must be able to withstand the torsional loads associated with driving the road wheels and the bending loads in both the horizontal and vertical planes plus the proportion of the weight of the vehicle on the wheels.

C. Three-quarter axle:

After semi-floating waves and full-floating waves are defined, the alternative between the two can be considered as 3/4-floating waves. This diagram shows a design with a single bearing mounted between the hub and housing. The main thrust load on the shaft is relieved, but all other loads must still be carried. Half shafts must withstand bending loads from side shifts when cornering and at the same time transmit drive torque.

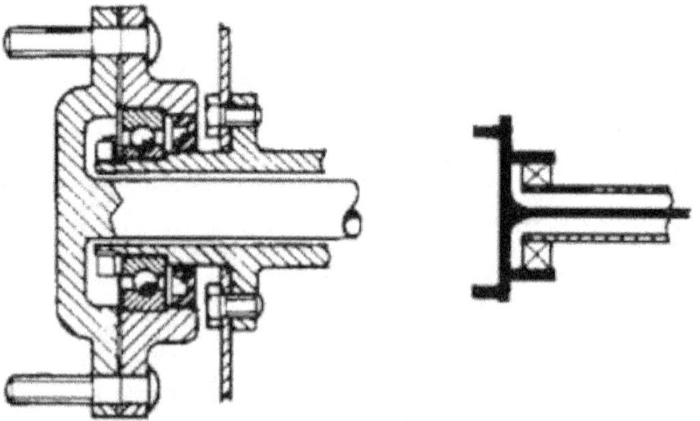

Figure 2.13: Representation of Three quarter Floating Axle

Steering Gear and Steering mechanism design

If the steering wheel were directly connected to the steering linkage, it would take a lot of effort to turn the front wheels. Therefore, a reduction system is used to support drivers. The steering gear is a device that converts the rotary motion of the steering wheel into the linear motion of the linkage with mechanical advantage. The steering gear is housed in a box called a steering gear.

Given below are the eight important steering gears:

A. Recirculating Ball Steering Gear

A recirculating ball gear is more like a worm or ball bearing than a steering gear. Balls are included in the half nut and transmission tube. As the cam or worm rotates, the balls move from one side of the nut to the transmission tube on the other side. Since the nut cannot rotate, the motion of the ball along the path of the cam carries the nut and rotates the rocker arm shaft.

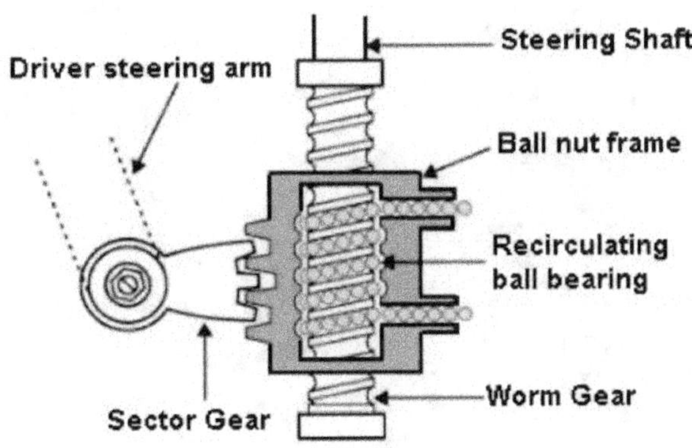

Figure 2.14: Recirculating ball steering gear

B. Rack and Pinion Steering Gear

A rack and pinion steering gear have a pinion attached to the end of the steering shaft. It works in conjunction with a steering rack that has ball joints at each end and allows the wheels to be raised and lowered. A road connects the ball joint to the stub excel. Turning the handle rotates the pinion and moves the rack sideways. The movement of this rack translates into wheels.

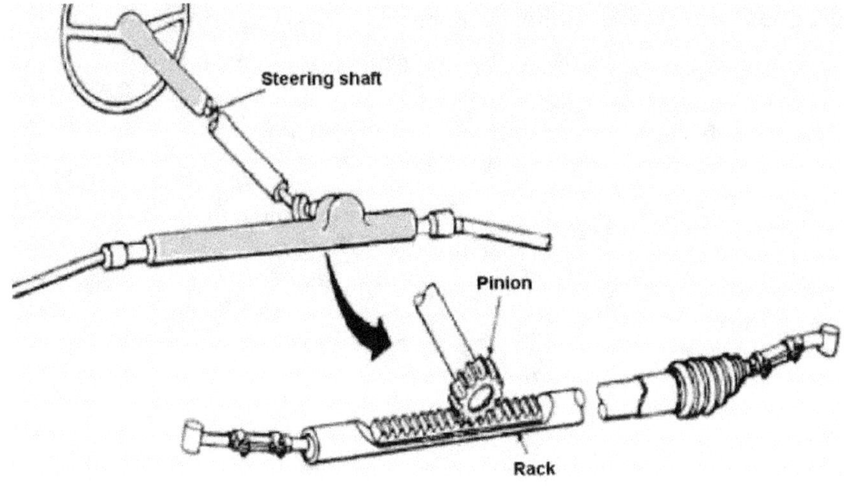

Figure 2.15: Rack and Pinion steering gear

C. Worm and Sector Steering Gear

In a worm sector steering gear, a worm at the end of the steering shaft meshes with a sector attached to the sector shaft. When you turn the handle to turn the worm, turning the sector shaft also turns the sector. That motion is transmitted to the wheels via the linkage. Sector shafts are also called pitman shafts, pitman shafts, roller shafts, steering arm shafts, and cross shafts.

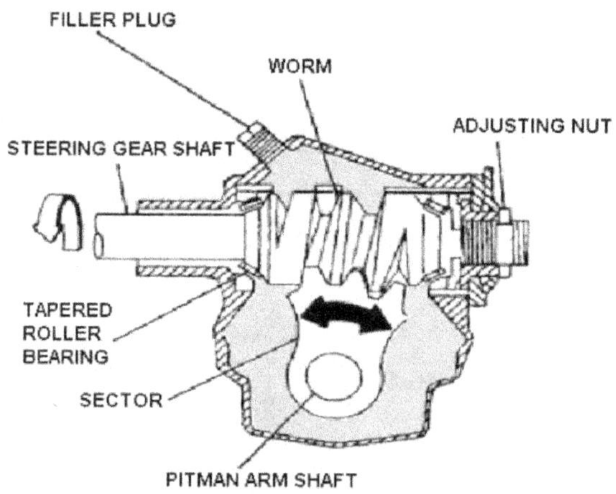

Figure 2.16: Worm and Sector Steering gear

D. Worm and Roller Steering Gear

In worm roller steering, a two-toothed roller is mounted on a sector or roller shaft to engage the threads of a worm wheel or shaft at the end of the steering shaft or steering tube. Rotating the worm shaft causes the rollers to move in an arc to rotate the roller shaft and at the same time rotate the pin that connects the roller and the shaft. The reel is mounted on ball bearings. The worm shaft is mounted on bearings designed to withstand both radial and end thrusts. This type of steering gear is widely used in American passenger cars.

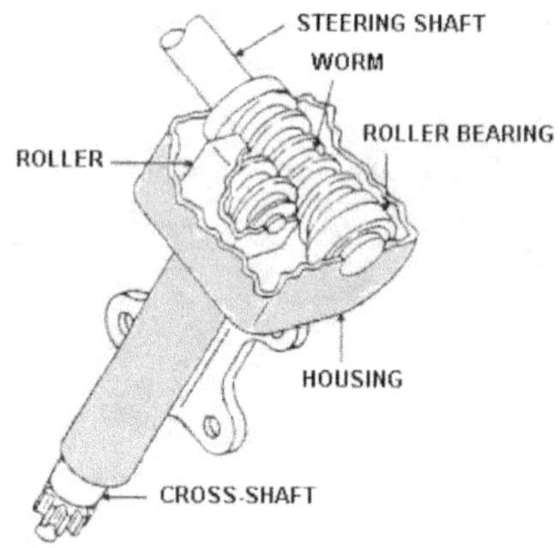

Figure 2.17: Worm and Roller steering gear

E. Worm and Ball Bearing Nut Steering Gear

Steering gear with a worm and ball bearing nut, in which a ball nut is attached to the worm of the steering shaft. The worm and nut have threaded grooves in which steel balls circulate, ensuring a frictionless drive between the worm and nut. Two sets of balls are used, each set working independently of the others. A ball return is attached to the outer surface of the nut. When the steering shaft is turned left and right, the ball rolls between the worm and the nut, causing the ball nut to move up and down. The sector gear attached to the sector shaft meshes with the ball nut and is moved by the ball nut.

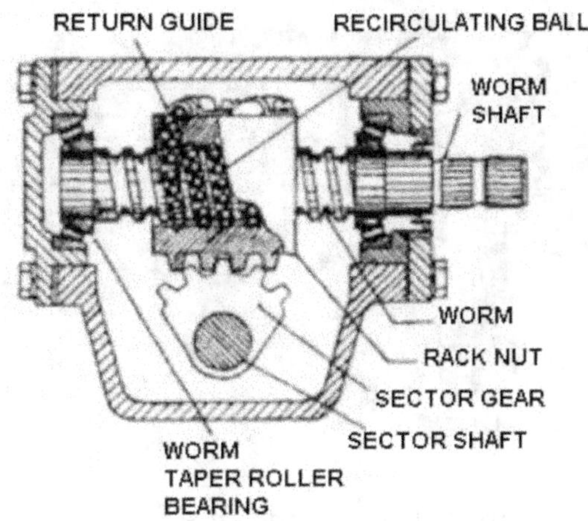

Figure 2.18: Worm and Ball bearing Nut Steering gear

F. Cam and Roller Steering Gear

In cam-and-roller steering, the cams mesh with the rollers. As the cam rotates, the rollers are forced to follow the cam, rotating the rocker arms shaft and moving the drop his arm. The cam profile is designed to mesh with the arc produced by the rollers, thus maintaining a constant depth of engagement and evenly distributing stress and wear between the mating pieces.

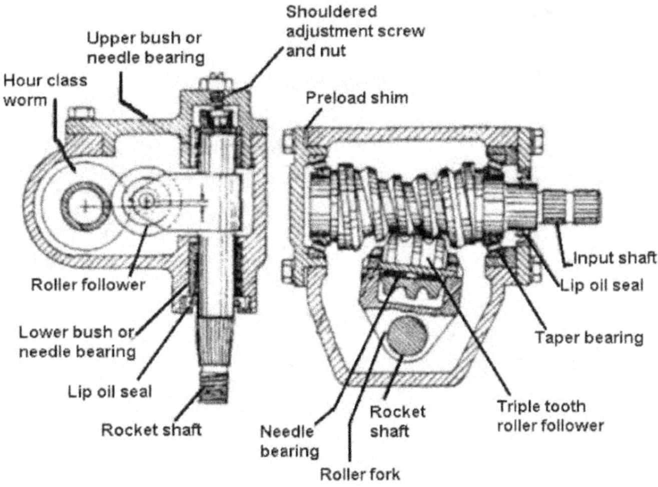

Figure 2.19: Cam and Roller steering gear

G. Cam and Peg Steering Gear

The rocker arm-mounted cam and trunnion steering gear has a tapered trunnion that engages the cam. As the cam rotates, the trunnion moves along the groove and rotates the rocker arm shaft.

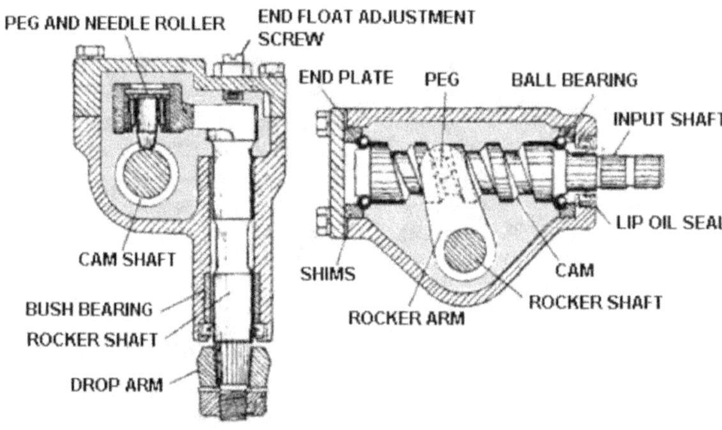

Figure 2.20: Cam and Peg Steering gear

H. Cam and Double Lever Steering Gear

In cam and double-lever steering gears, a special worm called a cam replaces the worm used in both worm sector gears and worm roller gears. The cam is cylindrical and its working part is a variable pitch groove, narrower in the center than at the ends. This provides irreversibility in the middle part of the cam where most of the autosteer occurs. The double lever is mounted on the cross shaft and positioned so that the stubs engage the cams laterally. As the cam rotates, the stub moves along the cam groove, the lever swings in an arc, and the cross shaft rotates.

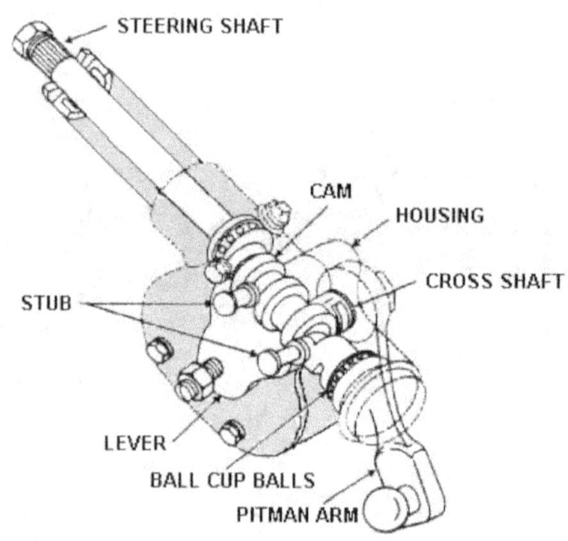

Figure 2.21: Cam and Double Lever Steering gear

Steering Mechanism design:

A steering mechanism is a combination of links and pairs that create a moment and change the direction of the vehicle. Steering is the guidance system of a machine or vehicle to achieve the desired direction or turn the vehicle to the desired side. Mechanisms used to steer or change the direction of a vehicle are called automotive steering mechanisms. There are two types of steering mechanisms in automobiles. They are:

A. Davis steering mechanism:

Davis Steering is one of those steering mechanisms that consist only of a pair of slides. This means that the pair slides in the mechanism while the vehicle is steered. Because Davis steering has more friction than a rotating pair, Davis steering wears quickly and becomes inaccurate after a period of time. This guy is mathematically accurate. The basic equations of this mechanism are satisfied at all positions. By this mechanism, the instantaneous point or intermediate point reaches the center of the wheelbase (l). Therefore, the equation

"$tan\ a = w\ /\ 2l$"

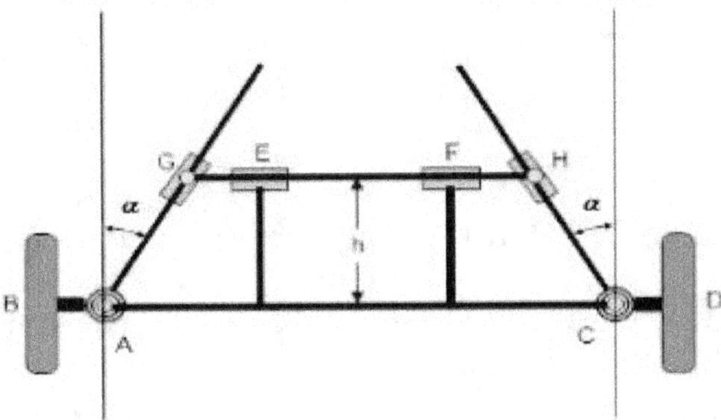

Figure 2.22: Davis steering gear mechanism

Advantage of the Davis steering mechanism:

1. Instead of sticking to a few turns, every position and turn satisfies the basic equation.
2. Davis Steering is a precision steering mechanism.
3. The setup is easy.
4. When turning the steering wheel, all the driver's power is transmitted to the wheels.

B. Ackermann steering mechanism:

Ackermann steering is another type of steering mechanism which have turning pairs and no sliding pairs unlike Davis Steering; because of those turning pairs, the Ackermann steering requires less effort when compared to Davis Mechanism. In this mechanism, the equation can be satisfied only at three given positions in a vehicle. The three positions are as follows:

- When the vehicle moves along a straight path
- When the vehicle is steering to the left correct angle
- When the vehicle is steering at the right correct angle

The mathematical equation for the mechanism is

"tan a = (sin a - sin b) / (cos b + cos a - 2)"

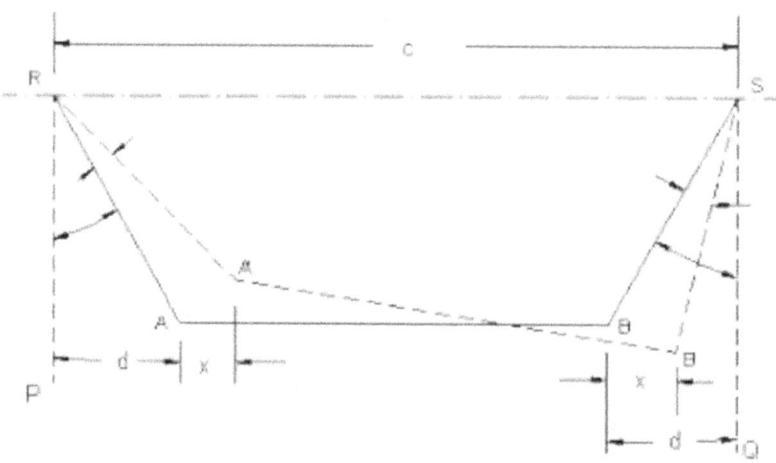

Figure 2.23: Ackermann steering gear mechanism

Ackermann Steering Mechanism, RSAB is a 4-bar chain as shown. Links RA and SB are of equal length and are rigidly connected to the steering knuckle. These links are interconnected via tie rods AB. When the vehicle is in a straight-ahead position, links RA and SB make an angle α equal to the centreline of the vehicle. The dotted line in the figure shows the position of the mechanism when the vehicle makes a left turn.

Let AB = 1 and RA = SB = r

PRA = QSB = α and in $ARA^1 = \theta$ & $BSB^1 = \emptyset$

That is, the knuckles of the inner and outer wheels rotate by angles θ and $\emptyset$ respectively. Ignoring the tilt of the tie rods at the pivot position, the horizontal motions of A and B can be considered equal (x).

"And, sin (α + $\emptyset$) = (d + x) / r and sin (α - $\emptyset$) = (d - x) / r"

"Addition, sin (α + $\emptyset$) + sin (α - $\emptyset$) = 2.d / r = 2.sin α -------- [1]"

The angle α can be determined using the formula above. The values of θ and $\emptyset$ used in this equation were determined for correct steering using the equations,

"cot $\emptyset$ − cot θ = w/L -----------[2]"

This mechanism provides precise steering in just three positions. One for θ = 0 and the other two for rotation to the right or left respectively (fixed rotation angles determined by Equation [1]). The correct values of $\emptyset$, [$\emptyset_c$] corresponding to different values of θ for correct steering can be determined using equation [2]. For a given dimension of the mechanism, the actual value of $\emptyset$ [$\emptyset_a$] can be obtained for different values of θ. The difference between $\emptyset_c$ and $\emptyset_a$ is very small for small angles of θ but large for large values of θ. Such a difference increases slip wear and shorten tire life.

But as the value of θ increases, the car has to turn sharper. Therefore, it moves slowly. At low speeds, tire wear is reduced. Therefore, a large difference between $\emptyset_c$ and $\emptyset_a$ is less of a problem for larger values of θ.

The mechanism uses only rotating couples, resulting in less friction and wear on the mechanism. Therefore, it is easy to maintain and is widely used in automobiles.

Advantages of Ackermann steering mechanism:

1. It requires less effort to operate due to its turning pairs.
2. It acquires fewer tear and wears problems.

• • •

CHAPTER III

Design of Brakes and Suspension

Brakes are mechanical devices used in mechanical systems to stop or reduce motion. Most brakes use a mechanism to convert kinetic energy into heat. Brakes are used to slow down or stop moving wheels, vehicles, or mechanical parts. Brakes come in a variety of styles and sizes, and the type you choose depends on your space, cost, and application.

Most brakes and braking systems act on rotating moving elements in mechanical systems. They reduce or stop the body by reducing or slowing movement. Brakes absorb kinetic energy in the body using either electrical, mechanical, or hydraulic methods. The kinetic energy of the moving parts is converted into heat energy when the brakes slow down the moving object. Because of this, the brakes may smoke in extreme situations. A regenerative braking system can later use this energy by converting some of the kinetic energy into electrical energy.

The most common type of braking system encountered is the mechanical braking system. A mechanical braking system absorbs the kinetic energy of a moving object and converts it into thermal energy. Brakes eventually wear out and need to be replaced because of the machinery. A mechanical link is attached from one end of the braking system to the other. In a car, when someone depresses the brake pedal, the braking system engages and exerts pressure on the spinning wheel discs or drums.

Factors Affecting Braking Effectiveness:

The effectiveness of braking is determined by the following factors:

Pressure: The friction that occurs between two contact surfaces depends in part on the applied force. In a vehicle, the fluid in the cylinder exerts the forces necessary to create friction. This force brings the brake shoe into contact with the handle drum.

Heat dissipation: When braking, the lost kinetic energy is converted into heat. The resulting heat must be dissipated. Failure to do so could damage the brake shoes and other nearby components. This heat is dissipated with the help of air flowing through the wheels.

Coefficient of friction: The amount of friction between two contacting surfaces depends on the friction coefficient. The higher the coefficient of friction value, the greater the amount of friction. However, the maximum friction coefficient is limited to 1 and depends on the material properties and surface roughness. Apply the brakes a few times to smooth out the surface. The coefficient of friction is reduced and the frictional force is reduced accordingly. In this case, replace the brake shoe with a new one with a rough surface. The coefficient of friction equals the force required to pull an object divided by its weight.

Contact area: The friction force depends on the contact area. The larger the contact area, the greater the force. The area can be increased by having larger rim brakes and placing them on all four wheels.

Types of automotive braking systems:

Automotive braking systems can be divided into the following categories:

- Mechanical brake
- Disc brake
- Hydraulic brake
- Power-assisted booster
- Air brake
- Electric
- Handbrake system

Internal Expanding shoe brake

Internal wheel brakes are used almost exclusively as wheel brakes but can be found on some cranes. This type of brake allows for a more compact and cost-effective design. The brake shoes and brake operating mechanism are mounted on a backing plate or backplate attached to the axle as shown in the diagram. Attached to the rotating wheel, the brake drum acts as a cover for the shoes and actuation mechanism, providing a friction surface for the brake shoes.

Construction of Internal expanding shoe brake:

The structure of the internal expanding shoe brake is shown in the figure. It consists of a shoe that pivots at one end and receives an actuation force P at the other end. A friction lining is secured to the shoe and the complete shoe, lining, and pivot assembly is inserted into the brake drum. Internal shoe brakes with two symmetrical shoes are used in all automobiles. Actuation force is typically provided by a hydraulic cylinder or cam mechanism. Internal shoe brake analysis is based on the following assumptions:

1. The normal pressure strength between the friction lining and the brake drum at any point is proportional to the vertical distance from the pivot.
2. Hard brake drums and shoes.
3. The centrifugal force acting on the shoe is negligible.
4. The coefficient of friction is constant.

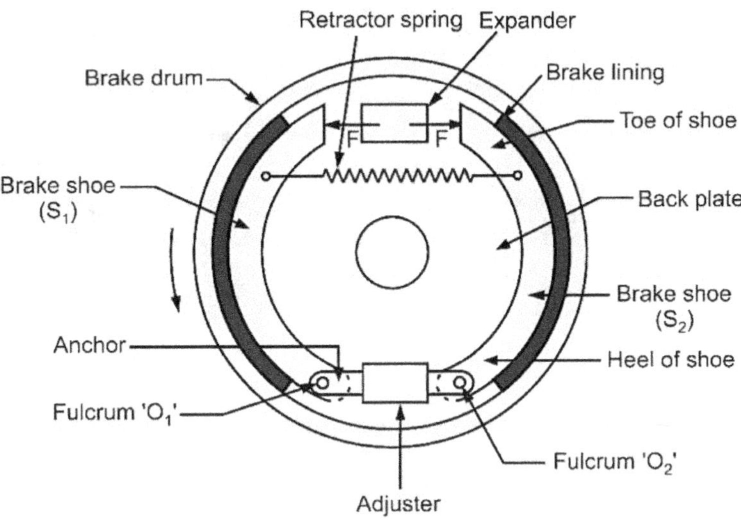

Figure 3.1: Architecture of Internal expanding shoe brake

The brake shoes of the internal extended brake are pressed outwards against the drum to create the braking effect. One end of the shoe is pivoted to the support plate by an anchor pin, while the other end is free and can be moved within the mount by an operating mechanism. When force is applied to the free end of the shoe by the operating mechanism, the shoe extends and brakes the wheel. A return spring returns the shoe to its original position when the brake is no longer needed, consisting of two shoes S1 and S2. The outer surface of the shoe is lined with a friction material to increase the coefficient of friction and prevent metal wear. Each shoe rotates about fixed pivot points O1 and O2 at one end and contacts a cam at the other end. As the cam rotates, the shoe presses against the rim of the drum. Friction between the shoe and the drum creates braking torque, slowing the drum. The shoe is normally held in the off position by a spring. The drum surrounds the entire mechanism and keeps out dust and moisture. This type of brake is commonly used on cars and light trucks.

Now let's look at the forces acting on such a brake when the drum rotates counterclockwise. When counterclockwise, the left shoe is called the front or primary shoe and the right shoe is called the rear or secondary shoe.

Design of Internal expanding shoe brake:

Consider an elemental area on the mechanical/friction lining located at an angle Ø and understand an angle dØ. The elemental area will be (RdØw)
, where w is the width of the lining to the brake drum axis.

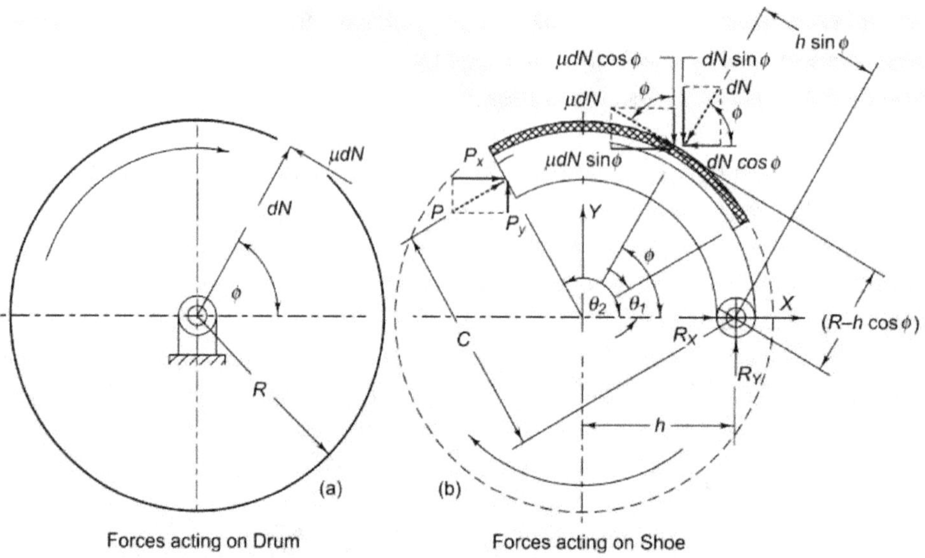

Figure 3.2: Free body diagram of all the forces

If p is the intensity of normal pressure, the normal reaction dN is given by,

$$\text{"}dN = pRwd\emptyset \text{ -------------(1)"}$$

As mentioned above, the normal pressure p is directly proportional to the vertical distance (RsinØ) of the elemental part from the pivot. Therefore,

$$\text{"}p\alpha sin\emptyset \text{ or } p = C1\ sin\emptyset \text{ --------------(2)"}$$

$$\text{"}Assuming\ p = p_{max}\ ,\ when\ \emptyset = \emptyset_{max}\ we\ have,$$
$$P_{max} = C1\ sin\phi_{max} \text{ -------------(3)"}$$

From equations (2) and (3),

$$\text{"}P = p_{max}\ sin\ \emptyset\ /sin\ \emptyset\ _{max}\text{"}$$

where p is the intensity of normal pressure.

Advantages of the internal expanding shoe brake:

Internal expanding shoe braking has the following advantages:

1. Simple structure with few parts. Inexpensive compared to other types of brakes.
2. The number of parts is small and the reliability is high.
3. Requires little maintenance;
4. With internal extended braking, a small actuation force can generate a large braking torque. (v) provide protection against foreign material intrusion.

Disadvantages of internal expanding shoe brakes:

The disadvantages of internal diffusion braking are:

1. Relatively low heat dissipation capability;
2. Self-locking due to wear if not properly designed.

Application of internal expanding shoe brake:

Internal extended brakes are mainly used for vehicles, conveyors, and hoists. Hydraulic braking systems are commonly used for automotive braking in passenger cars, trucks, and buses. It uses hydraulic fluid as the medium to transfer power from the brake pedal to the wheel brakes. Below are some guidelines for designing vehicle brakes.

- The maximum force exerted by a woman in the 5th percentile is 22 N, approximately 42 N for men. Therefore, from ergonomics, the braking system should be designed for maximum pedaling force, 22 degrees 25 degrees north latitude. With the booster, the pedal force is up to 11×17N.
- For ergonomic reasons, pedal travel should not exceed 150mm;
- The braking system should be designed to achieve 1g deceleration (i.e. 9.81m/s2) when fully loaded.

Braking conditions and calculations

A. Energy absorbed by brake:

The energy absorbed by the brakes depends on the type of motion of the moving body. Body motion can be either pure translation or pure rotation, or a combination of translation and rotation. The energy associated with movement is kinetic energy. Consider these requests as follows:

1. When body movement is a pure translation:

Imagine an object of mass (m) moving with a velocity of v1m/s. his speed decreased to v2m/s when braking. Therefore, the change in kinetic energy is the kinetic energy of the translation body or translation,

$$\text{``}E_1 = (1/2)m[v_1^2 - v_2^2]\text{''}$$

This energy must be absorbed by the brake. If the moving body is stopped after brakes are applied, then $v_2 = 0$,

$$"E_1 = (1/2)m(v_1)^2"$$

where E_1 is the change in kinetic energy after brakes are applied.

2. When body movement is a pure rotation:

Imagine a moment of inertia I (about a given axis) rotating about its axis with angular velocity ω_1 rad/s. Angular velocity can be reduced to ω_2 rad/s after braking. Therefore, the change in kinetic energy is the kinetic energy of a rotating body or rotation,

$$"E_2 = (1/2)I[(\omega_1)^2 - (\omega_2)^2]"$$

This energy must be absorbed by the brake. If the moving body is stopped after brakes are applied, then $\omega_2 = 0$,

$$"E_2 = (1/2)I[\omega_1]^2"$$

where E_2 is the change in kinetic energy of a rotating body after brakes are applied.

3. When body motion is a combination of translation and rotation:

Imagine an object that has both linear and angular motion. The driving wheels of a locomotive and the wheels of a moving car. In such cases, the total kinetic energy of the object is equal to the sum of its translational and rotational kinetic energies,

$$"W = E_1 + E_2"$$

where, W is the total kinetic energy

B. Heat dissipated during braking:

The energy absorbed by the brakes and converted to heat must be dissipated into the surrounding air to avoid excessive heating of the brake pads. Heating depends on the mass of the brake drum, braking time, and the heat dissipation capacity of the brake. Recommended maximum allowable temperatures for various brake pad materials are:

- For leather, textile, and wood top layers = 65 -70°C
- For lightly lubricated asbestos and metal surfaces = 90 −105 °C
- For car brakes with asbestos blocks = 180 − 225 °C

This is an important factor in brake design because the energy absorbed (or heat generated) at a given speed and the rate of brake pad wear depend on the normal pressure between the braking surfaces. The permissible normal pressure between the braking surfaces depends on the material of the brake linings, the coefficient of friction, and the maximum energy absorbed.

Mechanical Lining materials

Materials used for brake pads should have the following properties:

- High coefficient of friction and minimal fading. This means that the coefficient of friction must remain constant across the surface as the temperature changes.
- Low wear rate.
- The coefficient of thermal expansion should be small.
- High heat dissipation capacity.
- Sufficient mechanical strength is required.
- High heat resistance.

Classification of brakes

A. Mechanical brake:

These brakes are actuated by mechanical means such as pedals, springs, or levers. Mechanical brakes are the most commonly used type of braking system. Mechanical brakes are commonly used on equipment that rotates on fixed pads and rolling wear surfaces. There are mainly two types of mechanical braking systems in common use: drum brakes and disc brakes. Drum brakes used on some vehicles are rotating drums with brake shoes that expand with heat and scrape the inside of the drum. A disc brake is another type of mechanical brake that uses pads to hold a rotating disc in place.

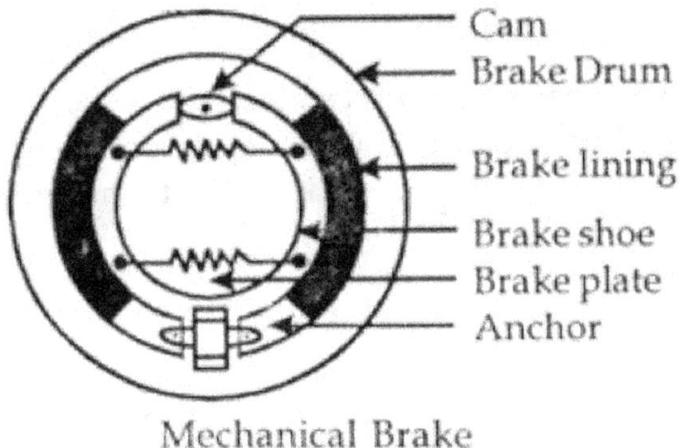

Figure 3.3: Architecture of Mechanical Brake

The capacity of mechanical brakes depends on the following factors:

- Uniform pressure between braking surfaces
- Brake heat dissipation capacity
- The contact area of the braking surface
- Machine factor
- Brake drum radius

Type of mechanical brake:

According to the shape of the mechanical material, mechanical brakes can be further classified:

- Block brake
- Disc brake
- External and internal shoe brakes

Advantages of mechanical brakes:

1. Easy structure and maintenance
2. Suitable for emergency braking and parking braking.
3. Inexpensive compared to hydraulic brakes

Disadvantages of mechanical brakes:

1. Uneven heat dissipation.
2. Wear occurs on the braking surface.
3. Less effective than hydraulic brakes.

B. Hydraulic and pneumatic brake

A brake system that uses brake fluid, cylinders, and friction. Pressure builds up in the system, creating a force that pushes against the brake pads and keeps the system from moving. Hydraulic systems are used in most automobiles today as they greatly reduce the chance of brake failure. This is due to the direct connection between the actuator and the disc/drum.

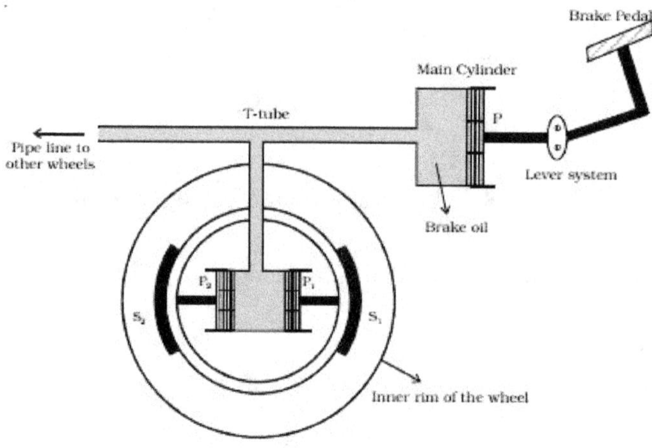

Figure 3.4: Architecture of Hydraulic brake

Advantages of hydraulic and pneumatic brakes:

1. More effective than mechanical brakes
2. More thorough heat dissipation than mechanical brakes
3. Durable due to low wear.
4. Each tire has the same braking power.

Disadvantages of hydraulic and pneumatic brakes:

1. Brake fluid may leak and damage the brakes.
2. Construction and maintenance are not as easy as mechanical brakes.
3. More expensive than mechanical brakes.
4. The fluid used must be compatible with the brake material.

C. Electric brake

These brakes work on the principle of electromagnetic force. These types of brakes are typically used when an electric motor is used as part of the machine. Eddy current brakes are a type of electromagnetic brake. They consist of a magnetic yoke with coils arranged along rails that are alternately magnetized between the north and south poles. As the magnet moves along the track, it creates an unsteady magnetic field. This creates a voltage that creates eddy currents. Eddy currents perturb the magnetic field and deflect the magnetic force in the opposite direction. This creates a horizontal force component that impedes the motion of the magnet. Since the electromagnetic brake does not contact the rail, it has the advantage of not generating rail wear, noise, or odor.

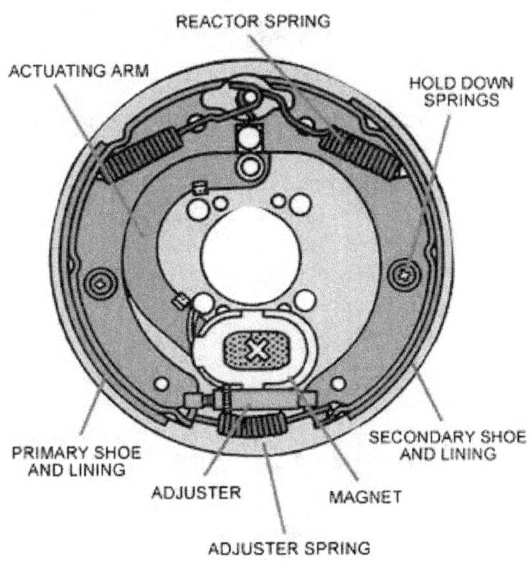

Figure 3.5: Architecture of Electric brake

Given below are the following types of electric brakes:

- Eddy's current braking
- Hysteresis brake
- Magnetic powder brake

Advantages of electric brakes:

1. They are fast
2. Low maintenance costs
3. Smooth operation

Disadvantages of electric brakes:

1. Works only while driving. This means that if you have to park your vehicle on downhill, you should use the mechanical brakes. Otherwise, the vehicle will descend downwards due to gravity.
2. High acquisition cost.
3. Not suitable for high temperatures.

Reasons for failure of brakes:

- Brakes can fail for many reasons. It is essential to take care of your braking system by performing maintenance and replacement as necessary. We'll look at the most common reasons why they can fail.
- Leaking brake fluid. A brake fluid leak is usually noticed by noticing a puddle of fluid under the vehicle or near the braking system. Do not use the vehicle or machine until the leak has been repaired and the brake fluid has been replenished.
- Defective parts can cause the braking system to fail. High-quality components should always be used within the braking system.
- *Brake wear:* Braking systems use friction to slow mechanical parts. Friction wears parts.
- The brake pads tear.
- Water ingress into the electric brake system.
- Lack of hydraulic oil.
- Broken or broken brake lines.

Design of Suspension

Springs are the basis of suspension systems. This allows the wheels to move up and down with minimal impact on the chassis and the rest of the vehicle. However, the spring's primary role is to hold the weight of the vehicle and its cargo. Springs, whether leaf, torsion, or coil, must compensate for road bumps, keep the suspension system at its specified height, and support the additional weight without excessive slack. Each of these features is critical to providing comfort, precise handling, and durability in modern vehicles.

The most common measurement for off-road vehicle springs is their spring rate. This is usually expressed in pounds per inch (lbs/in). Which defines how many pounds it takes to compress spring one inch. Spring frequency is another measure of springs, but it's not very useful to us as we rarely see aftermarket springs with frequency weighting. The higher the spring rate (higher number), the more weight it takes to compress the spring and the more weight the spring can hold. Spring rates can vary greatly for the same application and stroke.

The spring constant is determined mainly by the thickness of the steel used for the spring. The thicker the diameter of the coil spring, the higher the rate. Also, the thicker the individual leaves in the leaf spring package, the higher the rate. The grade of steel also affects the spring rate, but the use of special ones is not common for lift springs.

Historically, steel disc springs are one of the oldest and most widely used spring designs in suspension systems. Leaf springs have many advantages as they attach the axle directly to the chassis in addition to acting as a spring. Some applications use a single "mono leaf" spring. While leaf springs are typically used in truck applications with full-drive axles, transverse leaf springs can be combined with an independently suspended rear axle to form a lightweight rear suspension system for high-performance road vehicles. Leaf springs can also be tuned for different load capacities and ride control needs by changing the number, thickness, width, and length of the spring leaves.

Types of springs used in suspension system:

A. Leaf Spring

Leaf springs provide the vehicle's suspension system. Dating back to the Middle Ages, it was originally called the Carriage or Lamellar Spring. Leaf spring systems were tried and tested and were used on almost all vehicles until the 1970s. Today, leaf springs are most useful in trucks and vans that carry heavy loads.

Spring leaves are arched strips of steel stacked and bolted together using the same material in smaller sizes. Its structure creates a reinforced bow-like element. It is then attached to the rear axle and chassis. It supports the added weight of the vehicle and prevents it from buckling or breaking under extreme weight pressures that axles are not designed to withstand.

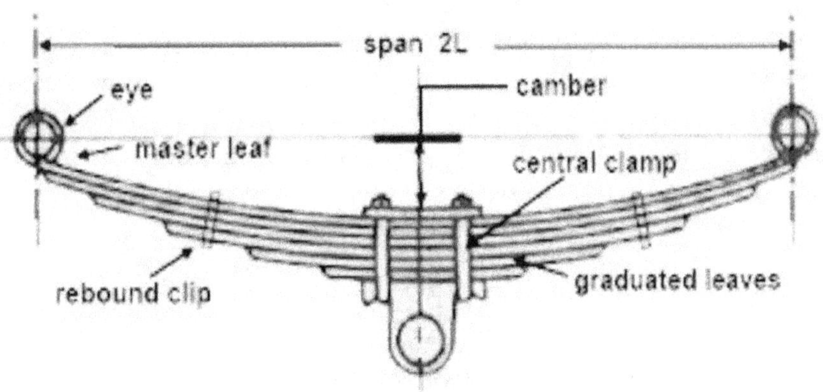

Figure 3.6: Illustration of Leaf Spring

A common purpose of leaf springs is to support a vehicle. It also provides a smoother ride and absorbs road bumps and potholes. In addition, leaf springs are used to position axles, control vehicle height, and align tires on the road. Leaf springs are in great demand due to their advantages. Unscheduled shipments are just one of the ways leaf springs have contributed to the transportation industry. Leaf springs are now popular in heavy-duty vehicles such as trucks, SUVs, and vans.

Advantages of leaf springs:

1. With so many layers of metal, leaf springs provide great support between the car's wheels, axles, and chassis. Due to the dense mesh structure, it can absorb very large vertical loads. As such, it is still used today in heavy-duty industries. Vertical loads are also distributed along the length of the leaf springs rather than abruptly through the small springs and dampers, which can create too much concentration in the suspension.
2. In cars, damping is a very important characteristic. With insufficient suspension damping, the car rolls and bounces after hitting a bump or pothole in the road. This was an important feature in cars that used coil springs before shock absorbers came along and were detrimental to the car when driven at real speed. It dealt with dumping much better. This made the car much more controllable with much faster reaction times after vertical flexing of the suspension.
3. Simpler in design and cheaper to manufacture than early springs and dampers, leaf springs were the go-to choice for cost-saving reliability when cars were fully mass-produced. . Monoleaf springs are the simplest design of the lot, consisting of spring steel that tapers from a thicker center to thinner ends (known as a parabolic leaf spring) for proper vertical load distribution.) was used. However, the single-leaf set-up could only be used on very light vehicles due to the lack of strength in the bars.

Disadvantages of leaf springs:

1. The main downside to the Leaf's setup is that it isn't great when it comes to suspension tuning. In racing and performance car applications, it is important to be able to manipulate the suspension set-up to suit driving conditions and different driving styles. This is a lot easier these days with adjustable ride heights. This lack of adjustability in the blade assembly means that the leaf spring ends are clamped to the chassis, allowing the blade to be shortened or lengthened. Emphasized by the fact that there is little room. Adjustments can therefore only be made through the strength and flexibility of the leaf spring material.
2. Also, while the blades cannot move in most directions and are actually designed to move vertically, manipulating the combination of springs and dampers allows them to have a much wider range of motion. The leaf springs are rigidly attached to the chassis, bolted, and clipped to the axle, leaving little to no room to move in other directions, resulting in excessive wear on the pivots and linkages that hold the setup together. may occur.
3. This connection with the live rear axle can cause the car to have strange dynamic characteristics compared to the more modern independent suspension that older Mustangs are famous for. The rear axle only bounces in high-speed corners as the suspension and axle are forced to move together, but the modern damping system makes the driving experience much more poised.
4. Compared to coil springs, leaf springs are generally much stiffer due to their steel construction and tight bolted package. Ride quality is therefore not a feature of vehicles using leaf springs after proper dampers were cost-effectively introduced into everyday vehicles in the 1970s.

B. Coil Spring

A coil spring is a helical mechanical device that is wound in a closed or open state. This is a helix or spiral of metal wire, usually made of steel. Spring is a mechanical device that absorbs weight or force from an object to prevent surface damage. Coil springs work by storing and releasing energy, absorbing shock, and maintaining force between two surfaces. Applying too much force can stretch the spring beyond its limits and permanently deform it.

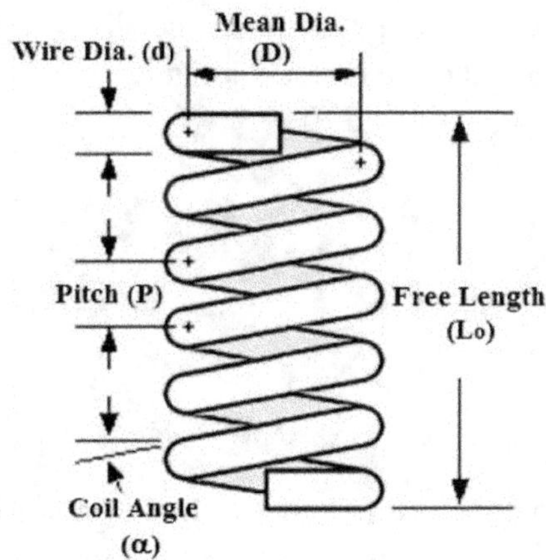

Figure 3.7: Illustration of Coil Spring

Compression coil springs are designed to push back against a surface upon contact. They provide resistance to compressive forces and are usually wound as cylinders of constant diameter or the same size as the spiral geometry. A telescopic spring pulls in two planes, like a screen door spring that closes a door after it has been opened. Coil springs are also called torsion springs. Coil springs come in many designs and use. In 1857, the first steel spiral spring was produced for an armchair. Today, coil springs are used in countless everyday items such as:

- Watch
- Automobile suspension systems and clutches
- Retractable pin
- Door handles, fans, toaster

Advantages of Coil Springs:

1. *Coil springs are lightweight:* Coil springs are surprisingly light for their performance. Coiled steel makes the spring stronger than metal if it retains its original straight shape. The heating and lapping process also helps strengthen the metal, allowing you to use less metal to hold more weight.
2. *Coil springs are cheap:* Most springs are made of steel or other cheap metals. These metals are easy to find everywhere and the cost of metal is low. With very little metal flowing into each spring, coil springs are one of the most economical alternatives for all types of applications.
3. *Coil springs are maintenance-free:* Coil springs are maintenance-free. Springs don't need to be lubricated, cleaned, specially coated, or cared for to work. The only problem that can arise with springs is that they can sometimes break. However, if the coil spring breaks, it can be easily fixed.
4. *Coil Springs Are Versatile:* There are hundreds of types of coil springs that coil spring manufacturers can use for a variety of applications. You can choose from tension springs, compression springs, and torsion springs according to your application. Each coil spring provides a unique service to your tool, making your tool or machine easier to work with.

Disadvantages of Coil Springs:

1. Due to the weight of the vehicle, it is not as suitable for large vehicles as leaf springs.
2. Prone to cracking and breaking under excessive pressure, especially if slightly corroded
3. Other improvements may be needed to make the coil last longer.

Types of materials used for Spring

Stainless steel:

- Commonly used in springs, this material is ideal for environments requiring greater corrosion or heat resistance. This steel alloy has a chromium content of at least 10.5% and at most 1.2%. There are several different grades of stainless steel, each with its own properties and types: austenitic, martensitic, and precipitation hardening.
- Austenitic stainless steel is hardened by cold working and is suitable for applications where corrosion resistance is required. Martensitic stainless steel also has good corrosion resistance, and low electrical conductivity, but strong magnetism. and precipitation-hardened stainless steels can crack under stress, but have high tensile strength and high fatigue resistance.
- It is a very popular and versatile spring alloy used in a variety of markets and sectors including architecture, arts, aerospace, chemical processing, food, and transportation.

High carbon steel:

- It is also a very popular alloy used to make feathers. Carbon steel has a maximum carbon content of 2.1%. The higher this percentage, the stronger the alloy. The properties of this material can provide excellent hardness and wear resistance, making it suitable for springs.
- Hardwire is cheaper for light-duty applications, but high tensile materials are best suited for heavy-duty applications and are more expensive.
- High-carbon steels are less ductile and more brittle than metals like steel, making them unsuitable for environments where flexibility is a concern.

Nickel alloy:

- Nickel is a versatile material that can be alloyed with a wide variety of metals, making it ideal for a variety of environments where resistance to corrosion and high temperatures is required.
- Nickel alloys typically offer high levels of strength and durability, maintaining reliability even in the most demanding environments such as chemical plants and oil platforms.
- Nickel-based alloys are also commonly found where sub-zero temperature applications are required, and their non-magnetic properties allow them to be used in gauges and gyroscopes.
- Cobalt-nickel alloys are often chosen when stainless steel is not sufficient. These alloys are strong, durable, ductile, corrosion, and wear-resistant.

Suspension system and linkages:

For many people who value ride comfort, the suspension system may look like just a set of springs and shock absorbers that connect the wheels to the vehicle's body. However, this is a very simplified aspect of the suspension system. is. A vehicle suspension system ensures that the wheels remain in contact with the ground, minimizing vehicle roll while providing a smooth ride over rough roads. A suspension system consists of three parts: the structure that supports the weight of the vehicle and determines the shape of the suspension, the springs that convert kinetic energy into potential energy and vice versa, and the shock absorbers, which are mechanical devices designed to absorb impacts. consists of one main part. Kinetic energy dissipates energy.

A vehicle's suspension connects the vehicle's wheels to the body while supporting the weight of the vehicle. Allows relative motion between the wheel and body. Theoretically, the suspension system should reduce the degrees of freedom (DOF) of the wheels from 6 to 2 at the rear and 3 at the front, but the suspension system should support propulsion, steering, braking, and related forces. there is. The relative motion of the wheels is vertical motion due to steering angle, rotational motion about the lateral axis, and rotational motion about the vertical axis.

As mentioned earlier, it's easy to think that the sole function of the suspension system is to absorb road bumps. However, due to various operating conditions, vehicle suspensions must meet many requirements with conflicting goals. The suspension connects the car body to the ground, so all forces and moments between the two pass through the suspension system. The suspension system therefore directly influences the dynamic behavior of the vehicle. Automotive engineers typically use three key principles to examine suspension system function.

Ride comfort: Ride comfort is defined based on how passengers feel in a moving vehicle. The most common task for suspension systems is road isolation. In other words, it isolates the car body from road disturbances. In general, ride comfort can be quantified by the level of vibration inside the vehicle. Vehicles have many internal and external sources of vibration. Internal sources of vibration include the vehicle's engine and transmission, while road bumps and aerodynamic forces are external sources. The vibration spectrum is divided into frequency ranges and classified as pleasant (0-25 Hz) or loud and harsh (25-20,000 Hz).

Handling: A good suspension system should ensure that the vehicle remains stable in any maneuver. But perfect handling is more than just stability. The vehicle must respond proportionally to driver input and smoothly follow braking, steering, and acceleration commands. Vehicle behavior must be predictable and behavior information must be communicated to the driver accordingly. Suspension systems can affect vehicle handling in a number of ways. It can minimize vehicle roll and pitch, control wheel angle, and reduce lateral load transfer when cornering.

Road holding: Forces at the point of contact between the wheels and the road act on the car body via the suspension system. One of the most important functions of a suspension system is load hold, as the magnitude and direction of forces determine vehicle behavior and performance. The lateral and longitudinal forces produced by tires are directly related to normal tire forces and aid in cornering, traction, and braking ability. These terms improve when normal tire load variations are minimized. Another function of the suspension is to support the static weight of the vehicle. Minimizing the rattling space requirements in the vehicle suffices to solve this challenge.

Components of suspension system:

The suspension system in a vehicle is made up of four components namely: mechanism, shock absorber, linkages, spring, and bushing. These components are explained in detail below:

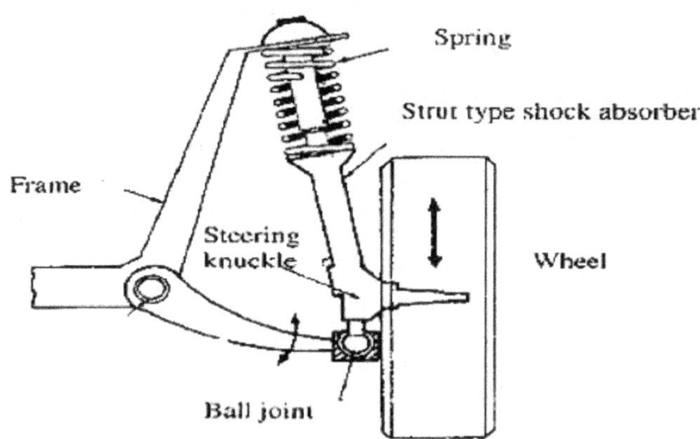

Figure 3.8: Main Components of Suspension System

Mechanism: Suspension mechanisms may include one or more arms that connect the wheels to the vehicle body. They transmit all forces and moments in different directions between the car body and the ground. Mechanisms determine some of the most important characteristics of suspension systems. This determines the shape of the suspension and the angle of the wheels and their relative movement. As the wheel angle changes during suspension travel, tire forces change, affecting road holding and vehicle handling. The main weight of the suspension system comes from its mechanics. Using heavier materials in its construction will reduce ride quality, while lighter materials will improve ride quality but are more expensive.

Shock Absorber: A shock absorber is a mechanical or hydraulic device designed to dampen impulses. High-damping shock absorbers instantly attenuate impacts at the expense of vehicle ride quality, improving handling and road-holding.

Spring: A spring is typically a coiled wire or series of metal strips that have elastic properties. It supports the weight of the vehicle and creates a suspension that the passengers can withstand. To best understand suspension behavior, the most important component to study is the spring. However, there is a contradiction in meaning. With stiffer springs, the vehicle exhibits good road holding and handling, but ride comfort is significantly reduced. This creates a constraint on choosing a suitable spring constant. The weight and size of the spring can also make this adjustment difficult.

Bushings: Bushings prevent direct contact between two metal objects, isolating noise and minimizing vibration. Soft materials such as rubber are used for insulating bushings. In fact, they are a type of anti-vibration device used to connect various moving parts to the car body or suspension frame. There are many types of bushings, classified according to the degrees of freedom between the two connecting parts they support. Swivel joints are the most common type of bushing.

Linkages: The rigid links used in suspension systems to connect the vehicle's main frame to the steering knuckles of the wheels with mechanical fasteners are known as control arms. The rigid links used in suspension systems to connect the vehicle's main frame to the steering knuckles of the wheels with mechanical fasteners are known as control arms.

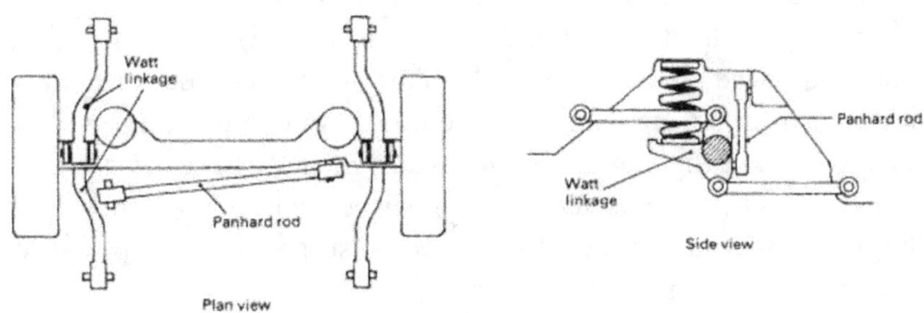

Figure 3.9: Overview of Linkages

1. *Wishbone or A-arm:* It is a type of A-shaped mechanical linkage, where the pointed end of the A-arm is attached to the steering knuckle, and the other two ends of the A-arm are attached to the vehicle's main frame. Single A-arms or dual A-arms are used, depending on the vehicle application.
2. *Rigid axle or rigid axle:* This is the type of linkage used to connect the vehicle's main frame to the steering knuckle of the wheel. This is a robust axle housing that supports the total weight of the vehicle.
3. *Multiple linkages:* Instead of double wishbones and solid axle linkages, various luxury vehicles use multi-link suspension. It uses several solid links to connect the vehicle's main frame to the wheel knuckles.

Types of Suspension System:

A. Independent suspension system

This system means that the suspension is set so that the left and right wheels move up and down independently when driving over uneven surfaces. The same vehicle has no mechanical connection between the two hubs, so forces acting on one wheel do not affect the other.Independent suspension mainly consists of a linkage that connects the wheel carrier to the vehicle body, coil springs, and shock absorbers. The left and right suspensions of the axle are mirror images of each other. A strut mount allows the shock absorber to also act as part of the linkage, greatly reducing the number of components required. In general, independent wheel suspension allows the wheels to move nearly vertically in response to road disturbances. Springs and shock absorbers act as control devices with the competing functions of reducing body acceleration, improving drivability, and keeping the tires on the ground to improve drivability. Other effects on the ride and handling include wheel position and wheel travel settings, and how the suspension reacts to cornering, braking, riding, and bump loading.

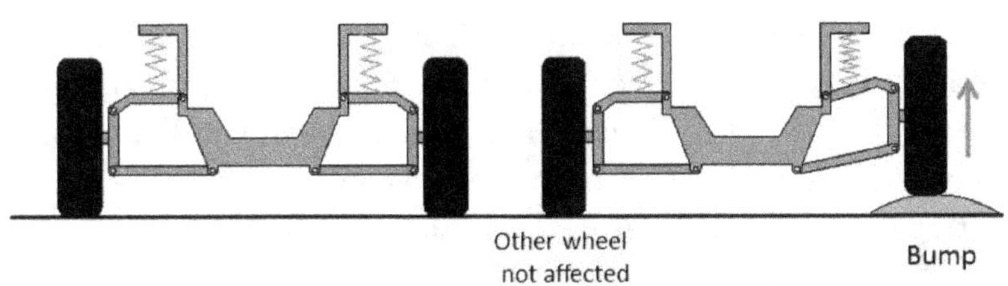

Figure 3.10: Independent Suspension System

Furthermore, in road vehicles, at least the front wheels are steered, so the suspension allows one of the links to be steered through a steering mechanism (usually a rack and pinion), while the remaining link of the steered suspension is steered. should be placed on the wheels around the desired steering axis. The connecting joint is usually a cylindrical rubber bushing if isolation from the road is required. B. A connection that allows rotation of the steering wheel. Independent suspension is not the only option for road vehicles. However, due to its excellent performance, it has been adopted by most market segments. This type of suspension typically has less unsprung mass, resulting in better ride and handling. The main advantages of independent suspension are space-saving, maneuverability, and low weight. An example of an independent suspension is

1. Double wishbone suspension: An independent suspension system that uses two wishbone arms (called A-ARM in the US and WISHBONE in the UK) to position the wheels. Each wishbone or arm has two mounting points on the chassis and a pivot on the steering knuckle. Angular motion of the compression and rebound wheels can be accommodated by using arms of different lengths. The main advantage of double wishbone suspension is the ability to easily adjust characteristics such as camber and toe-in. This type of suspension increases negative camber gain up to maximum travel. On the one hand, it takes up more space and is a bit more complicated than other systems like MacPherson struts. It also gives you fewer design options.

2. McPherson strut suspension: This type of independent suspension got its name from Earle S. Mr. McPherson who developed this design. The MacPherson strut is a developed version of the double wishbone suspension. McPherson's main advantage is that he can combine all the parts that provide suspension and wheel control into one assembly. Facilitates installation on horizontal engines. This design is quite popular due to its low manufacturing cost and simplicity. The downside is that it is difficult to block out street noise. This requires upper strut bearings and should be separated as much as possible.

B. Dependent suspension system

Dependent suspension is a fixed connection between her two wheels on the same axle. Forces acting on one wheel also act on the other wheel, and each time the road surface causes the wheels to move, the associated wheel is also affected by bumps.

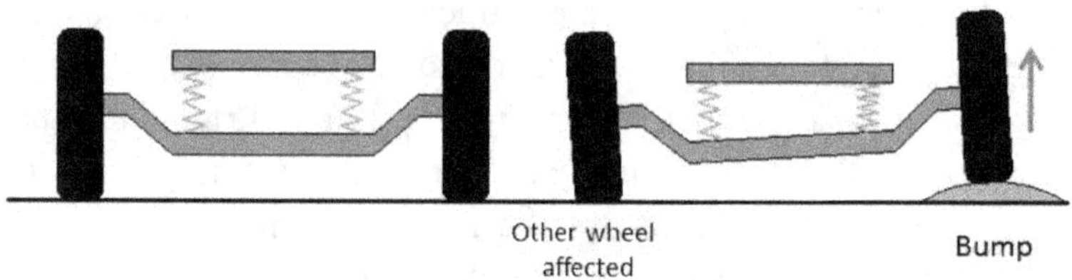

Figure 3.11: Dependent Suspension System

Mainly used for large vehicles. It has a greater capacity to withstand impacts than an independent suspension. An example of this system is

Solid axle: A live or beam axle is a dependent suspension. This is mainly used on the rear wheels, where the rear axle is supported by her two leaf springs. The vertical movement of one wheel affects the other. They are cheap and easy to manufacture. They are very stiff and tire wear is less because tread width, toe-in, and camber do not change on a full bump. The main drawback is that the mass of the beam is included in the vehicle's unsprung weight, which reduces ride comfort. Cornering is also bad with zero camber angle.

C. Semi-independent system

This type of system has characteristics of both dependent and independent suspension. In semi-independent suspension, the wheels move relative to each other like independent suspension, but with twisted suspension parts because the position of one wheel affects the other.

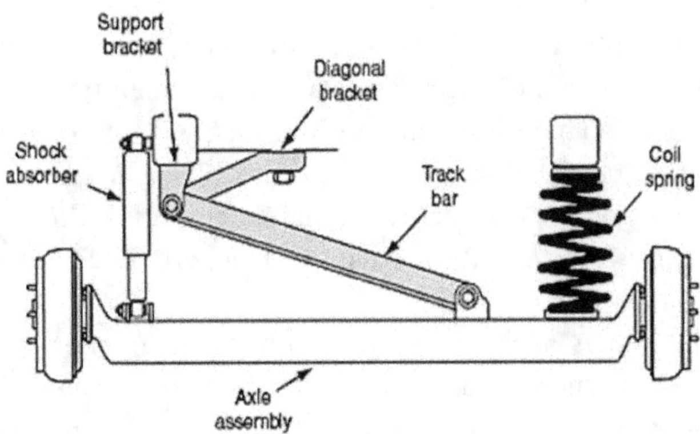

Figure 3.12: Semi-Independent Suspension System

Twist beam: A torsion beam axle is also called a torsion beam axle. These are mainly based on C-shaped or H-shaped beams. An H-shaped cross member holds the two trailing arms together and gives the suspension roll stiffness. It is mainly used for the rear wheels of automobiles. Due to its low price, it is very inexpensive and has excellent durability. It has a simple design and is very light. However, on the other hand, the camber angle is limited and the roll rigidity is not very high.

• • •

CHAPTER IV

Introduction to Hybrid and Electric Vehicles

Automobiles are essential to everyone's life, but their emissions are a major source of urban pollution that contributes to the greenhouse effect that leads to climate change. The world's reliance on oil as the primary source of energy for passenger vehicles has economic and political implications that will undoubtedly worsen as the world's oil supply dries up. The development of clean, efficient, and sustainable vehicles for urban transport is driven by both environmental and economic concerns. Powered by alternative energy sources and enabled by highly efficient electric motors and controllers, electric vehicles (EVs) provide a clean, efficient, and environmentally friendly urban transportation system.

Additionally, renewable energy sources such as water, wind, and solar energy can be used to power electric vehicles. EVs and HEVs present many new and increasingly complex design challenges not encountered in conventional automotive technology or transportation systems. The automotive industry invests significant resources in developing electric vehicles to meet increasingly stringent standards for fuel efficiency, economy, vehicle safety, performance, and environmental protection. This chapter will help you gain knowledge about electric and hybrid vehicles, including their associated benefits and design issues.

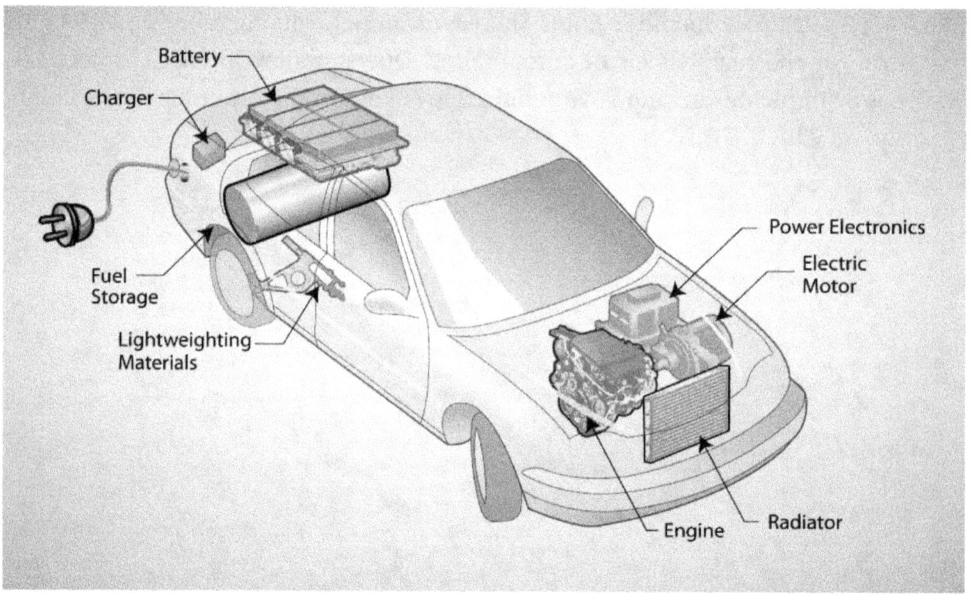

Figure 4.1: Pictorial representation of Electric Vehicle

Electric vehicles have been around for quite a long time. It continues to capture the imagination of people from all walks of life and is gaining traction across industries. But they struggle to compete with our great love, the internal combustion engine, for our position on the highway), and even a hobby (all kinds of motorsport). Entire industries, including aftermarket parts, maintenance services, and the custom car customization industry, not to mention automakers and fuel suppliers, exist solely to support this fascination with internal combustion engines. The power plant put up an uphill battle to overthrow the reigning champions of personal transport for many reasons. One of the main reasons is that the energy storage, batteries, and fuel cells that provide onboard energy to drive electric motors have not approached the range and payload characteristics of internal combustion engines common today. Another fundamental problem that has hampered the growth of electric vehicles is refueling.

Working principle of an Electric vehicle:

When you step on the pedals of a car, then:

- The controller obtains and regulates electrical energy from the battery and inverter
- When the controller is set, the inverter sends a certain amount of electrical energy to the motor (depending on how hard the pedal is pressed).
- Electric motors convert electrical energy into mechanical energy (rotation).
- The rotation of the engine's rotor turns the gearbox, which turns the wheels and moves the car.

Note: The above operating principles apply to Battery Electric Vehicle (BEV) types.
Electric vehicles are classified into four different types namely:

A. Battery Electric Vehicle (BEV)

A Battery Electric Vehicle (BEV), additionally known as All-Electric Vehicle (AEV), runs totally on a battery and electric drive train. These types of electric-powered automobiles no longer have an ICE. Electricity is stored in large compact battery packs which are charged with the aid of using plugging into the strength grid. The battery pack, in turn, gives power to at least one or more electric motors to run the electric vehicle.

Architecture and Main Components of BEV:

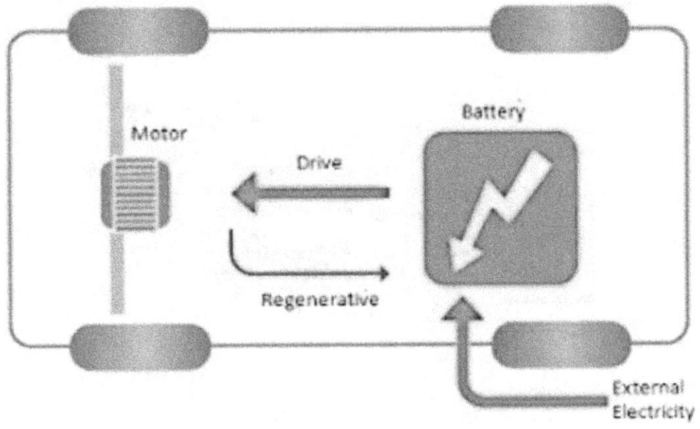

Figure 4.2: Architecture of BEV

- Electric motor
- Inverter
- Drive train
- Battery
- Control Module

Working Principles of BEV:

1. Power is transformed from the DC battery to AC for the electrical motor.
2. The accelerator pedal sends a sign to the controller which adjusts the vehicle's velocity with the aid of using converting the frequency of the AC energy from the inverter to the motor.
3. The motor connects and turns the wheels via a cog.
4. When the brakes are pressed or the electrical automobile is decelerating, the motor turns into an alternator and produces energy, that is despatched again to the battery.

Examples of BEV:

Volkswagen e-Golf, Mitsubishi i-MiEV, Tesla X, Toyota Rav4, Tesla Model 3, Chevy Spark, Nissan LEAF, Ford Focus Electric, BMW i3, Chevy Bolt, Hyundai Ioniq, Karma Revera, Kia Soul.

B. Hybrid Electric Vehicle (HEV)

This type of hybrid vehicle is often referred to as a standard hybrid or parallel hybrid. HEVs have both internal combustion engines and electric motors. In these types of electric vehicles, the internal combustion engine gets energy from fuel (gasoline or some other type of fuel) and the motor gets power from the battery. A petrol engine and an electric motor simultaneously rotate a gearbox that drives the wheels.

The difference between BEVs, HEVs, and PHEVs is that HEV batteries can only be charged by ICE, wheel movement, or a combination of both. There is no charging port, so the battery cannot be charged from outside the system, such as mains power.

Architecture and main components of HEV:

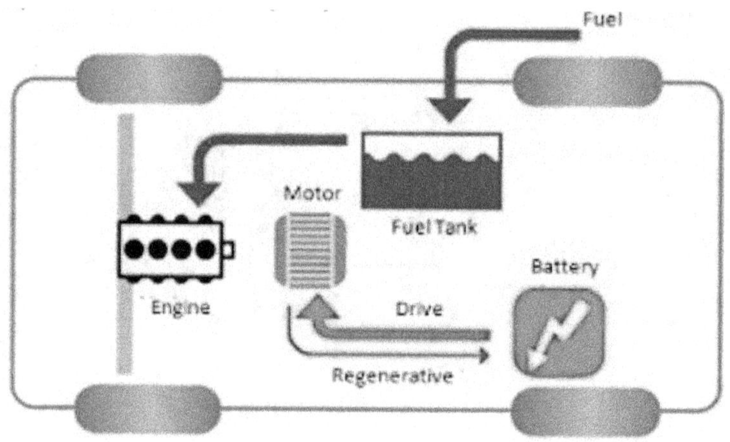

Figure 4.3: Architecture of HEV

- Engine
- Electric motor
- Control module
- Battery pack with controller and inverter
- Fuel tank

Working principle of HEV:

1. Has a fuel tank to feed the engine like a normal car
2. There is also a set of batteries to power the electric motor
3. The internal combustion engine and the electric motor can rotate the gearbox at the same time

Examples of HEV:

Honda Civic Hybrid, Toyota Camry, Hybrid, Toyota Prius Hybrid, Honda Civic Hybrid

Plug-in hybrid electric vehicles (PHEVs)

A PHEV is a type of hybrid vehicle with both an internal combustion engine and an electric motor, also known as a series hybrid. This type of electric vehicle has a choice of fuel. This type of electric vehicle can run on conventional fuels (such as gasoline) or alternative fuels (such as biodiesel) and rechargeable battery packs. The battery can be charged by plugging it into an electrical outlet or electric vehicle charging station (EVCS).
A PHEV can typically operate in at least two modes.

- Full electric mode where the motor and battery provide all the energy for the vehicle.
- Hybrid mode using both electric and petrol. Some PHEVs can travel over 70 miles on electricity alone.

Architecture and main components of PHEV:

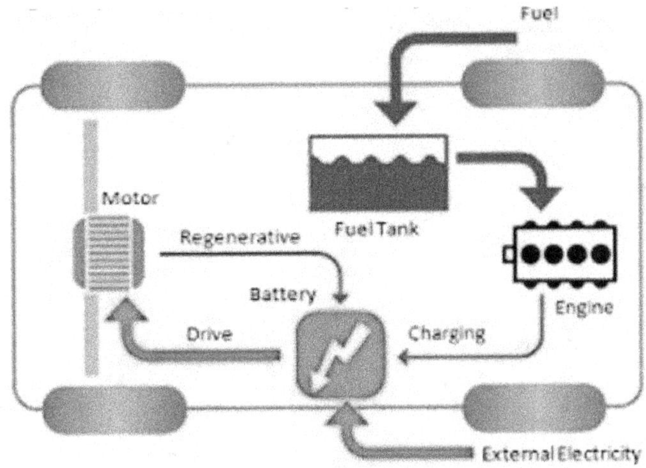

Figure 4.4: Architecture of PHEV

- Electric motor
- Engine
- Battery

- Fuel tank
- Converter
- Control module
- Battery charger (for onboard models)

Working principles of PHEV:

1. PHEVs typically start in all-electric mode and run-on electricity until the battery pack is empty. Some models switch to hybrid mode when they reach highway cruising speeds, typically more than 60 or 70 miles per hour. When the battery dies, the engine takes over and the vehicle operates as a traditional non-plug-in hybrid.
2. A PHEV's battery can be charged by the internal combustion engine or regenerative braking as well as connected to an external power source.
3. When braking, the electric motor acts as a generator and uses energy to charge the battery. An electric motor complements the power of the engine.
4. As a result, smaller engines can be used, making vehicles more fuel efficient without sacrificing performance.

Examples of PHEVs:

Porsche Cayenne S E-Hybrid, Mercedes GLE550e, Mini Cooper SE, Ford C-Max Energi, Ford Fusion Energi, Chevrolet Volt, Chrysler Pacifica, Mercedes C350e, Mercedes S550e.

Fuel Cell Vehicles (FCEV):

A fuel cell electric vehicle (FCEV), also known as a fuel cell vehicle (FCV) or zero-emission vehicle, is a type of electric vehicle that uses fuel cell technology to generate the electricity needed to run the vehicle. In this type of vehicle, the chemical energy of the fuel is converted directly into electrical energy.

Architecture and main components of FCEV:

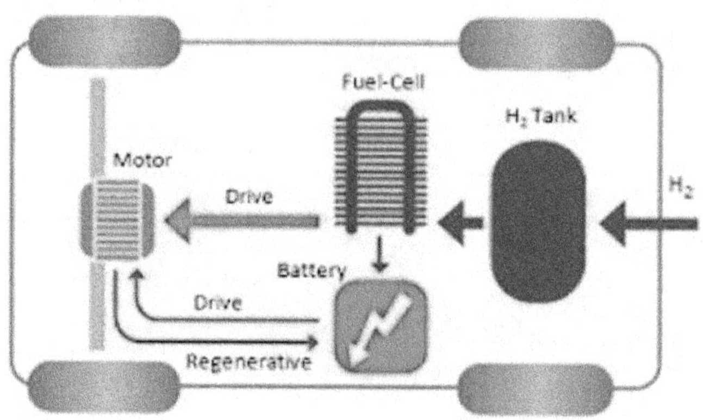

Figure 4.5: Architecture of FCEV

- Electric motor
- Hydrogen storage
- Fuel cell pack
- Battery with converter and controller

Working Principle of FCEV:

The operating principle of a "fuel cell" electric vehicle is different from that of a "plug-in" electric vehicle. This type of electric vehicle is because the FCEV generates the power required to operate this vehicle inside the vehicle.

Examples of FCEVs:

Toyota Mirai, Riversimple Rhasa, Hyundai Tucson FCEV, Honda Clarity Fuel Cell, Hyundai Nexo.\

Hybrid Electric Drivetrain

A hybrid vehicle's powertrain transmits power to the drive wheels of the hybrid vehicle. Hybrid vehicles have multiple power sources. Hybrids come in many configurations. For example, hybrids can burn oil for energy, but switch between an electric motor and an internal combustion engine.

Electric vehicles were primarily used in railroad locomotives, but like diesel-electric powertrains, they have a long history of combining internal combustion engines with electric transmissions. Diesel-electric powertrains fall short of the hybrid definition. This is because the electric drive transmission directly replaces the mechanical transmission rather than being an additional source of power. One of the earliest forms of hybrid land vehicles was the "trackless" trolleybus of the 1930s, which used traction, usually supplied by wires. Trolleybuses were commonly equipped with an internal combustion engine (ICE), which either directly propelled the bus or independently generated electricity. This allowed the vehicle to avoid obstacles and broken overhead wires.

The drivetrain contains all the components for converting stored potential energy. Powertrains can be either chemical, solar, nuclear, or dynamic and are available for propulsion. The oldest examples are galleys with sails and oars. A common modern example is an electric bicycle. Hybrid electric vehicles combine batteries or supercapacitors supplemented with ICE that can charge the battery or power the vehicle. Other hybrid drivetrains use flywheels to store energy.

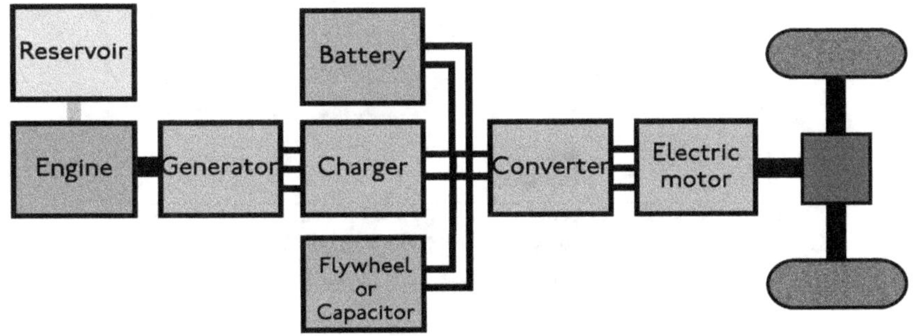

Figure 4.6: Design of Hybrid Electric Drivetrain

A hybrid propulsion system was designed to compensate for the lack of battery technology. Since batteries can only provide enough energy for short trips, an onboard generator with an internal combustion engine can be installed and used for long trips. The technology consists of three main components:

1. propulsion unit,
2. energy storage system,
3. and power unit.

Power units include fuel cells, conventional internal combustion engines, and turbine engines. The energy storage can be a battery or flywheel system and the propulsion unit can take the form of an electric motor. These components can be combined in a variety of ways, including completely from the electric motor (series configuration) or with direct mechanical input from the motor with the electric motor (parallel configuration). A hybrid electric vehicle indicates that the energy source is provided by an electric motor. HEVs come in many types, including:

- Gasoline ICE and Battery
- Diesel ICE and battery
- Battery and flywheel
- Battery and FC
- Batteries and capacitors
- Battery and battery hybrid.

Hybrids, while not as clean as pure electricity, may offer the market an effective mechanism to significantly reduce air pollution. Engines can be sized for average load rather than peak load, thus reducing weight beyond the onboard payload. Significantly improved fuel efficiency (estimated from 40mpg minimum to 80mpg maximum) and greater design freedom throughout the vehicle. It can also be supported by existing infrastructure designed to enable effective migration strategies to cleaner vehicles. In terms of overall energy efficiency, the conceptual advantages of hybrids over conventional vehicles are:

Regenerative Braking: One of the key advances impacting HEVs is the availability of effective and affordable regenerative braking systems. Hybrids can recover some of the energy normally lost to mechanical braking as heat by using the electric traction motor in generator mode to brake the vehicle. This is a way to recover and reuse energy that would normally be expended as heat or friction.

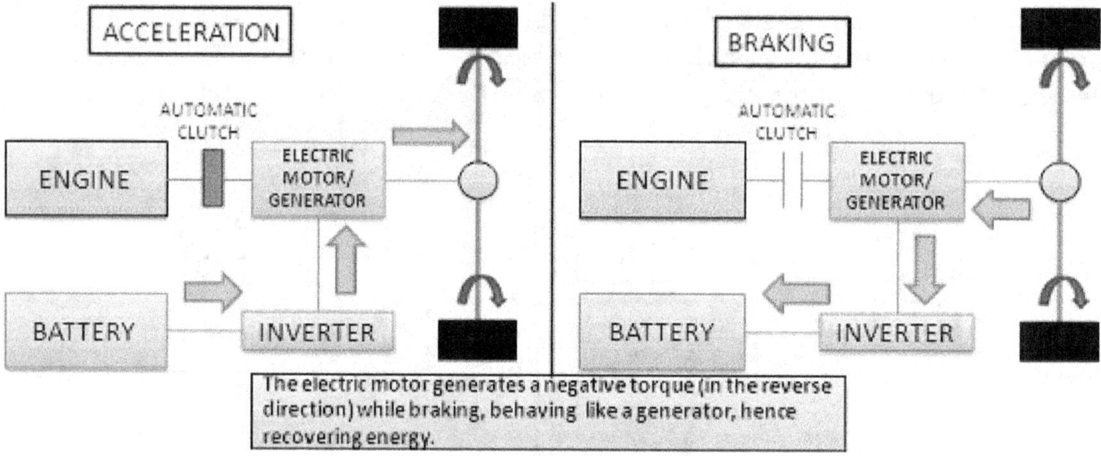

Figure 4.7: Working of Regenerative Braking

In a conventional vehicle, when the driver applies the brakes to slow down the vehicle in motion, the brake pads engage the drum or disc, slowing the vehicle. Regenerative braking uses a portion of the energy from the moving vehicle to spin the onboard generator, and the electricity generated by the generator is returned to the battery to achieve "regenerative braking".

Idling reduction: Hybrids use energy storage devices to absorb, increase or replace some of the engine's power output, thereby reducing the energy losses associated with engine operation at speed and load combinations where the engine is inefficient. can avoid some of the

Miniaturization of ICE: The HEV ICE can be miniaturized because the storage device can bear part of the load. ICEs may be designed for continuous loads rather than for very high short-term accelerated loads. This allows the ICE to operate at a higher percentage of rated power for most operations, generally improving fuel efficiency.

Another key advancement supporting this technology is the availability of advanced onboard control systems that can constantly monitor the power demands of the wheels and redirect system resources to meet specific needs. Changes in vehicle construction materials have also contributed significantly to the development of this technology. High-strength, lightweight body, and frame components, along with an engine built with alloys and materials that are significantly lighter than the cast-iron blocks of previous engines, all help improve his HEV's power-to-weight ratio. As a result, driving performance approaching that of conventional automobiles has been achieved.

Countervailing factors that reduce the energy advantage of hybrids include:

Higher weight potential: A hybrid vehicle's fuel-driven energy source is generally less powerful and lighter than a conventional vehicle's engine of similar power output, but the total weight of a hybrid vehicle can be greater than the conventional vehicle it replaces. there is. Additional weight storage devices, electric motors (EV), and other components.

Electrical loss: Individual components in electric powertrains are very efficient for unidirectional energy flow, but in many hybrid configurations current flows back and forth through.

Tractive efforts in normal driving

Conventional engine-powered vehicles use the engine to convert fuel energy into shaft power and direct most of that power through the drive train to turn the wheels. A heat engine has a theoretical efficiency limit, so much of the heat produced by combustion cannot be used for work and is wasted. Furthermore, it is impossible to reach the theoretical efficiency limit because

- Some of the heat is lost from the cylinder wall before it can work.
- Fuel is also burned when the engine is under negative load (when braking) or when the vehicle is coasting or stationary and the engine is idling.

Vehicle performance is usually expressed in terms of maximum cruising speed, climbing ability, and acceleration. Traction is defined as the force on the rim or outer edge of the driving wheels of a moving train. So, this is the sum of traction and rolling forces on the road. Traction is provided by locomotives on long-distance trains and rail cars on S-trains. Drawbar force is the horizontal force available to the vehicle to pull a load. This force is less than the tractive effort required to move heavy-duty vehicles i.e., locomotives. The maximum allowable tractive force that can be applied without the wheels slipping is

$$\text{``}F_m = 9.810\mu M_d N\text{''}$$

where μ is the adhesion coefficient and M_d is the adhesion weight or drive wheel weight.

Tractive effort vs. speed characteristics

Traction motors used for traction purposes include DC series motors, separately excited DC series motors, three-phase induction motors, synchronous motors, and permanent magnet synchronous motors. Whatever the source or principle of operation of the traction motor, all offer traction characteristics that meet traction resistance and provide acceleration.

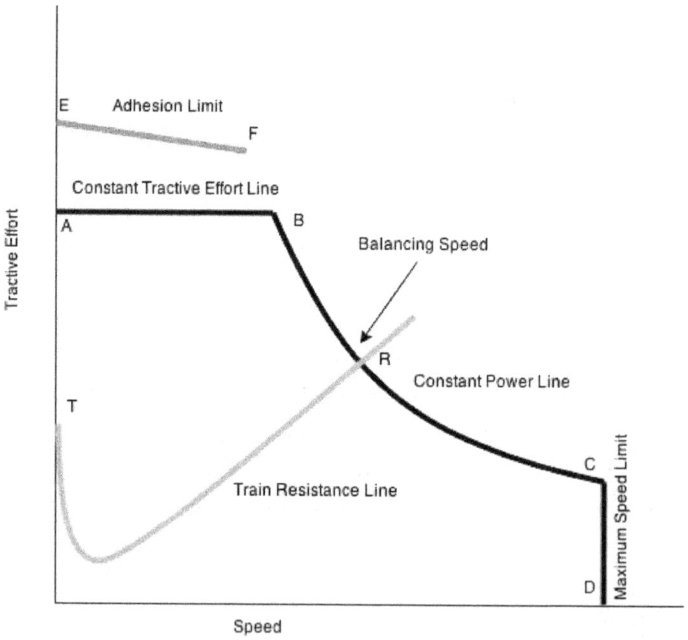

Figure 4.8: Graph representing tractive effort vs speed

AB - This is generally constant towline up to 30-50 km/h. Point B is the maximum power point. OA is determined based on continuous traction motor evaluation and grip limits. This curve is lifted upwards by overloading the traction motor using the heat capacity of the traction motor.

BC - This is a constant line of force where the pulling force decreases inversely with increasing velocity. For passenger locomotives, the tractive power required is small relative to speed, so the tractive power characteristic is at the low end with low horsepower.

The CD maximum speed limit is imposed by the mechanical design of the traction motor and mechanical transmission.

TR - This is the pull resistance curve. The point of intersection determines the speed at which drag equals drag. The accelerator reserve is up to the intersection. The curve TR rises and falls while traveling uphill and downhill.

EF - This line specifies the hold weight limit and the pulling force must be within this limit.

Thermal overload of the traction motor

The motor can be momentarily overloaded because the temperature rises slowly compared to the time required for acceleration. This period ranges from 2, 10, and 30 minutes with overload capabilities of 150, 120, and 110%, during which the temperature rise is within the insulation class for which the traction motor is designed. This is useful when starting a motor that needs to develop significant traction when the current drawn is higher than the continuous power, and to provide higher acceleration for some time thereafter.

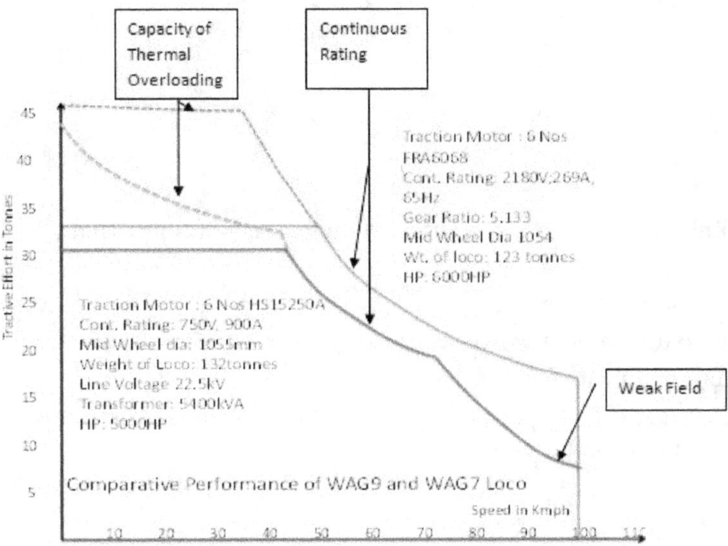

Figure 4.9: Thermal overload of the tractive motor

The function of the Tractive Effort:

Below are the functions performed by the traction force on the vehicle:

1. Tractive effort (in N) is required to horizontally accelerate the train mass with an acceleration of à
   Fa1 = (1000M) x (à x 1000)/3600 = 277.8Mà, N
   where M is the mass in tons
2. Traction required to accelerate the rotating part:
   The rotating part consists of the gears, axles, wheels, and rotors of the motor. The moment of inertia of the wheel is expressed by the following formula.

$$\text{``}J_1 = 2N_xJ_w\text{''}$$

where J_w is the wheel moment of inertia, kgm^2, and N_x is the number of wheel axles.
   N – Drive motor number.
   n_1 – number of teeth on the motor gear wheel
   n_2 – number of teeth on the Axle gear wheel

$$\text{``}\grave{a} = n_1 / n_2 = whole\ speed\ /\ motor\ speed\text{''}$$

J_m – Moment of inertia of the motor, kg-m^2
Then the moment of inertia of the motor relative to the wheels

$$\text{``}J_2 = NJ_m / \grave{a}^2$$
$$Acceleration = (\grave{a} \times 1000)/3600R,\ meter/second^2\text{''}$$

where, R - wheel radius, m

3. Traction required to overcome force due to gravity:

When going uphill, the driver must apply traction to overcome gravity. The pulling force required to overcome gravity is

$$^{``}F_g = 1000M \times (G/1000) \times g, N$$
$$F_g = 9.81MG, N$$
$$F_g = MG, kg\,^{"}$$

For railroads, uphill or downhill gradients are expressed in meters as gradients that are 1000 m line lengths and are denoted by G.

4. Traction required to overcome train resistance:

Train drag is primarily due to different types of friction. The three basic friction types that contribute to drag are Coulomb friction, viscous friction, and air friction.

Coulomb friction is caused by the relative motion of two surfaces. Viscous friction is directly proportional to train speed, air friction is independent of speed squared.

$$^{``}F_r = rM, N$$
$$F_r = rM/9.81, kg\,^{"}$$

where V is the train speed and A, B, and C are constants.

5. The total tractive force required to move the train:

$$^{``}F_r = F_a + F_g + F_r$$
$$F_r = 28.3M_e\grave{a} \pm MG + M_r, N$$
$$F_r = 277.8M_e\grave{a} \pm 9.81MG + M_r, N\,^{"}$$

A positive sign is used for the uphill of the train and a negative sign for the downhill.

Electric Drives:

An all-electric vehicle (EV) runs entirely on electricity. They are powered by more than one electric motor through rechargeable battery packs. Electric vehicles have several advantages over conventional vehicles:

Energy efficiency: Electric vehicles convert more than 77% of electrical energy from the grid into electricity at their wheels. Conventional gasoline vehicles can only convert about 12-30% of the energy stored in gasoline to power the wheels.

Environmentally Friendly: Electric vehicles do not emit pollutants through their exhaust pipes, but power plants that generate electricity can. Electricity from nuclear, hydro, solar, or wind power plants does not cause air pollutants.

Performance benefits: Electric motors offer quiet, smooth operation, and quick acceleration, and require less maintenance than internal combustion engines (ICEs).

Reduced energy dependency: Electricity is a household energy source.

On the other hand, Electric vehicles have some drawbacks compared to gasoline vehicles:

Driving range: EVs have a shorter range than most traditional vehicles, but EVs have a better range. In most electric cars he can drive over 100 miles on a single charge, and in some models, he can go over 200 or 300 miles.

Charging time: It takes 3 to 12 hours to fully charge the battery pack. Even a "fast charge" to 80 Pac can take 30 minutes.

Energy Consumption

Electrical energy consumption is the form of energy consumption that uses electrical energy. Electricity consumption is the actual energy demand of existing power sources for transportation, residential, industrial, commercial, and various other purposes. There are many ways to calculate the energy consumption of an electric vehicle, but the most common method is to use kilowatt hours/100 km. It shows how much electricity (in kilowatt-hours) the vehicle consumes per 100 km traveled. First, determine your average daily mileage and vehicle battery size.

Once you have the information, you can use the following formula:

"Battery size (kilowatt hours) x average mileage per day / 100 = kilowatt hours/mile"

For example, if you drive about 30 km per day and have a 40-kWh battery, the calculation would be:

40 kWh x 30 km / 100 = 12 kWh per 100 km. Calculations show that an electric vehicle consumes 12 kWh of energy for a 100 km trip. While the numbers can vary depending on many factors, this gives a clearer picture of how much energy an electric vehicle is using.

When it comes to energy consumption, the difference between electric and petrol cars is even more dramatic. Electric vehicles can have a utilization rate of as much as 30 kWh per 100 miles, while conventional vehicles consume about 40+ kWh to travel the same distance. This indicates that electric vehicles can save at least four times more than gasoline vehicles.

Factors Affecting Electric Vehicle Power Consumption:

Driving dynamics play an important role in determining the estimated energy consumption of electric vehicles. Vehicle dynamics is the science of how vehicles behave: powertrain, driver, tires, car weight, and shape. These factors affect a car's energy consumption. Below are several factors that can affect the power consumption of electric vehicles.

Aerodynamic resistance: Most electric cars are specifically designed to be as aerodynamic as possible, which makes them look different than their traditional models. Extreme wind conditions may reduce the distance you can drive before needing to recharge.

Weight: Perhaps the most important factor is the weight of the vehicle. The more stuff you load your car with, the more momentum you need to accelerate. If she's the only driver, a single charge can take and the whole family farther in the car. Heavy objects require more energy to move, so they consume more power when driving. Consider vehicle weight when purchasing an electric vehicle.

Rolling resistance: Rolling resistance, or the friction experienced by a tire as it rolls on the ground. The higher the rolling resistance, the more energy it takes to keep the car moving. If you want an efficient electric car, choose tires with low rolling resistance.

Average speed: Average speed means that the faster you drive, the more energy you expend. If you want to save energy, it is recommended to drive at a moderate speed.

How to reduce the energy consumption of electric vehicles:

With the surge in demand for electric vehicles, finding ways to reduce energy consumption is beneficial. By following the tips below, you can ultimately save money and reduce your carbon footprint:

Drive slower: Driving more slowly is best to minimize energy consumption. Going faster means electric cars work harder and consume more energy.

Avoid using air conditioning: Avoid using air conditioning as much as possible to reduce energy consumption. Electric car air conditioning consumes a lot of energy and should be avoided as much as possible. Instead, try opening the windows and enjoying the fresh air.

Keep the air in the tires: Finally, make sure your tires are properly inflated. Electric vehicles consume more energy when their tires are flat, especially when driving on rough roads.

Concept of Hybrid electric powertrain:

A hybrid electric vehicle indicates that the energy source is provided by an electric motor. Hybrid vehicles use two or more different types of energy, such as:

1. Internal combustion engines and batteries or ultracapacitors in diesel hybrid vehicles.
2. Fuel cells and batteries in fuel cell hybrid vehicles.
3. Electric overhead lines and batteries of a trolley hybrid bus.

The diagram below shows the hybrid powertrain concept and possible energy flow paths. Different possibilities for combining power flows according to driving requirements are:

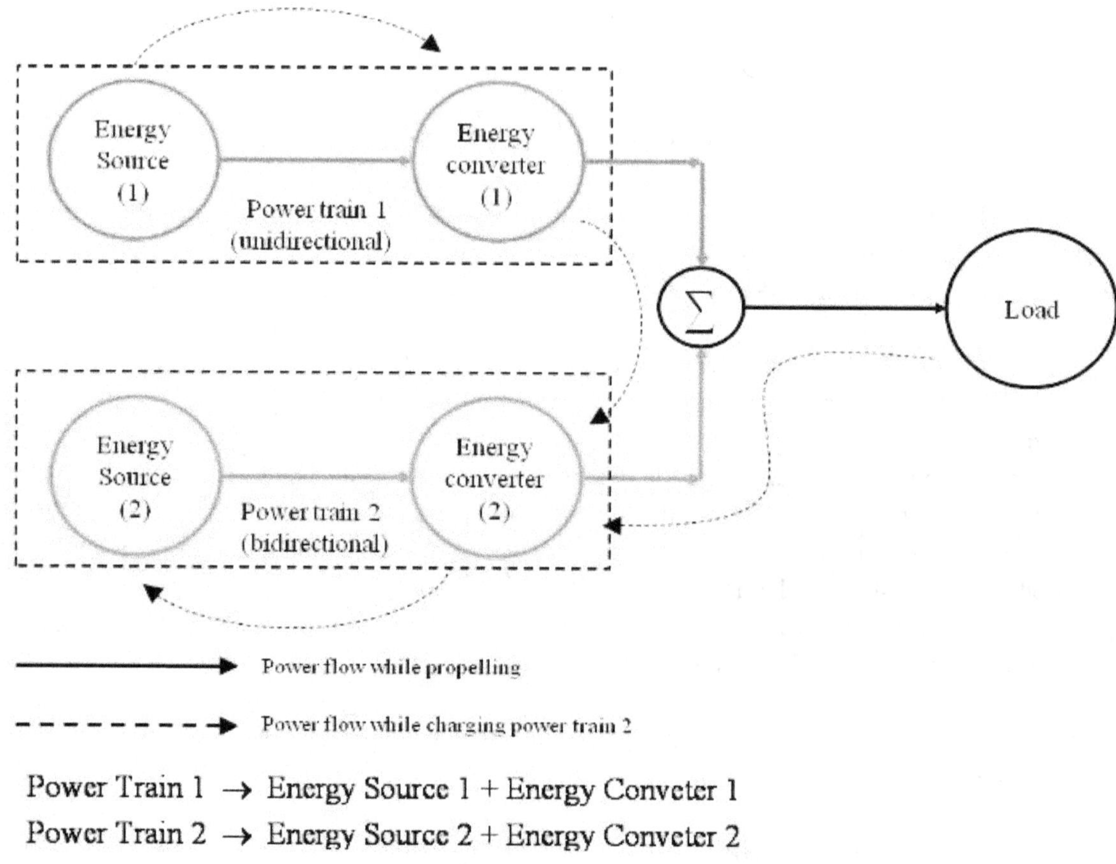

Figure 4.10: Concept of Hybrid powertrain

- Power with only powertrain 1
- Power with only powertrain 2
- Both powertrains 1 and 2 power the load at the same time
- Powertrain 2 receives power from Powertrain 1
- Powertrain 2 receives power from the load (regenerative braking)
- Drivetrain 1 simultaneously powers drivetrain 2 and the load

- Drivetrain 1 powers drivetrain 2, and drivetrain 2 powers the load.
- Driveline 1 powers the load and the load powers driveline 2.

The charging performance of the vehicle during actual driving varies randomly due to frequent acceleration/deceleration and uphill slopes. Performance requirements for common driving scenarios are listed below.

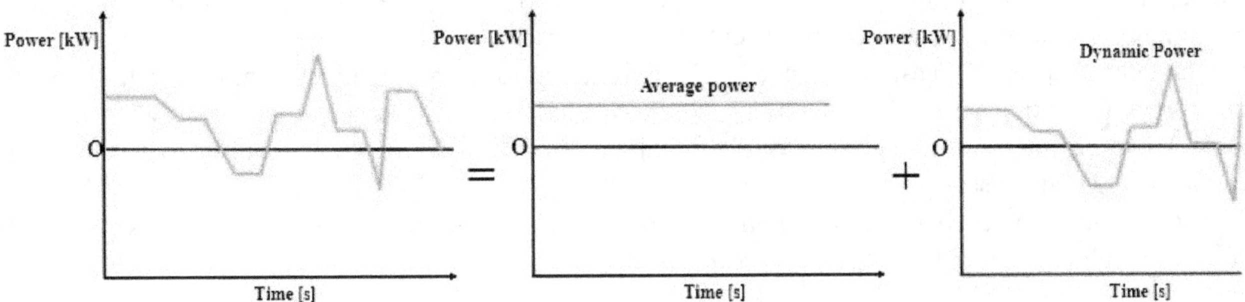

Figure 4.11: Classification of load power

The load power can be classified into two parts.
1. Steady power, power with a constant value
2. Dynamic value, a power whose average value is zero
In hybrid electric vehicles, the powertrain prefers steady-state operation i.e., ICE or fuel cell. Whereas, other HEV powertrain is used to deliver dynamic performance. The total energy output of dynamic powertrains is zero throughout the drive cycle.

The architecture of Hybrid Electric Drivetrain:

To understand how HEVs can save energy, we must first look at how conventional vehicles use energy. The breakdown of vehicle energy consumption is as follows:
To maintain motion, the vehicle must generate forces at the wheels to overcome:

- Drag (air friction on the car body surface combined with compressive force due to airflow)

1. Rolling resistance (resistance force between tire and road surface)
2. Gravitational drag when climbing a slope

- In addition, the vehicle must have inertia in order to accelerate. Most of the energy consumed during acceleration is lost as heat in the brakes when the vehicle comes to a stop.
- The vehicle must have power accessories such as heater fans, lights, power steering, and air conditioning.
- Finally, the vehicle must be able to provide power to accelerate with little deceleration when the driver presses the gas pedal.

Traditional engine-powered vehicles use the engine to convert fuel energy into shaft power and send most of that power through the drive train to turn the wheels. A heat engine has a theoretical efficiency limit, so much of the heat produced by combustion cannot be used for work and is wasted. Moreover, it is impossible to reach the theoretical efficiency frontier for the following reasons.

1. Some heat is lost through the cylinder wall before it operates.

2. Part of the fuel is burning below the maximum possible pressure
3. Fuel is also burned when the engine is under negative load or when the vehicle is idling or stopped and the engine is idling.

Although there will be some motor losses under all circumstances, motors in conventional powertrains are sized to provide very high peak horsepower for the acceleration capabilities consumers expect, so 10 Approximately 10 times the horsepower required for a km/h cruising speed is required. However, motors most of the time run at a fraction of their peak power and are very inefficient at these operating points.

Such a large engine also increases the amount of fuel required to keep the engine running while the vehicle is stationary, or while braking or coasting, increasing engine weight losses and reducing rolling resistance. increase the inertia loss. Even the gradeability requirement requires about 60 or 70% of the power required to accelerate from 0 to 100 km/h in less than 12 seconds.

This diagram shows the conversion of fuel energy into work at the wheels of a typical medium-sized vehicle on city streets and highways. From the diagram you can see that:

1. At best, only 20% of his fuel energy reaches the wheels and is available to overcome traction. This is on the highway, with minimal idling loss, rare braking loss, and far less common gear changes.
2. Braking and idling losses are very high during urban driving and even higher in heavy traffic areas. B. Inner city during rush hour. Loss of brakes accounts for 46% of all traction losses in urban traffic. Idling losses account for approximately one-sixth of the fuel energy in this cycle.
3. Drag losses account for less than one-fifth of traction losses in city traffic, but more than half of highway traction losses.

Series Hybrid Electric Drive Trains

A series powertrain is the simplest hybrid configuration. In a series hybrid, the electric motor is the sole means of powering the wheels. The engine receives power from a battery pack or a generator powered by a gasoline engine. The computer decides how much power will come from the battery or the motor/generator. Both the motor/generator and the use of regenerative braking recharge the battery pack. Series hybrids perform best in stop-and-go traffic where petrol and diesel engines are less efficient. The vehicle's computer can choose to power the engine using only the battery pack, thus saving the engine in more efficient situations.

Engines are typically smaller in series powertrains because they only need to meet specific performance requirements. Battery packs are generally more powerful than parallel hybrids to meet remaining power needs. This larger battery and motor, along with the alternator, increase the cost of the vehicle, making series hybrids more expensive than parallel hybrids.

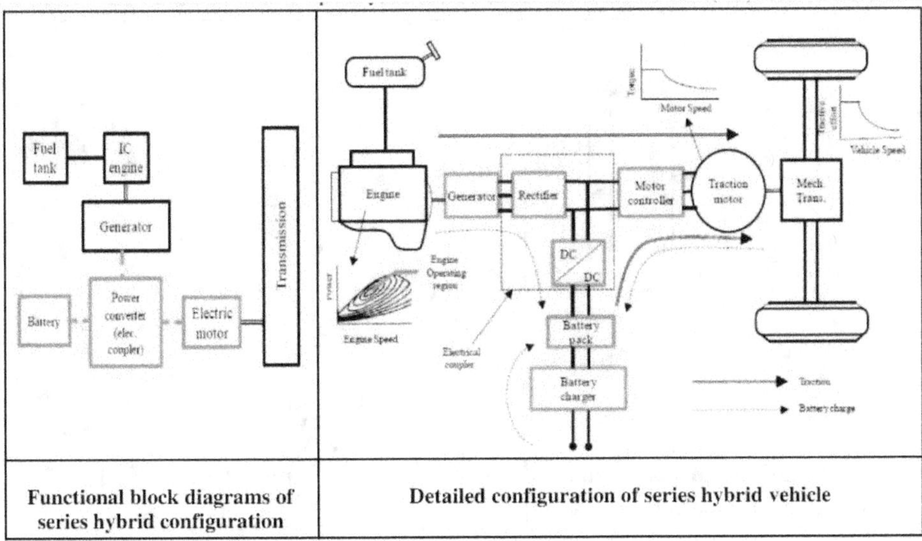

Figure 4.12: Series hybrid Vehicle

Advantages of Serial Hybrid Drives:

1. The mechanical separation between the internal combustion engine and the drive wheels allows the internal combustion engine to operate within a very narrow optimum range.
2. The nearly ideal torque/speed behavior of electric motors eliminates the need for multi-speed gearboxes.

Disadvantages of Serial Hybrid Drives:

1. The energy converts twice (mechanical to electrical and then mechanical), resulting in lower overall efficiency.
2. A large traction motor is required as it requires two electric machines and is the sole source of torque for the driven wheels.

Parallel Hybrid Electric Drive Trains

In a vehicle with a parallel hybrid powertrain, the internal combustion engine and electric motor work together to produce the power to drive the wheels. Parallel hybrids tend to use smaller battery packs than series powertrains and rely on regenerative braking to keep them charged. When power requirements are low, parallel hybrids also use the motor as a generator for additional charging, much like a conventional car's alternator.

The engine is connected directly to the wheels in a parallel powertrain, eliminating the inefficiencies of converting mechanical power to electricity and back, making these hybrids more efficient on the highway. This reduces but does not eliminate, the efficiency advantages of electric motors and batteries in stop-and-go traffic.

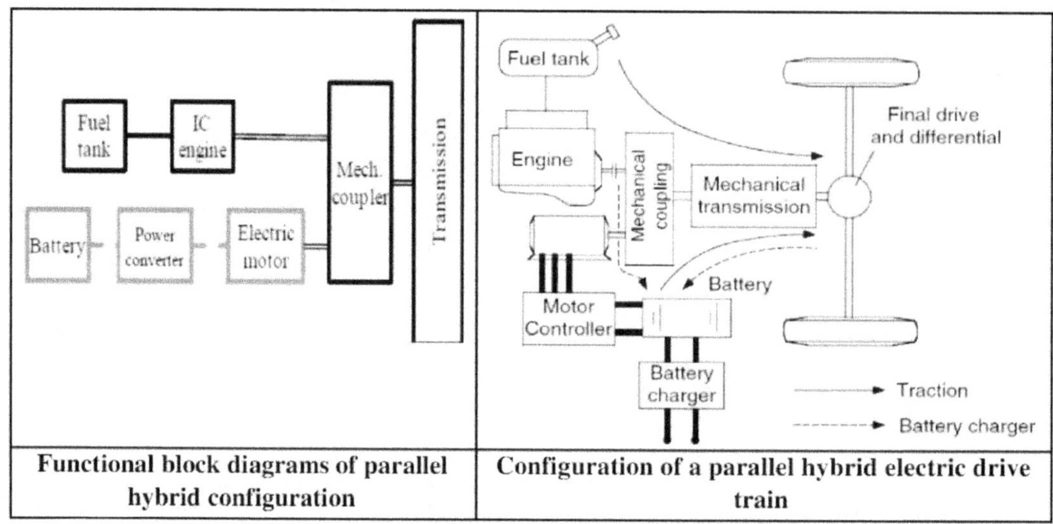

Figure 4.13: Parallel hybrid vehicle

Advantages of Parallel Hybrid Drives:

1. Low energy loss as both the internal combustion engine and the electric motor deliver torque directly to the drive wheels and there is no energy format conversion
2. Compactness that does not require miniaturization of generators and traction motors.

Disadvantages of Parallel Hybrid Drives:

1. Due to the mechanical coupling between the motor and drive wheels, the operating point of the motor cannot be specified over a narrow speed range.
2. Complex mechanical configuration and control strategy compared to serial hybrid powertrains.

Electric Propulsion unit

The critical subsystem required for an electric vehicle is the propulsion system, which provides the tractive force that drives the vehicle. A purely electric drive system (Electric Vehicle, EV, or Battery Electric Vehicle (BEV)) is characterized by an electrical energy conversion chain upstream of the drive train. Broadly speaking, it consists of a battery (or another power storage device), an electric motor, and its controller. The resulting vehicle is not autonomous because the energy density of the battery does not provide sufficient driving autonomy. Moreover, the time required for recharging is usually not negligible and is certainly longer than the typical refueling time of an internal combustion engine vehicle. An electric vehicle's drive system consists of an energy storage system, a power converter, a drive motor, and associated controls. Batteries are widely used as energy storage systems and charging is an integral part of EV systems.

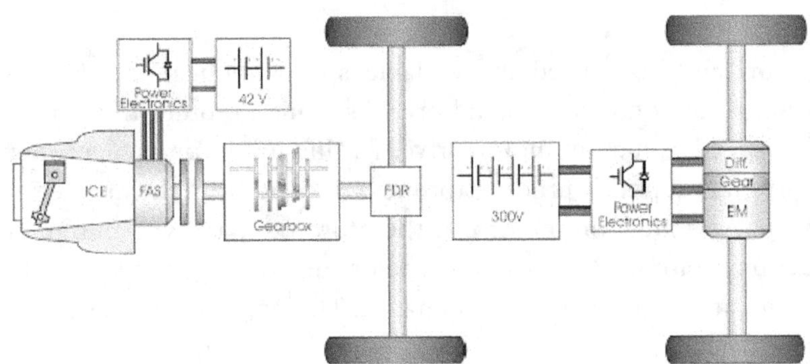

Figure 4.14: Components of electric vehicle propulsion system

Electric propulsion has many advantages over fossil fuel-based propulsion. This includes the extremely quiet operation of such engines. It also has a large diameter, low-speed propeller, and is relatively quiet. This is in contrast to the noisy piston or gas turbine engines and propellers associated with conventional equipment. As long as the propeller is balanced, the operation of the electric motor is virtually vibration-free. None of the other usual annoyances of a petrol engine. There is no residue, odors, or dirt associated with running an engine like this - they are very clean.

Other benefits include extremely easy and reliable starting and running of the engine. The engine itself is a very reliable device that requires minimal maintenance compared to piston engines. No tune-ups or expensive overhauls are required. Another important aspect is pilot and passenger safety. There is no need to worry about carbon monoxide poisoning as it does not use fossil fuels. Another advantage is that it can be charged simply by plugging it into a household outlet, and charging is inexpensive during this period. Electric aircraft are also environmentally friendly and emit no greenhouse gases, but this is offset by the fact that in many places power generation releases harmful greenhouse gas chemicals into the environment. This applies to electricity from oil- or coal-fired power plants. Renewable energy, of course, is the answer, offering unique possibilities for electric aircraft as a green mode of transport.

Configuration and control of DC Motor drives:

The DC motor drive is a type of power modulator or amplifier that integrate between the DC motor and a controller. It takes the low current and converts it into a high current which is suitable for the motor. The DC motor drive also provides high current torque which is 400% more than the rated continuous torque. The main applications of DC motor drives are paper mills, rolling mills, mine winders, machine tools, hoists, traction, printing presses, textile mills, excavators, and cranes.

Types of DC Motor Drives:

Non-regenerative DC Drive: The Non-regenerative DC drive rotates only in one direction and is hence also called a single quadrant drive. This type of DC motor drive does not have any inherent braking capability. The DC motor is terminated only by removing the supply. This type of drive is used where a strong natural brake or high friction load requires.

Regenerative DC Drive: The regenerative DC drive is a four-quadrant drive, and it controls the direction, speed, and torque of a motor. Under the braking condition, this drive converts load and mechanical energy into electrical energy which is returned to the power source.

Induction Motor Drives

DC motor drives have historically been used for variable speed applications. However, this motor has some drawbacks, such as the presence of commutators and brushes, which require frequent maintenance. This problem is overcome with a variable speed induction motor drive. An induction or asynchronous motor is an AC electric motor in which the rotor current required to produce torque is derived from the magnetic field in the stator windings by electromagnetic induction. An induction motor can therefore be made without an electrical connection to the rotor. The rotor of an induction motor is either wound type or squirrel cage type. Induction motor drives are cheap, lightweight, compact, efficient, and require little maintenance. The only drawback of induction motor drives is their high cost.

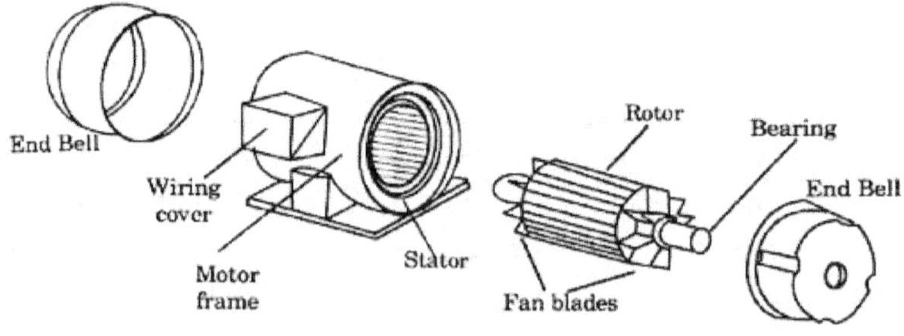

Figure 4.15: Diagram of Induction motor drives

Induction motor drives have many applications including fans, blowers, mill discharge tables, crane conveyors, and traction. The induction motor drive will start automatically. In other words, we can say that when the motor is powered, it will start spinning without any external power source. Since the initial resistance of the power supply is zero, a large current will flow through the motor, damaging the motor windings. Various starting methods are used to reduce the starting current flow. These methods keep the magnitude of the inrush current within predetermined limits so as not to cause overheating.

Induction motors are known to self-start. That is, when the electric motor is powered, it will start spinning without any external help. Since induction motors initially have no resistance (i.e. during starting), when they start, they tend to draw huge currents in the rotor circuit, which can permanently damage the circuit.

Permanent Magnet Motor drives

Permanent magnet synchronous motors (PMSM) are typically used for high-power, high-efficiency motor drives. High-performance motor control features smooth rotation throughout the motor's speed range, perfect torque control at zero speed, and rapid acceleration and deceleration. Vector control technology for PM synchronous motors is used to achieve such control. Vector control schemes are also commonly referred to as Field Oriented Control (FOC). The basic idea of vector control algorithms is to decompose the stator current into a magnetic field-producing part and a torque-producing part. Both components can be controlled individually after disassembly. And the motor control (vector control) structure is almost the same as that of a separately excited DC motor, which simplifies the control of permanent magnet synchronous motors.

The magnetic field in a synchronous machine can be provided by using permanent magnets of neodymium-boron-iron, samarium-cobalt, or ferrite in the rotor. In some motors, these magnets are glued to the surface of the rotor core so the magnetic field is directed radially across the air gap. In other designs, the magnets are set on the surface of the rotor core or in slots just below the surface. Another form of permanent magnet motor has circumferentially oriented magnets placed in radial slots to supply magnetic flux to the iron poles, which establishes a radial magnetic field in the air gap increase.

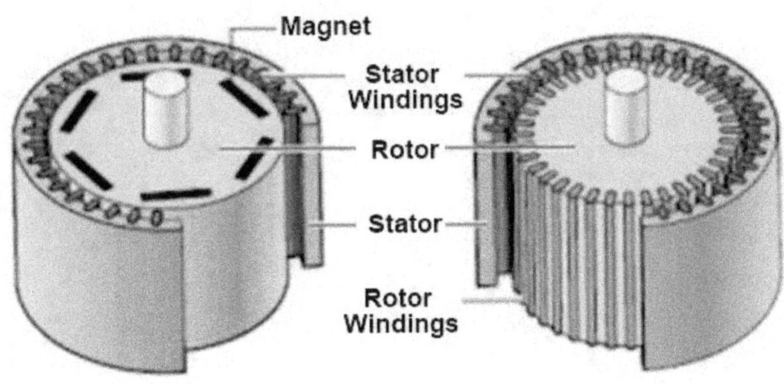

Figure 4.16: Components of Permanent Magnet and Induction

The main application of permanent magnet motors is variable speed drives, where the stator is powered by an electronically controlled variable frequency and voltage source. Such drives are capable of precise speed and position control. They are also very efficient as they lose less power in the rotor compared to induction motor drives.

Permanent magnet motors can be designed to operate at synchronous speed from a constant voltage and frequency source. Magnets are embedded in the rotor iron and damper windings are placed in slots on the rotor surface to provide the starting function. However, such motors have no means of controlling the stator power factor.

Torque Generation:

The reactive torque in a PMSM is generated by the interaction of two magnetic fields, one in the stator and one in the rotor. The stator magnetic field is expressed as flux/stator current. The magnetic field of the rotor is represented by the magnetic flux of the permanent magnet and is constant except for the field-weakening field. You can think of these two magnetic fields as two-bar magnets. Because we know that the forces tending to attract or repel these magnets are greatest when they are perpendicular to each other. This means that the stator current should be controlled so that the stator vector is perpendicular to the rotor magnets. As the rotor rotates, we need to update the stator currents to keep the stator flux vector always at 90 degrees to the rotor magnets. The reactance torque of an indoor PM-type PMSM (IPMSM) when the magnetic fields of the stator and rotor are perpendicular is

$$\text{``}Torque = 32pp\lambda_{PM}.I_{qs}\text{''}$$

pp = Number of pole pairs

λ_{PM} = Magnetic flux of the permanent magnets

I_{qs} = Amplitude of the current in the quadrature axis

As shown in the previous equation, when the magnetic field is vertical, the reactance torque is proportional to the amplitude of the q-axis current. The MCU must control the phase stator current magnitude and phase/angle simultaneously, which is not as easy a task as DC motor control.

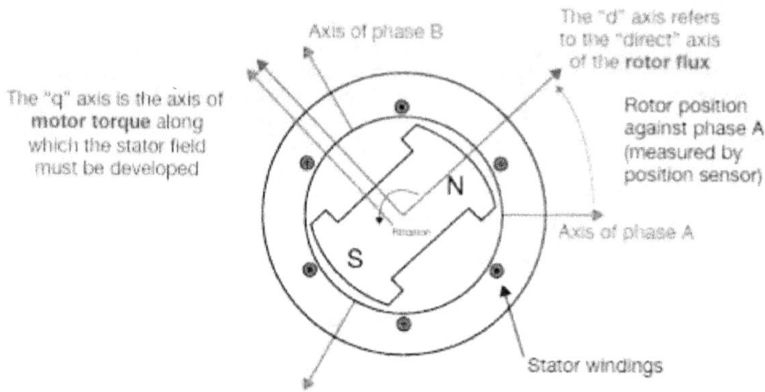

Figure 4.17: Diagram of Permanent magnet synchronous motor (PMSM)

Switched reluctance motor

Electric motors like SRM (Switched Reluctance Motor) work through reluctance torque. Unlike traditional brushed DC motors, power can be transferred to the windings inside the stator instead of the rotor. Another name for this motor is VRM (Variable Reluctance Motor). A switching inverter is used for better operation of this motor. The control characteristics of this motor are the same as an electronically commutated DC motor. These engines are applicable where size and horsepower (HP) to weight ratio are important.

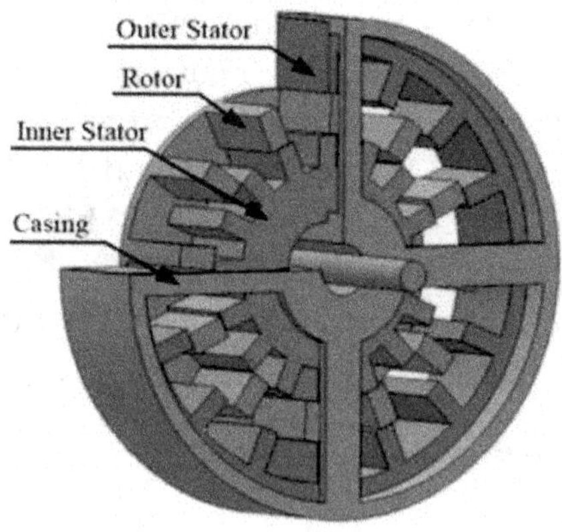

Figure 4.18: Components of switched reluctance motor

This motor simplifies mechanical design and limits current flow to rotating parts. However, it complicates the design by requiring the use of some sort of switching system to transfer power to the various windings. This mechanical structure can also be used for generators. The load can be switched to the coils, in turn, to adjust the current flow due to rotation. Compared to traditional motor types, these generators can also operate at high speeds. This is because the armature is made like a slotted cylinder like a single magnetizable material.

Working principle:

The working principle of a switched reluctance motor is to work on the principle of variable reluctance. In other words, the rotor of this motor always tries to align through the least reluctance track. A rotating magnetic field can be created through a circuit of power electronics. The reluctance of the magnetic circuit mainly depends on the air gap. So by changing the air gap between the rotor and stator, we can also change the reluctance of this motor.

Here reluctance can be defined as the resistance to magnetic flux. For electrical circuits, reluctance is a combination of resistance and magnetic circuits.

The architecture of SRM:

The architecture of a switched reluctance motor is shown below. This motor contains 6 stator poles and 4 rotor poles. The stator design can be done with silicon steel stampings inside the protruding poles. The number of stator poles can be odd or even. Most electric motors have an even number of poles in the stator with field coils. If the poles are opposite, the field coils are connected in series. So, their magnetomotive forces, called phase windings, add up. A set of coils or a single coil can include phase windings. Each winding can be connected to a motor terminal and these are appropriately connected to the o/p terminals of the power semiconductor circuit. Its input is a DC power supply.

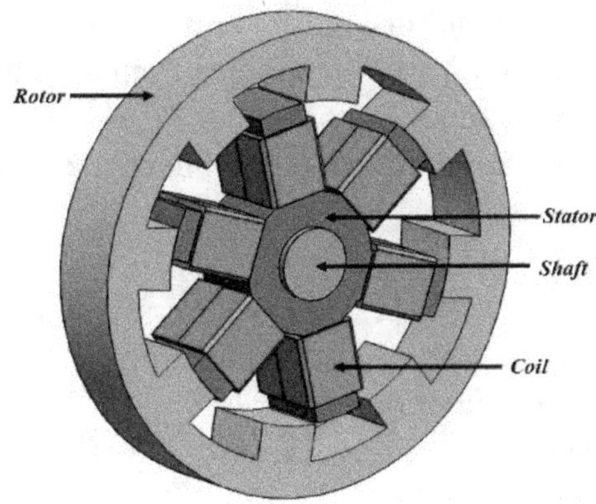

Figure 4.19: Architecture of SRM

The rotor design can be done with Si steel stamping through the outwardly projecting poles. The rotor poles are different from the stator poles. In most existing motors, the rotor poles are 4 or 6 based on the number of stator poles. The rotor shaft holds the position sensor. Therefore, the operation of various devices within the power semiconductor circuit is primarily controlled by the signals received from this sensor.

In this motor, both the stator and rotor contain salient poles made of soft iron and silicon stampings used to reduce hysteresis losses. The stator of the motor contains field windings, but the rotor does not. In the stator, each winding in series can be connected with opposite poles to increase the magnetomotive force of the circuit.

Types of SRM:

Switched reluctance motors can be classified based on construction such as linear SRM and rotary SRM.

Linear SRM: Linear SRM or linear switched reluctance motors are known in the market as servos. It contains a single-stage stator and rotor.

Rotary SRM: SRM rotary or rotary switch reluctance motor has two types: radial field and axial field. Axial field SRMs are classified into two types: single-stack and multi-stack. This rotating SRM contains more than a rotor and stator.

Features of SRM:

The features of the switched reluctance motor are as follows.

1. This type of reluctance motor can be 1-phase or 3-phase.
2. Controlling the speed of this motor is easy.
3. Speeding up is possible by changing the trigger circuit
4. Operates on the DC power supply used in the inverter.
5. Different speeds can be achieved by being able to change the firing angle of any switching device.
6. Control of one phase is independent of her other two phases. Wasted energy supplied to the motor can be recovered using feedback diodes. This improves efficiency.

Advantages of SRM:

1. These motors are very simple and the rotors in this motor are very strong.
2. VFD (Variable Frequency Drive) for this motor is a bit simpler compared to his traditional VFD.
3. They are cheap because they have no permanent magnets.
4. This motor does not require an additional ventilation system if both the stator and rotor slots are protruding. This keeps the airflow between the slots.
5. Self-starting without additional precautions
6. Highly fault tolerant
7. This motor works with a simple 2-phase or 3-phase pulse generator.
8. An open phase does not change the operation of the motor.
9. These motors are suitable for high-speed applications.
10. As soon as the phase sequence is changed, the direction of rotation of the motor is changed. inertia ratio or high torque

Disadvantages of SRM:

1. Switched reluctance motors have low torque capacity and typically these motors are noisy.
2. High noise level
3. They are suitable for low-cost, medium to high-speed applications where controllability and torque ripple or noise are not critical.
4. Uses external rotor position sensor
5. This motor generates torque ripple at high-speed rotation.
6. This motor generates harmonics when rotating at high speed. To reduce this, you should install a larger capacitor. Due to the lack of permanent magnets, SRMs must carry high i/p currents, increasing the need for converter KVA.

Applications for SRM:

1. These types of motors are used as replacements for asynchronous motors in a variety of applications where the operating conditions for that motor are not compatible.

2. For textile machines such as towel looms and rapier looms
3. Mining equipment such as belt conveyors, shears, winches, ball mills, drills, and coal crushers.
4. Used in electric vehicles
5. Oilfield equipment such as beam pumps, vertical pumps, well testers
6. Used for all mechanical presses such as screw presses.

• • •

CHAPTER V

Energy Source Battery

Batteries convert the energy stored in the chemical bonds of materials into electrical energy through a series of oxidation/reduction reactions (commonly abbreviated as redox). A redox reaction is a chemical reaction in which electrons are required or produced by the chemical reaction. It contains two substances that cannot undergo a redox reaction directly, but if electrons are allowed to move from one substance to the other through an external circuit, the ions can move through the cell at the same time. move. In a primary battery, this is a one-way process. Chemical energy is converted into electrical energy, but this process is irreversible and electrical energy cannot be converted into chemical energy. This means that primary batteries cannot be charged.

An example of a primary battery is a consumer alkaline battery used in things like flashlights. In secondary batteries, the conversion process between electrical and chemical energy is reversible. Chemical energy is converted into electrical energy, and electrical energy is converted into chemical energy, so the battery can be charged. All batteries used in photovoltaic systems must be rechargeable or secondary. Common examples of secondary batteries are lead-acid and lithium-ion batteries, which are used in high-power consumer electronics such as laptop computers, camcorders, cell phones, and some digital cameras.

Cell vs Battery:

A "cell" is the basic electrochemical unit. It has a voltage (or "potential") defined by its chemistry. A "battery" consists of more than one cell connected in parallel or series.

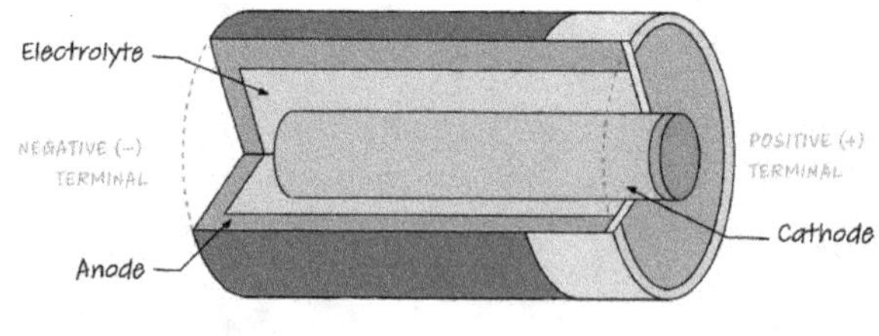

Figure 5.1: Representation of Battery

In its basic form, a cell typically consists of three main components: two electrodes and an electrolyte, plus terminals, separators, and a container. Speaking of electrodes, there are two types of electrodes: anode and cathode. The anode is the negative electrode (also known as the fuel electrode or reduction electrode). It releases electrons into an external circuit and is oxidized in an electrochemical reaction.

On the other hand, the cathode is the positive electrode (also called the oxidation electrode). It absorbs electrons from the perpetual cycle and is reduced in an electrochemical reaction. Energy conversion in batteries is therefore based on electrochemical redox reactions.

The third important part of the cell is the electrolyte. The electrolyte acts as a medium for charge transfer in ionic form between two electrodes. Therefore, electrolytes are sometimes called ionic conductors. An important point to note here is that electrolytes are not electrically conductive, only ionic conductive.

Batteries often consist of one or more "cells" electrically connected in series or parallel to provide the required voltage and current ratings.

Applications of Battery:

Over the past few decades, the use of small sealed batteries in consumer applications has grown exponentially. Small form factor primary or rechargeable batteries are used in a wide variety of devices. Some of them are listed below.

- Portable electronics: watches, cameras, mobile phones, laptops, camcorders, calculators, test equipment (multimeters).
- Entertainment: radios, MP3 players, CD players, all IR remotes, toys, games, keyboards.
- Household items: clocks, alarms, smoke detectors, flashing lights, UPS, emergency lights, toothbrushes, clippers and razors, blood pressure monitors, hearing aids, pacemakers, and portable power tools (drills, screwdrivers).

Different types of batteries:

- Basically, all electrochemical cells and batteries can be divided into two types.
- Primary (non-rechargeable)
- Secondary (rechargeable)

There are several other classifications of these two battery types, but these two are the basic types. Primary batteries are non-rechargeable batteries i.e., it cannot be recharged. While the secondary battery is a rechargeable battery i.e., these can be charged.

Primary battery

Primary batteries are one the simple and convenient power sources for a wide variety of portable electronic and electrical devices such as lamps, cameras, watches, toys, and radios. Since it cannot be charged, it is a type of "use and discards after discharging".

Primary batteries are typically inexpensive, lightweight, small, very easy to use, and require relatively little or no maintenance. The majority of primary batteries used in domestic applications are single cells, usually cylindrical in configuration (although they are very easy to manufacture in a variety of shapes and sizes).

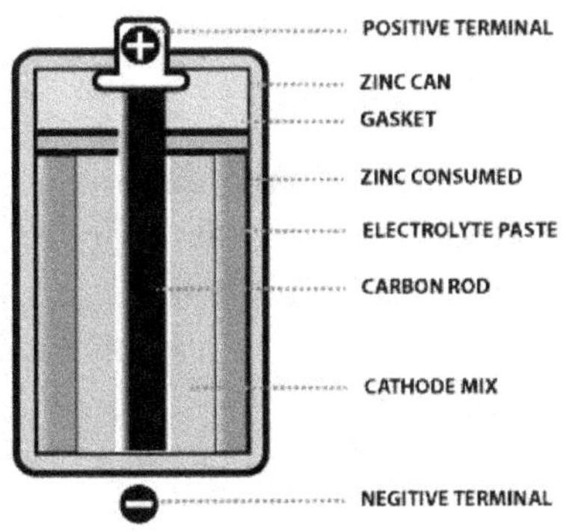

Figure 5.2: Representation of Primary Battery

Types of common primary batteries:

1. Until the 1970s, zinc anode-based batteries were the predominant primary battery type. During and after World War II, zinc-carbon-based batteries weighed an average capacity of 50Wh/kg. The most important developments in battery technology took place between 1970 and 1990. It was during this period that the famous zinc/alkaline manganese dioxide battery was developed, slowly replacing the older zinc-carbon type as the primary battery.
2. Mercury oxide and mercury cadmium oxide batteries were also used during this period, but environmental concerns about the use of mercury led to the phasing out of these battery types.
3. Around this time, the development of batteries with lithium as the negative electrode active material began. This is considered a major achievement due to the higher specific energy and longer shelf life of lithium batteries compared to conventional zinc batteries.
4. Lithium batteries are manufactured as button and button cells for specific applications (watches, memory backups, etc.), but larger cylindrical batteries are also available. The table below shows the types of primary batteries and their characteristics and applications.

Secondary battery

Secondary batteries are also called secondary batteries because they can be charged with electricity after being discharged. The chemical state of an electrochemical cell can be "recharged" back to its original state by passing a current through the cell in the opposite direction of the discharge.

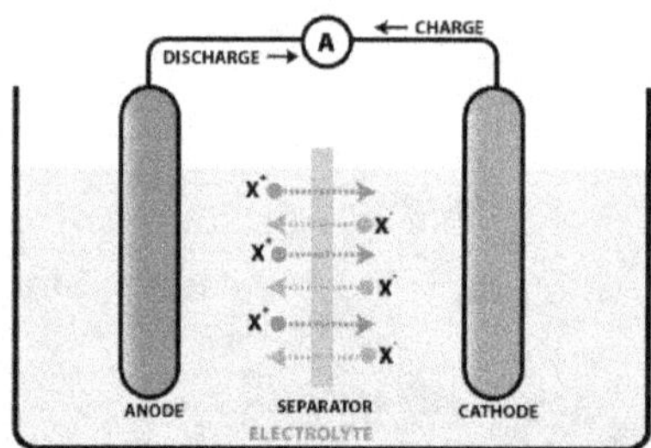

Figure 5.3: Representation of Secondary Battery

Basically, secondary batteries can be used in two ways:

1. In the first category of applications, secondary batteries are basically used as energy storage, electrically connected to the main energy source to be charged and also supplied with energy when needed. Examples of such applications include hybrid electric vehicles (HEV) and uninterruptible power supplies (UPS).2.
2. The second application category for secondary batteries is applications where the battery is used as a primary cell and discharged. A fully (or nearly fully) discharged battery is recharged using an appropriate charging mechanism rather than being discarded. Examples of such applications are modern portable electronic devices such as mobile phones, laptops, and electric vehicles.

The energy density of secondary batteries is relatively lower than that of primary batteries, but it has excellent characteristics such as high power density, flat discharge curve, high discharge rate, and low-temperature performance.

Types of common secondary batteries:

In fact, two of the oldest batteries are lead-acid batteries developed in the late 1850s and secondary batteries called nickel-cadmium batteries developed in the early 1900s. Until recently, there were only two types of secondary batteries. The first and most commonly used rechargeable battery is called a lead-acid battery, which is based on the electrochemical pair lead-lead dioxide (Pb-PbO2). The electrolyte used in these types of batteries is the widely used sulfuric acid.

The second type of rechargeable battery is called a nickel-cadmium battery. They are based on nickel oxyhydroxide (nickel oxide) as the positive electrode and a negative electrode based on cadmium metal. An alkaline solution of potassium hydroxide is used as the electrolyte.

Two new types of rechargeable batteries have emerged in the last few decades. Nickel-metal hydride batteries and lithium-ion batteries. Of these two, the lithium-ion battery proved to be the breakthrough, becoming commercially superior with its high specific energy and energy density values (150 Wh/kg and 400 Wh/L).

The main four types of Secondary batteries are:

Lead acid battery

1. Lead-acid batteries are the most popular and commonly used rechargeable batteries. They are his successful products for over a century. Lead-acid batteries are available in a different range of configurations, from small cells with a capacity of 1 Ah to large cells with a capacity up to 12,000 Ah.
2. One of the main uses of lead-acid batteries is in the automotive industry, primarily as SLI (Start, Light, Ignite) batteries.
3. Other uses for lead-acid batteries include energy storage, backup power, electric vehicles (including hybrid vehicles), communication systems, and emergency lighting systems.
4. The wide use of lead-acid batteries is attributed to their wide voltage range, variety of shapes and sizes, low cost, and relatively easy maintenance. Compared to other secondary battery technologies, lead-acid batteries are the most cost-effective option for all applications and offer exceptional performance.
5. Lead-acid batteries have an electrical efficiency of 75-80%. These efficiency values are suitable for energy storage (uninterruptible power supply - UPS) and electric vehicles.

Nickel-cadmium battery

1. Along with lead-acid batteries, nickel-cadmium batteries or simply Ni-Cd batteries are one of the oldest types of batteries available today. They have a very long service life and are very reliable and robust.
2. One of the main advantages of Ni-Cd batteries is that they can be exposed to high discharge rates and operate over a wide temperature range. The Ni-Cd battery life is also very long. These batteries cost more per watt-hour than lead-acid batteries, but less than other types of alkaline batteries.
3. As mentioned earlier, Ni-Cd batteries use nickel oxyhydroxide (NiOOH) as the cathode and metallic cadmium (Cd) as the anode. The online voltage of a typical consumer battery is 1.2V. In industrial applications, Ni-Cd batteries are second best in low-temperature performance, flat discharge voltage, long life, low maintenance, and good reliability. -Acid battery.
4. Unfortunately, Ni-Cd batteries have an important property called the "memory effect," which is their only drawback. When Ni-Cd cells are partially discharged and then recharged, they gradually lose capacity. H. Cycle to cycle. "Conditioning" is the process by which the lost capacity of the battery can be restored. The cell is fully discharged to zero volts and then fully charged again.

Nickel metal hydride battery

1. These are a relatively new type of battery, an advanced version of Ni-MH electrode batteries used only for aerospace (satellite) applications. The positive electrode is nickel oxyhydroxide (NiOOH) and the cell's negative electrode is a metal alloy in which hydrogen is reversibly stored.
2. During charging, metal alloys absorb hydrogen to form metal hydrides, and during discharging, metal hydrides release hydrogen. The main advantages of Ni-MH batteries compared to Ni-Cd batteries are their high specific energy and energy density. Sealed nickel metal hydride batteries are commercially available as small cylindrical batteries and are used in portable electronic devices.

Lithium-ion battery

1. The advent of lithium-ion batteries over the last few decades has been pretty amazing. More than 50% of his consumer market adopts the use of lithium-ion batteries. Especially laptops, mobile phones, cameras, etc.
2. Lithium-ion batteries have a very high energy density, high specific energy, and long service life. Other major advantages of lithium-ion batteries are their slow self-discharge rate and wide operating temperature range.

Charging/Discharging of Lead acid battery:

Construction:

The different parts of a lead-acid battery are shown below. Canisters and plates are the main parts of lead-acid batteries. Chemical energy is stored in the container and converted into electrical energy with the help of plates.

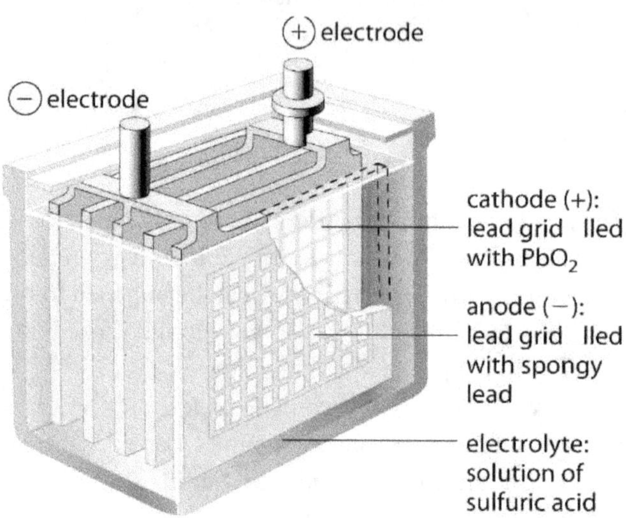

Figure 5.4: Construction of the Lead acid battery

Container:

The lead-acid battery container is made of glass, lead-lined wood, ebonite, and hard rubber made from bitumen, ceramic materials, or molded plastic, and is placed on top to prevent electrolyte leakage. will be killed. The bottom of the container has four ribs, two of which support the positive plate and the rest of the negative plate. The prism acts as a support for the plate and at the same time protects the plate from short circuits. Battery container materials must be resistant to sulfuric acid and must not deform, become porous, or contain impurities that damage the battery electrolyte.

Plates:

The plates of lead-acid batteries are designed in a variety of ways, all of which consist of some kind of grid composed of lead and active material. Grids are essential for conducting and evenly distributing current to the active material. If the current is not evenly distributed, the active material will peel and fall off.

The grid is made of an alloy of lead and antimony. These are usually made with transverse ribs that cross the spot at right angles or diagonally. The grids for the positive and negative plates are constructed identically, but the grid for the negative plates is less important for uniform conduction of current, so it is lighter.

Active Materials:

The materials in the cell that actively participate in chemical reactions (absorbing or generating electrical energy) during charging or discharging are called the cell's active materials. The active element of lead acid is

- Lead Peroxide (PbO_2) – Forms the positive electrode active material. PbO_2 is the color of dark chocolate.
- Sponge Lead - It forms the negative electrode active material
- Dilute sulfuric acid (H_2SO_4) – It is used as an electrolyte. Contains 31% sulfuric acid.
- Lead peroxide and sponge lead, which constitute the negative electrode active material and the positive electrode active material, have low mechanical strength and can be used alone.

Separator:

A separator is a thin sheet of non-conductive material, made of chemically treated leadwood, porous rubber, or fiberglass mat, placed between the positive and negative to insulate them from each other. The separator is vertically grooved on one side and smooth on the other side.

Battery Terminals:

The battery has two terminals, positive and negative. The positive electrode is 17.5 mm in diameter at the top, slightly larger than the 16 mm diameter negative electrode.

Working Principle:

How lead-acid batteries work is all about chemistry, and it's very interesting to know about. A large number of chemical processes are involved in the charge/discharge state of lead-acid batteries. Dilute Sulfuric Acid - H_2SO_4 The molecule splits into two parts as the acid dissolves. Positive ions $2H^+$ and negative ions SO_4^- are generated. As previously mentioned, two electrodes, an anode, and a cathode are connected as plates. The anode traps negative ions and the cathode attracts positive ions. This binding at the anode and cathode of SO_4^- and $2H^+$ exchanges electrons and further reacts with H2O or water (dilute sulfuric acid, sulfuric acid + water).

Operation during charging:

When sulfuric acid dissolves, its molecules break down into positive hydrogen ions (2H+) and negative sulfate ions (SO4−) and are free to move. When two electrodes are immersed in a solution and connected to a DC power supply, the hydrogen ions are positively charged and migrate to the electrodes, connecting them to the negative terminal of the power supply. Negatively charged SO4- ions migrated to the electrode connected to the positive terminal (ie, anode) of the feed line.

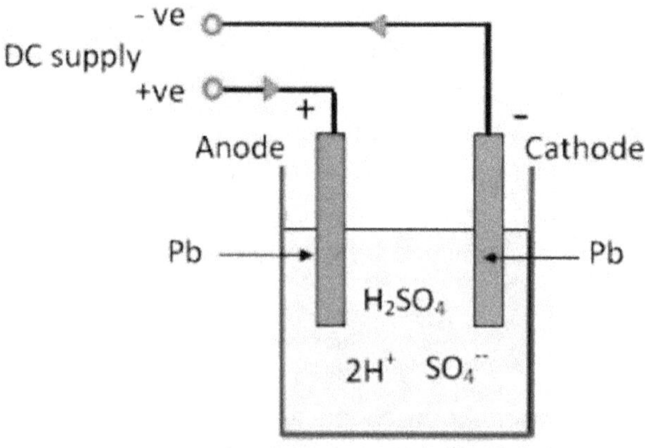

Figure 5.5: Charging of Lead Acid Cell

Each hydrogen ion receives an electron from the cathode and each sulfate ion receives two negative ions from the anode and reacts with water to produce sulfuric acid and hydrochloric acid.

Oxygen from the above formula reacts with lead oxide to form lead peroxide (PbO2). During charging, lead cathodes remain lead, while lead anodes convert to chocolate-colored lead peroxide. When the DC power supply is disconnected and a voltmeter connects between the electrodes, the potential difference between the electrodes is displayed. When wires connect the electrodes, current flows from the positive plate to the negative plate through an external circuit. This means that the cell can supply electrical energy.

Operation during discharging:

When the cell is fully discharged, the anode is made of lead peroxide (PbO2) and the cathode is made of sponge metal (Pb). If the electrodes are connected through a resistor, the cell will discharge and electrons will flow in the opposite direction to when charging.

Hydrogen ions move to the anode, reach the anode, receive electrons from the anode, and become hydrogen atoms. Hydrogen atoms attack lead sulfate (PbSO4) to form it comes in contact with PbO2, resulting in a whitish color and water according to the chemical formula.

$$PbSO_4 + 2H = PbO + H_2O$$

$$PbO + H_2SO_4 = PbSO_4 + 2H_2O$$

$$PbO_2 + H_2SO_4 + 2H = PbSO_4 + 2H_2O$$

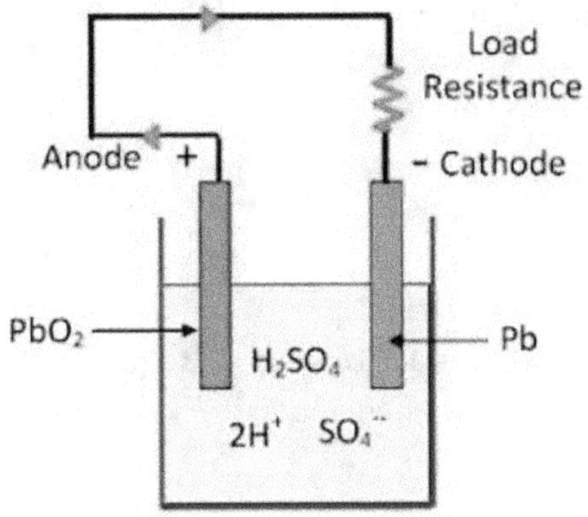

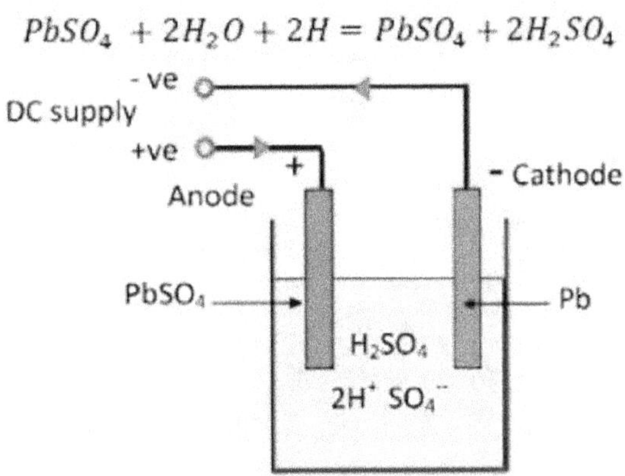

Figure 5.6: Discharging of Lead Acid Cell

Each sulfate ion (SO4-) moves to the cathode, where it gives up two electrons, becomes a radical SO4, and attacks the metallic lead cathode, forming whitish-colored lead sulfate according to the chemical formula.

Operation during recharging:

For recharging, the anode and cathode are connected to the positive and negative poles of the DC power network. A molecule of sulfuric acid breaks down into 2H+ and SO4- ions. A positively charged hydrogen ion moves to the cathode, from where it receives two electrons and forms a hydrogen atom. Hydrogen atoms react with the lead sulfate cathode to form lead and sulfuric acid according to the chemical formula.

$$PbSO_4 + 2H_2O + 2H = PbSO_4 + 2H_2SO_4$$

Figure 5.7: Recharging of Lead Acid Cell

The SO4- ion moves to the anode, gives up its two extra electrons, becomes the radical SO4, and reacts with the lead sulfate anode, forming lead peroxide and lead sulfate according to the chemical formula.

Advantages:

1. Inexpensive and easy to manufacture Low cost per watt hour.
2. Suitable for high specific power and high discharge current.
3. Excellent performance at low and high temperatures.
4. No need for block-by-block or cell-by-cell BMS.

Disadvantages:

1. Low specific energy; poor weight-to-energy ratio.
2. *Slow charging:* Fully saturated charging takes 14-16 hours. Requires storage while charging to avoid sulfation, limited lifetime, and repeated deep cycling will shorten battery life flooding-type watering needs.
3. Submerged type transport restrictions.
4. Negative impact on the environment.

Charging/Discharging of Nickel-cadmium battery:

Construction:

Nickel-cadmium batteries behave like any other battery. Nickel and cadmium are used to improve performance. Since a battery is a DC voltage source, it requires two points of potential, positive and negative, commonly known as anode and cathode. Nickel-cadmium batteries maintain a coating of nickel oxide NiO_2 around the redox.

This nickel oxide coating acts as the cathode. A coating of KaOH is maintained over the nickel oxide layer and acts as a separator. Please note that this separating layer must be wet or moist. Its goal is to supply the OH negative ions needed for chemical reactions. Cadmium is mounted on top of the divider. In nickel-cadmium batteries, the cadmium coating acts as the anode. A schematic of a nickel-cadmium battery is shown below.

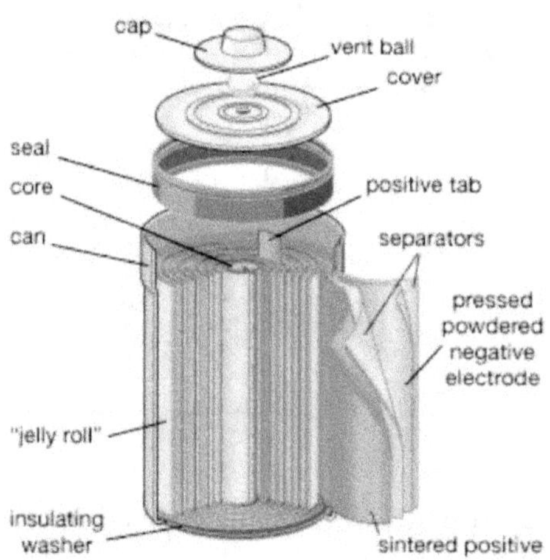

Figure 5.8: Construction of nickel-cadmium battery

As shown in the figure, the nickel layer acts as the positive current collector and the cadmium layer acts as the negative current collector. KOH or NaOH is used as a separating layer between two layers. Its role is to provide OH ions. A safety valve, sealing cushion, insulating ring, insulating gasket, and outer housing complete the package.

The role of the insulator ring is to separate the two layers from each other by insulating them. The isolator seal is where the isolator ring is at hand. This ring is attached to the divider. The outer case serves to protect the inner layer from external factors such as battery failure or mishandling. Keep in mind that handling batteries can be dangerous due to the chemical reaction that takes place inside the battery. The battery compartment is never opened, so all layers are visible and may cause injury to the user. It is often a good idea to remove the battery when the device is not in use.

Nickel-cadmium batteries are similar in construction to lead-acid batteries. It consists of three basic layers. First the nickel layer, then the separator layer, then the cadmium layer. The nickel layer acts as the positive current collector and the cadmium layer acts as the negative current collector. KOH or NaOH is used as a separating layer between two layers. Its role is to provide OH ions. A safety valve, sealing cushion, insulating ring, insulating gasket, and outer casing complete the package. The role of the insulator ring is to separate the two layers by an insulator. The isolator seal is where the isolator ring is at hand. A ring is attached to the partition plate.

The outer case serves to protect the inner layer from external factors such as battery failure or mishandling. Keep in mind that handling batteries can be dangerous due to the chemical reaction that takes place inside the battery. The layers, in combination with the separating layers, produce the required chemical reactions and potential differences.

Operation during discharging:

A battery has two electrodes that are immersed in an electrolyte. When an external load is connected to these two electrodes, an oxidation reaction starts at one electrode and a reduction reaction takes place at the other electrode at the same time. At the electrode where oxidation occurs, there is an excess number of electrons. This electrode is called the negative electrode or anode.

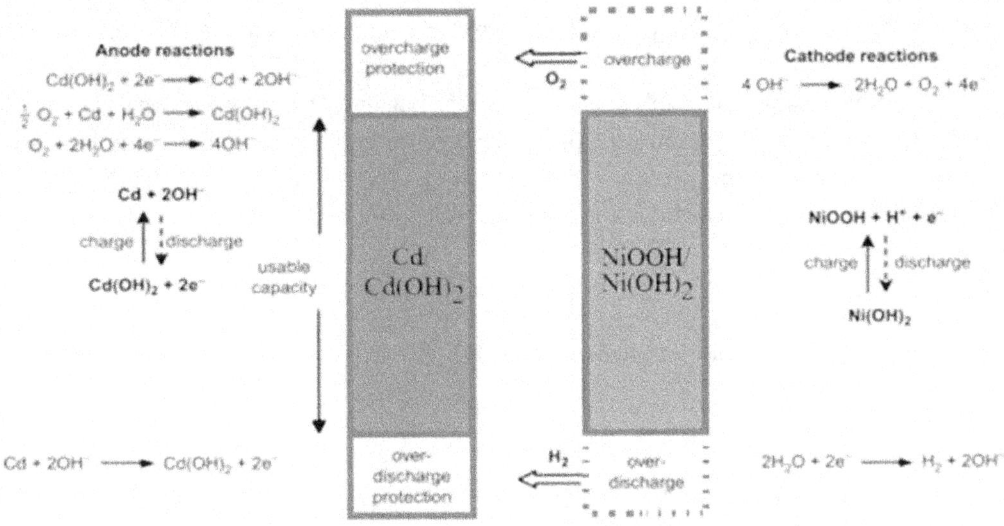

Figure 5.9: Discharging & Charging of Nickel-Cadmium battery

Meanwhile, during battery discharge, the other electrode participates in a reduction reaction. This electrode is called the cathode. Extra electrons at the anode flow to the cathode due to external stress. These electrons are absorbed by the cathode. That is, the cathode material participates in the reduction reaction.

Here, the products of the oxidation reaction at the anode are positive ions or cations that flow through the electrolyte to the cathode, while the products of the reduction reaction at the cathode are negative ions or cations that flow through the electrolyte to the anode. It is an anion.

To illustrate battery discharge, let's look at a real-world example. Consider a nickel-cadmium cell. Here cadmium is the anode or cathode. Cadmium metal reacts with OH – ions during oxidation at the anode, releasing two electrons and becoming cadmium hydroxide.

$$\text{``} Cd + 2(OH) = Cd(OH)_2 + 2e \text{''}$$

The cathode of this battery is made of simply nickel oxide, and nickel oxyhydroxide.

$$\text{``} NiOOH + H_2O + e = OH^- + Ni(OH)_2 \text{''}$$

A reduction reaction occurs at the cathode, and the nickel oxyhydroxide receives electrons and becomes nickel hydroxide through this reduction reaction.

Operation during charging:

An external DC power supply is applied to the battery during battery charging. The negative terminal of the DC power supply is connected to the negative plate or anode of the battery, and the positive terminal of the power supply is connected to the positive plate or cathode of the battery.

An external DC power supply injects electrons into the anode. The reduction reaction takes place at the anode, not at the cathode. In fact, when the battery is discharged, a reduction reaction takes place at the cathode. This reduction reaction causes the anode material to regain electrons and return to its previous state when the battery was not discharged.

Since the positive terminal of the DC power supply is connected to the cathode, electrons from that electrode are attracted to this positive terminal of the DC power supply. As a result, an oxidation reaction occurs at the cathode, returning the cathode material to its previous state (when not discharged). This is the general basis for charging batteries.

Now let's look at an example of a rechargeable nickel-cadmium battery. When the battery is charging, the negative and positive terminals of the charger's DC power supply are connected to the negative and positive terminals of the battery. Now at the anode, due to the presence of electrons from the negative electrode with direct current, a reduction occurs, cadmium hydroxide turns back to cadmium, releasing hydroxide ions (OH-) into the electrolyte.

$$\text{``} Cd(OH)_2 + 2e = Cd + 2OH^- \text{''}$$

At the cathode or cathode, nickel hydroxide oxidizes to nickel oxyhydroxide, releasing water into the electrolyte.

$$\text{``} Ni(OH)_2 + OH = NiOOH + H_2O + H_2O + e \text{''}$$

During battery charging, the secondary battery returns to its original state of charge, ready for further battery discharge.

Advantages:

1. Provides high output current.
2. Relatively tolerant to overcharging.
3. Withstands up to 500 charging cycles.

Disadvantages:

1. Mature technology with low overcharge resistance.
2. Cadmium is harmful to the environment.
3. Remarkable loading memory effect.

Alternative Batteries:

In recent years, the demand for lithium-ion batteries (LIB) has increased significantly. This growth is due to cost reductions and technology improvements. Despite their advantages, there are concerns about LIB energy density and lifetime, safety, resource-intensive manufacturing, and cost.

Several technologies, such as sodium-ion batteries, solid-state batteries, and flow batteries, are already in various stages of deployment and development. However, cost parity should not be the only metric, other parameters should also be evaluated before choosing a technology for your use case. Some of the important factors are listed below.

1. Energy and power density (especially for mobile applications)
2. Technical Readiness Level (TRL) or Maturity
3. Safety under various conditions of use
4. Existing production capacity
5. Durability
6. Incremental costs of use cases
7. Recyclability

With these considerations, a few alternative replacements to current batteries could be:

*Aluminum:*Aluminium is one of the most abundant metallic materials on earth. Recent research shows that aluminum-based batteries are cheaper, lighter, and easier to procure than their lithium counterparts.

Salt: The salt is very similar to lithium in its chemical composition. However, the environmental impact is minimal. Some have suggested sodium-ion batteries as a solution to the lithium problem. A viable method has not yet been developed, and sodium-ion batteries are heavier and have lower power output than lithium batteries due to the higher density of sodium.

*Iron:*Iron flow batteries are much larger than lithium batteries. As such, it is not suitable for phones or electric vehicles, but may be suitable for practical grid storage.

Silicon: Silicon can't completely replace lithium in batteries, but adding silicon to a lithium battery makes the battery cheaper and lasts longer. Currently, lithium-ion batteries contain graphite as a major component. But lithium seeps through the gaps in the stacked carbon layers of graphite, causing the battery to lose its reserves over time. Using silicon instead of graphite reduces this leakage and creates a lighter battery.

Magnesium: Magnesium can theoretically carry a larger +2 charge than lithium or sodium. For this reason, researchers say, batteries made from this material will have a higher energy density, higher stability, and lower cost than the lithium-ion batteries currently in use. A lithium atom can lose only one, while it can lose two electrons. This means that magnesium has the potential to transfer twice as much energy as lithium. However, research in this area is still in a relatively early stage.

Battery Parameters:

The basic parameters of battery are explained below:

Battery capacity:

This determines the number of hours the battery can be discharged with constant current to the defined cut-off voltage. The units are expressed in coulombs SI (amperes per second), but since these units are usually very small, the unit ampere hours (Ah) are used instead (1 Ah equals 3600°C).

The value of this capacity depends on ambient temperature, battery age, and discharge rate. The higher the discharge rate, the lower the capacity, but the impact on each battery technology is different. In addition to units of ampere-hours, storage capacity can also be specified in watt-hours (Wh=V x Ah). where 1 Wh is equivalent to 3600 J.

Specific power:

This parameter is defined as the power capacity per kilogram of battery (W/kg). Some battery technologies have high energy densities but low specific power, so they can store large amounts of energy, but can quickly supply only small amounts of power. When it comes to transportation, this means vehicles can travel long distances at low speeds. On the other hand, batteries with higher specific power usually have lower energy density. This is because high discharge currents typically deplete the available energy quickly (e.g., high acceleration).

Cell voltage:

The cell voltage is determined by the thermodynamic equilibrium reactions taking place within the cell, but this value is often difficult to measure, so instead, the open circuit voltage (OCV) measured between the anode and cathode terminals is will be used. For some battery technologies (such as lead-acid), OCV can be used as a basic estimate of the state of charge (SoC). Another commonly used measure is the quiescent current-voltage (CCV). This depends on the cell's load current, state of charge, and usage history.

Energy density:

Energy density is the amount of energy stored per cubic meter of battery volume, expressed in watt-hours per cubic meter (Wh/m3). This is a very important parameter when choosing a specific battery technology for transportation applications where space availability is critical.

Charge/discharge current:

During the battery discharge process, electrons flow from the anode to the cathode through the load, providing the required current and completing the circuit in the electrolyte. During charging, a charging current is supplied from an external power supply, oxidation occurs at the positive electrode and reduction occurs at the negative electrode. For convenience, the term C-rate is used to describe charge or discharge current relative to rated capacity. For example, a discharge rate of 1 C means that the battery will be fully discharged in 1 hour.

Self-discharge:

This parameter defines the reduction in battery energy capacity when the battery is idle (i.e. idle) as a result of internal short circuits or chemical reactions. This parameter can be affected by environmental conditions such as temperature and humidity, as well as battery DoD and charge/discharge history. Also, this parameter is especially important for long-term battery storage.

Round trip efficiency:

Due to internal losses and material degradation, discharging cannot recover all of the energy put into the battery during charging. The amount of energy that can be extracted from the battery during the discharge process via the supplied energy determines the round-trip efficiency. This efficiency is sensitive to charge and discharge currents. As the current increases, heat loss increases, and efficiency decreases.

State of charge:

State of charge (SoC) defines the amount of stored energy relative to the battery's total energy storage capacity. Different methods are used to estimate this value, depending on the battery technology.

Depth of Discharge:

This parameter, often called DoD (%), represents the discharged battery capacity relative to the maximum capacity. Each battery technology supports a different maximum recommended DoD value to minimize the impact on overall cycle life.

Cycle Life:

Cycle life determines the number of charge/discharge cycles a battery can go through before reaching a given energy capacity or other performance criteria. The current rate at which the battery is charged/discharged, environmental conditions (such as temperature and humidity), and DoD can affect this number as it is initially calculated by the manufacturer based on the specific charge and discharge conditions.

Battery Pack Design

A battery pack is a device that stores electrical energy to power electrical systems such as electric vehicles (EVs) and energy storage systems (ESS). Energy is stored in cells, all interconnected within the battery pack. To provide sufficient power, battery packs require a minimum voltage that cannot be achieved with a single cell. Therefore, we connect several cells in series to increase the voltage. Some designs use small-capacity cells. To achieve the required battery energy, cells are connected in parallel to increase capacity. Cells connected in parallel deliver power as if they were a single large cell.

A battery pack is made up of multiple smaller sections called battery modules (or sub packs). These modules contain a small number of cells connected in series and parallel. They usually have low voltages that are safe to handle. The module facilitates servicing when only a few cells are defective and can be replaced without replacing the entire battery. EV batteries typically consist of 4 to 40 modules connected in series.

Main components of Battery Pack:

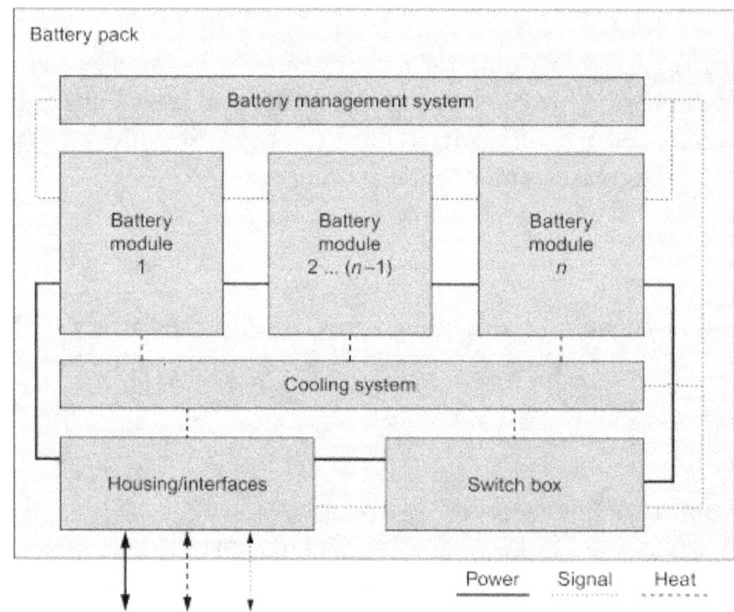

Figure 5.10: Main components of Battery Pack

*Cells:*Cells are the most important component of battery packs. The mixture of materials that make up a cell is called chemistry. Different battery types can achieve different performances and specifications. There are two types of cells: power cells and power cells. There are also many variations that offer the perfect compromise depending on the application. Li-ion cells are the most widely used chemistries in the EV industry. Alternative chemicals may also be used, such as Nickel Metal Hydride (NiMH). Slightly longer service life.

*Electrical connectors:*Electrical connectors such as bus bars, wires, or other power distribution conductors are used to connect cells and groups of cells in series or in parallel. These connections are typically made by ultrasonic bonding or laser welding. Busbar connections between modules can also be made mechanically using fasteners.

*Thermal Interface Materials:*Thermal interface materials (TIMs) such as pastes, adhesives, and gap fillers are inserted between battery components to mechanically connect them while enhancing thermal properties between surfaces. With the advent of structural battery packs, TIMs are becoming an integral component.

*Battery Management System:*Battery Management System "BMS" monitors critical parameters such as voltage, current, and temperature to protect cells. It is responsible for cell balancing (to maintain optimal cell performance at the correct voltage) and communicates with multiple systems such as engine management and temperature control. It also includes protection that can shut off the battery if necessary.

*Battery Thermal Management System:*The Battery Thermal Management System (BTMS) controls thermal energy inside the powertrain and electric vehicle, providing cooling or heating as needed to meet the thermal demands of the battery and protect the cells. BTMS includes components such as heat exchangers, tubes, hoses, cold plates, pumps, valves, and temperature sensors.

Contactor system:The contactor system is a switch controlled by the battery management system. The electrical connection between the main battery and the high voltage bus that powers the traction motor and other high voltage components may be broken.

*Housing:*The case is a hard case that protects the battery from environmental elements such as water, dust, and salt. It helps maintain precise temperature and electrical insulation within the battery, preventing damage such as rust and slow short.

*Communication System:*A communication system ensures communication with other components of the electric vehicle. The most commonly used protocol is the CAN bus.

Ragone Plots:

The Ragone plot is a chart used to compare the energy density of various energy storage devices. In such diagrams, the values of specific energy (W·h/kg) are plotted against specific power (W/kg). Both axes are logarithmic, allowing us to compare the performance of very different devices. Ragone plots can provide information about gravimetric energy density, but not details about volumetric energy density.

The Ragone diagram was first used to compare battery performance. However, it is useful for comparing energy devices such as engines, gas turbines, and fuel cells, as well as any energy storage device. The plot was named after David V. Ragone.

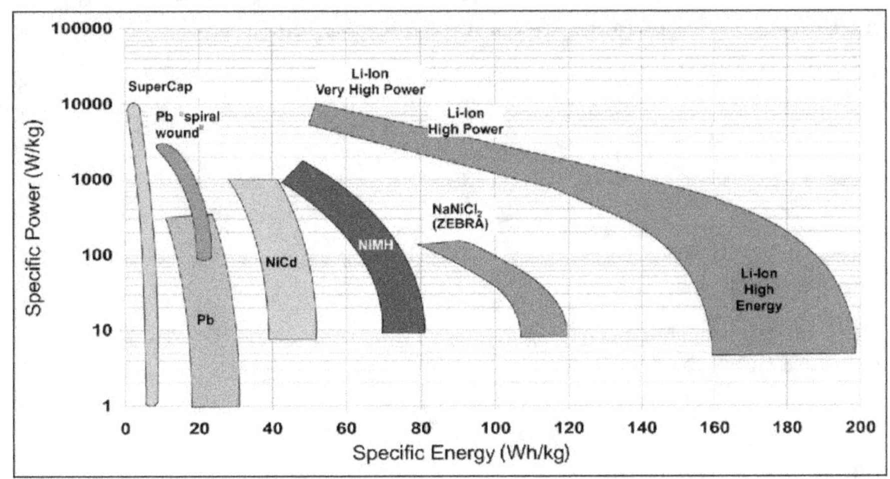

Figure 5.11: Representation of Ragone Plots

Conceptually, the vertical axis represents the amount of energy available per unit mass, while the horizontal axis shows how quickly that energy can be delivered, also known as power per unit mass. A point on a Ragone diagram represents a particular energy device or technology. The amount of time (in hours) that a device can operate at rated power is expressed as the ratio of specific energy (y-axis) to specific power (x-axis). This is true regardless of the overall size of the device. Because as devices get bigger, both power and power increase proportionally. Therefore, the isocurve (constant operating time) of the Ragone plot is a straight line.

For the electric system, the equation is relevant to:

"specific energy = (V x I x t) / m,
specific power = (V x I) / m,"

where V is voltage (V), I electric current (A), t time (s), and m mass (kg).

Battery Modelling

Battery models have become an essential tool in the design of battery-powered systems. Its applications include battery characterization, system-level optimization, state-of-health (SOH) and state-of-charge (SOC) estimation, algorithm development, and real-time simulation for battery management system design.

A battery model based on an equivalent circuit is suitable for system-level development and control applications due to its relative simplicity. Engineers model the thermoelectric behavior of batteries using equivalent circuits and parameterize the nonlinear elements using correlation techniques that combine models and experimental measurements through optimization.

Importance of battery modeling:

1. Mathematical modeling of batteries is important for the following reasons:
2. Development of efficient BMS.
3. Essential for improving charging/discharging technology and increasing battery capacity;
4. We need to understand the effect of power consumption on the battery.
5. To prevent serious damage to the battery due to overcharging or over-discharging;
6. A faster and safer way to study battery behavior under different operating conditions.
7. Identify operating limits to achieve optimum life for a particular application;

Types of Modelling:

- Electrochemical Modelling of a Battery
- Mathematical Modelling of a Battery
- Circuit-Oriented Modelling of a Battery
- Combined Modelling of a Battery

Constant current Discharge Approach:

1. Batteries exist because they store and release energy. This is done in a safe and controlled manner at set times. To ensure that these batteries can deliver the specified capacity of stored energy when needed, it is important to test them at full load on a regular basis.
2. The importance of constant current discharge in this context is that when using test equipment to perform load tests on energy storage units, the current does not need to be constantly adjusted during the test. A constant current load bank keeps the current stable as the voltage drops during the test. This allows less intervention during testing.
3. The rate of charge and discharge of the battery is governed by the C rate. Battery capacity is usually expressed in 1C. This means that a fully charged 1Ah battery can deliver 1A in 1 hour. The same battery discharged at 0.5C will deliver 500mA in 2 hours and 2A in 30 minutes at 2C. Losses in fast discharge reduce discharge time and these losses also affect charge time.
4. The main purposes of using constant current discharge load banks are:

- Discharge test (also called load test or capacity test)
- Acceptance test
- Engineering testing
- Testing battery capacity and
- Battery maintenance

C-Rating Definition:

A battery's C rating is defined by the time it takes to charge and discharge. You can increase or decrease the C rating. This affects how long it takes to charge or discharge the battery. C-Rate charge or discharge time varies depending on the rating. 1C is equivalent to 60 minutes, 0.5C is up to 120 minutes, and 2C is equivalent to 30 minutes.

The formula is:

"$t = Time$

$Cr = C\ Rate$

$t = 1\ /\ Cr$ *(to view in hours)*

$t = 60\ minutes\ /\ Cr$ *(to view in minutes)*"

When discharging a battery with a battery analyzer that allows different C-rates, a higher C-rate will result in a lower capacity value and vice versa. By discharging a 1Ah battery at a faster 2C rate or 2A, the battery should ideally provide full capacity in 30 minutes. The total should be the same because the same amount of energy is released in less time. In practice, internal losses turn some of the energy into heat, resulting in a capacity reduction of about 95% or less. Discharging the same battery at 0.5C or 500mA for 2 hours can increase the capacity by more than 100%.

Small batteries are rated for a 1C discharge rate. Due to its slow behavior, lead acid is rated at 0.2 °C (5 hours) and 0.05 °C (20 hours).

Lead- and nickel-based batteries can be discharged quickly, but protection circuitry prevents lithium-ion power cells from discharging above 1C. Power cells with Nickel, Manganese, and Phosphate active materials can withstand discharge rates up to 10°C with correspondingly higher current thresholds.

Fractional Depletion Model

With the introduction of fractional-order elements, fractional depletion models have received much attention due to their robustness and high fitting accuracy for complex dynamic processes. Electrochemical impedance spectroscopy (EIS) is analyzed for structural identification and parameter estimation of the fractional depletion model. Applied to optimize fractional order α and polarization response parameters.

Model Explanation:

- A battery electrochemical model (ECM) can be obtained from EIS analysis and provides insight into the electrochemical system and depicts the internal dynamic processes of the battery.
- The diagram shows the corresponding relationship between the battery ECM and the EIS. The dotted line representing the EIS is divided into three regions according to different frequency domains, corresponding to different electrochemical reactions.

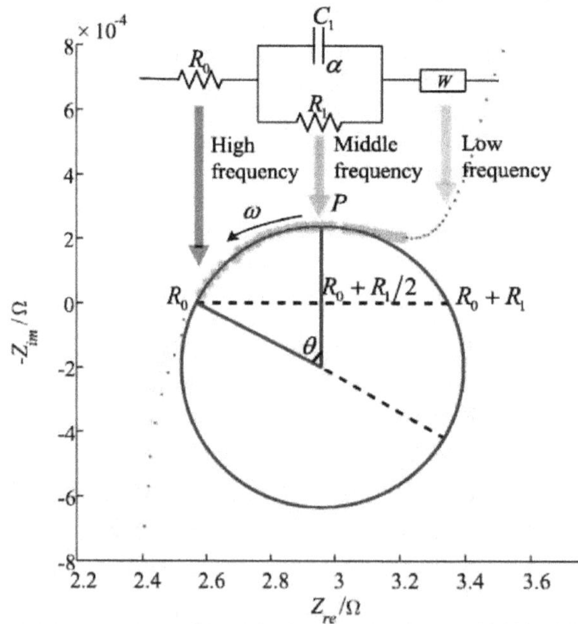

Figure 5.12: Representation of Fractional Depletion Model

- In the low-frequency range, typically below 1 Hz (rightmost red dashed slope curve), EIS describes the diffusion process of the electrochemical reaction and is expressed as the Warburg impedance.
- In the intermediate frequency range (marked with green dots), typically between 1 Hz and 1 kHz, EIS describes the electric double layer effect in batteries and the charge transfer process of lithium ions and electrons in conducting junctions. It will be -Zim=0 in the top circle. This creates a resistance and a double layer capacitance represented as an RC pair.
- The high-frequency range, generally above 1 kHz (leftmost red dashed curve), represents the movement of charge transported through the electrolyte and current collector to the external circuit. In this region, the battery behavior is modeled by an ohmic resistance due to the intersection point R0 between EIS and -Zim=0.
- A fractional-order equivalent circuit model (FO-ECM) will consist of all equivalent circuit elements within the above range. An H. Ohm resistor, an RC pair, and a Warburg impedance are connected in series. The impedance of the polarization capacitance is expressed as:

$$\text{``}Z_1(j\dot\omega) = 1 \,/\, C_1(j\dot\omega)^{\dot\alpha}\text{''}$$

where C_1 is the fractional order capacity defined as a constant.

(The units of C_1 are F·sec à −1 to meet the dimension requirements. The physical meaning of C_1 in the disordered elements indicates the process of electric double layer effect and transfer reaction on the electrode surface.)

j is an imaginary number,

ὼ is the angular frequency,

and à is the fractional order of the polarization capacity.

Standard Driving Cycle

A standard drive cycle typically represents a series of vehicle speed points versus time. Used to evaluate vehicle fuel economy and battery drain in a normalized way so that different vehicles can be compared. The drive cycle is run on a chassis dynamometer where emissions from the vehicle's tailpipes are collected, analyzed, and evaluated for emissions.

In the commercial vehicle domain, drive cycles are performed on engine dynamos rather than vehicle dynamometers and are evaluated using a series of engine torque and speed points rather than vehicle speed points.

There are two types of driving cycles: modal cycles like the standard European NEDC or his 10-15 mode in Japan, and transient cycles like FTP-75 or Artemis cycles. The main difference is that the modal cycle is a composite of a period of linear acceleration and a period of constant speed and does not represent real driver behavior, whereas the transient cycle exhibits many speed fluctuations typical of on-road driving conditions.

Factors impacting driving conditions on EV Battery pack lifecycle are:

- Environmental data (temperature, elevation, etc.)
- Vehicle data (speed, throttle, etc.)
- Battery data (voltage, current, temperature, SoC)
- Heating circuit data (indoor temperature, heating power, etc.)

Types of Standard driving cycles:

European driving cycles:

A. The NEDC

NEDC is used in Europe and some other countries as the reference cycle for vehicle homologation up to the Euro6 standard. It consists of four repeated inner-city sections called ECE and a suburban section, EUDC.

This cycle has been criticized by experts for not representing real driving conditions. Acceleration is actually very smooth. There are many constant speed cruises and many idle events. This makes it impossible to obtain certified values when driving the vehicle in real conditions. For these reasons, European authorities are considering alternative solutions to NEDC. A new cycle called the Worldwide Harmonized Light Vehicle Test Procedure (WLTP) will appear in the upcoming Euro7 standard.

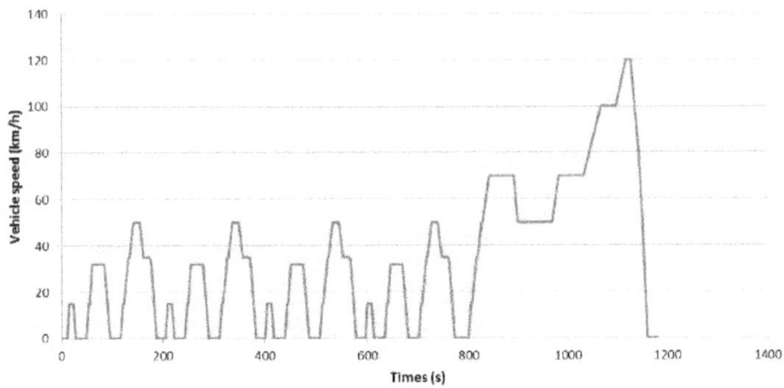

Figure 5.13: The NEDC *(New European Driving Cycle)*

B. The Artemis driving cycle

This cycle is based on statistical research carried out in Europe as part of the so-called Artemis project. It consists of 3 different configurations plus additional variants: city bike, country bike, highway 130 km/h, and highway 150 km/h.

The Artemis cycle is not used for emissions or fuel economy certification. However, automakers use this type of cycle to better understand real-world driving conditions and assess the real-world performance of their vehicles.

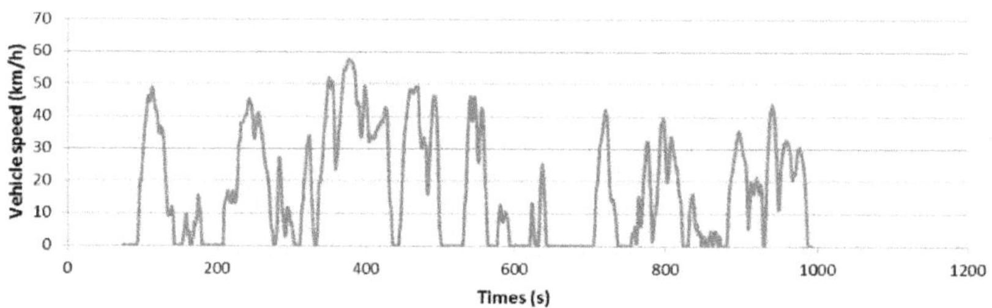

Figure 5.14: Urban Artemis Cycle

American driving cycles:

A. FTP-75 cycle

The FTP (Federal Test Procedure) cycle was developed by the US EPA (Environmental Protection Agency) and describes a vibration cycle that includes part city driving with frequent stops and part highway driving.

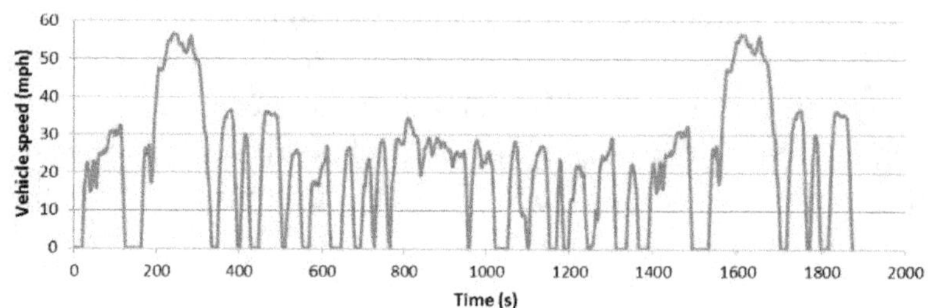

Figure 5.15: FTP-75 Cycle

B. Highway Fuel Economy Test Cycle

The Highway Fuel Economy Test (HWFET) is used to evaluate fuel economy during highway driving cycles.

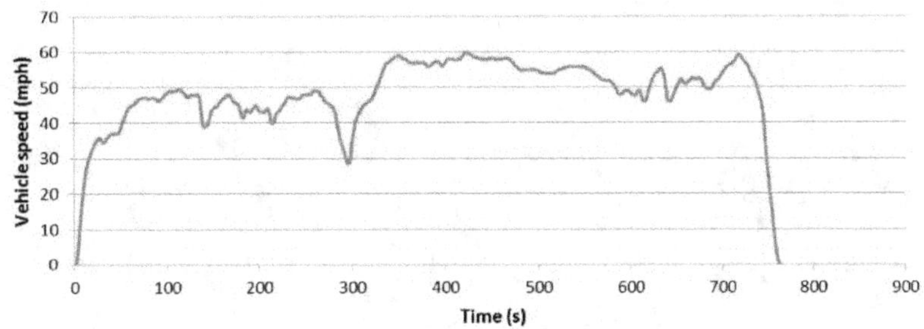

Figure 5.16: Highway fuel economy test cycle

Japanese driving cycle:

A. The 10-15 mode cycles

The Japanese 10-15 cycle mode is used for emissions and fuel economy certification in Japan. Simulate both city and highway cycles including idling, accelerating, driving, and decelerating. Measurements are taken on a hot engine using standard warm-up procedures.

Since this cycle has the same drawbacks as NEDC, Japanese authorities and manufacturers have decided to switch to a more realistic cycle, the JC08 cycle, from 2011 onwards.

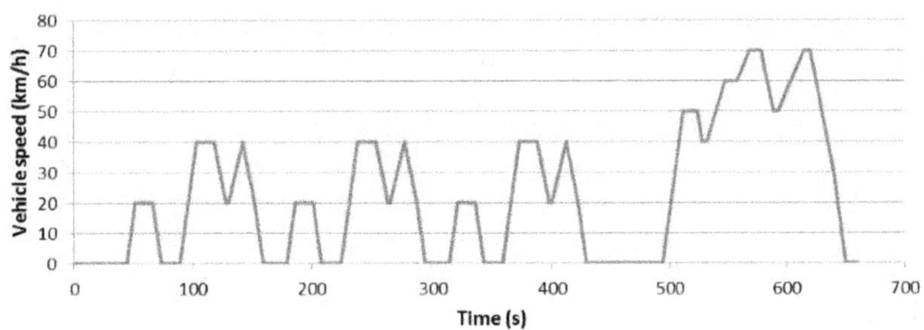

Figure 5.17: The 10-15 mode cycles

B. The JC08 cycle

JC08 is a much more severe transient cycle than the 10-15 mode cycle. It runs on both cold and warm starts and represents driving in heavy traffic with heavy acceleration and deceleration.

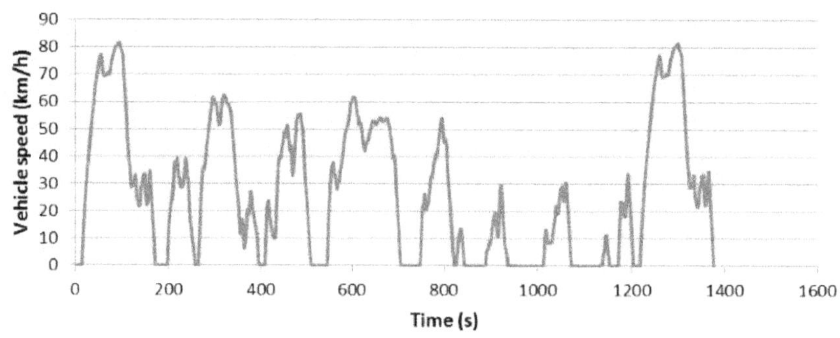

Figure 5.18: The JC08 cycle

Global harmonized driving cycle:

As with previous cycles, the Worldwide Harmonized Light Vehicles Test Procedures (WLTP) are tests performed on a chassis dynamometer. Evaluate pollutants, emissions, and fuel consumption as well as the electrical range of light commercial vehicles (cars and vans). Developed by experts from Europe, Japan, and India to replace the NEDC cycle from 2013 to 2014.

The test procedure he divided into three cycles according to the ratio of power to the mass of the vehicle tested. This power-to-mass ratio (PMR) is defined as the rated power (W) divided by the curb weight (kg).

A. Class 3 cycle

Class 3 cycle consists of four speed zones: a representative zone for city driving, a zone for suburban driving, a zone for suburban driving, and a highway.

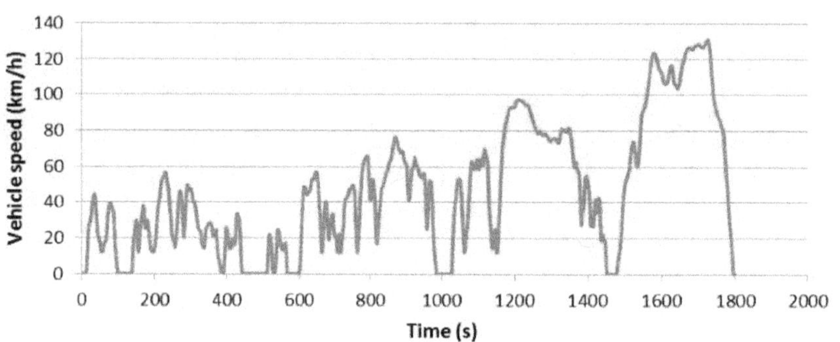

Figure 5.19: The WLTC Class 3 cycle

B. Class 2 cycle

Class 2 cycles represent low, medium, and relatively high vehicle speeds and are intended for Indian, low-power European, and Japanese vehicles.

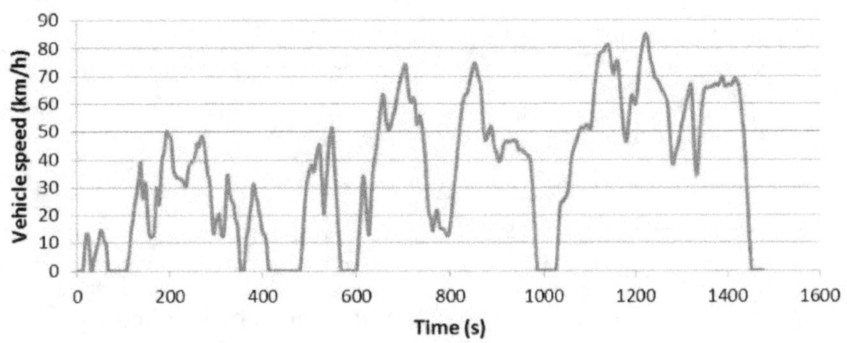

Figure 5.20: The WLTC Class 2 cycle

C. Class 1 cycle

This cycle consists of a low-speed zone and a medium-speed zone. This is typical of low-powered automobiles found in India.

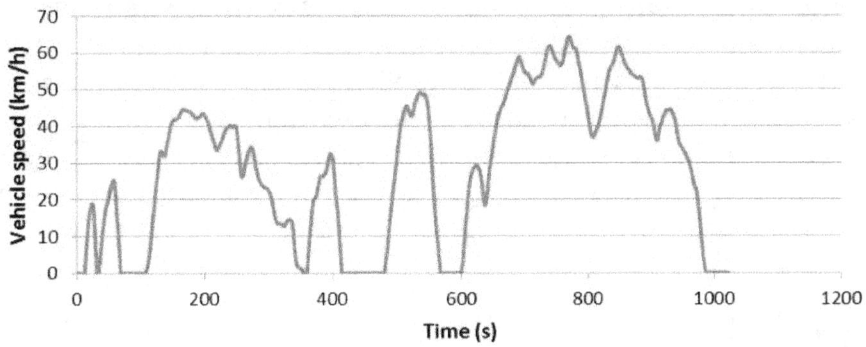

Figure 5.21: The WLTC Class 1 cycle

Power Density Approach:

In the context of energy management, power density serves as a measure of the amount of energy that can be handled in a given space or area. Power density is the amount of energy processed per unit area. Various units are used to measure power density, but it is usually expressed in watts per cubic meter (W/m3) or watts per cubic inch (W/in3).

$$\text{``}Power\ Density = (V_0.I_0)\ /\ x.y.z\text{''}$$

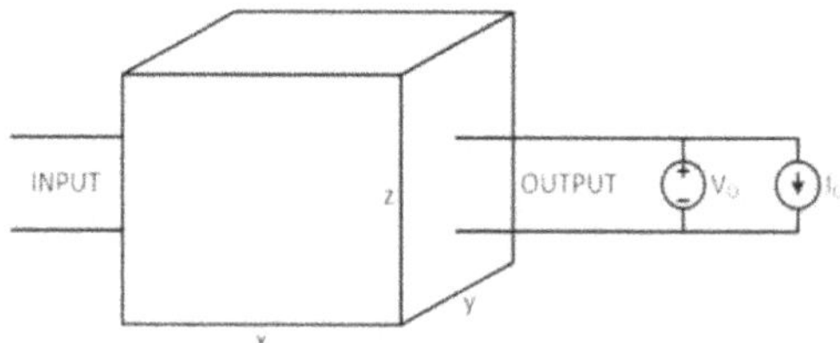

Power density is important because it indicates how much power can be handled in a given space. This is the key to achieving more performance in a smaller space while cutting costs with the latest economical technology. Some power system designers consider power density to be a major concern in the design process.

Before applying any power density solution, it is important to recognize its limitations and trade-offs. In some cases, there may be line losses or switch on/off points. Other converter performance degradation can be attributed to thermal issues, reverse recovery, and charging

Although limited, designers can still achieve high power densities if they focus on certain factors. For example, the switch must have low switching and conduction losses. Converters must be able to operate at high switching frequencies and provide good thermal performance. Another strategy is to integrate multiple semiconductor chips into a system. This is for passive integration of power and control processes.

Design and Application of the Battery Management System

Battery Management System "BMS" is an electronic controller that monitors and controls battery charging and discharging. Various types of battery management systems are used in most devices that use rechargeable batteries. It is also common in data centers where a UPS (uninterruptible power supply) keeps servers online. Cars, especially electric vehicles, have battery management systems, as do everyday portable devices such as MP3 players and smartphones.

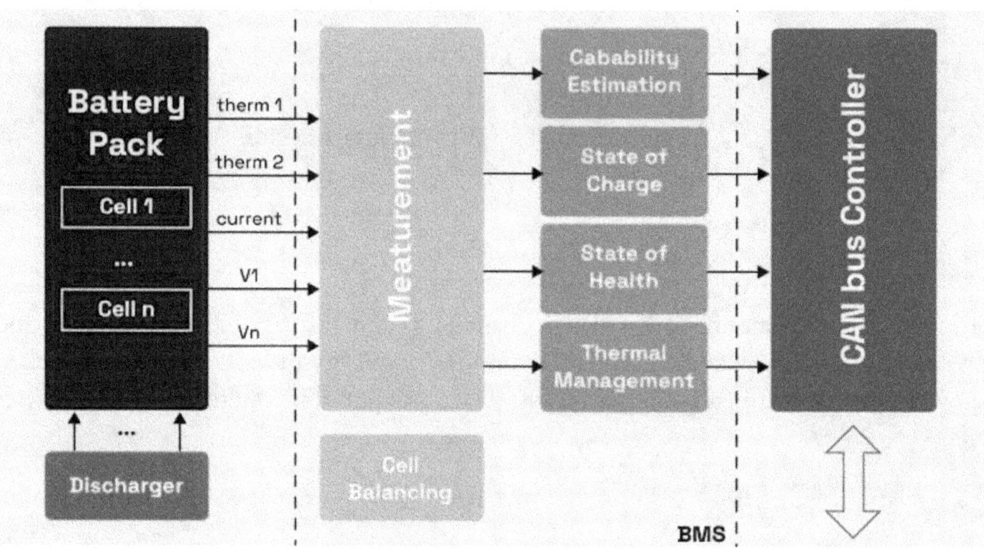

Figure 5.22: Components of Battery Management System

A battery management system can be as simple as an electronic device that measures voltage and stops charging when the desired voltage is reached. At that point, they were able to stop the current flow. In the event of an irregular or dangerous situation, an alarm may be issued. A more complex BMS monitors many factors that affect battery life and performance to ensure safe operation. Single-cell or multi-cell battery systems can be monitored. A multi-cell system can monitor and control the state of individual cells. Some systems connect to your computer for advanced monitoring, logging, email alerts, etc. Elements monitored and controlled by the battery management system include:

- Power-supply voltage.
- Battery or cell voltage.
- Charge rate and discharge rate.
- Battery or cell temperature.
- Battery and cell status.
- Cooling water temperature and flow rate for air or liquid cooling.

Functions of Battery Management System:

Battery management is much more stringent in EVs and HEVs than in portable batteries. It needs to interface with various other in-vehicle systems, need to operate in real-time under rapidly changing charge/discharge conditions as the vehicle accelerates and brakes, and perform in harsh and uncontrolled environments.

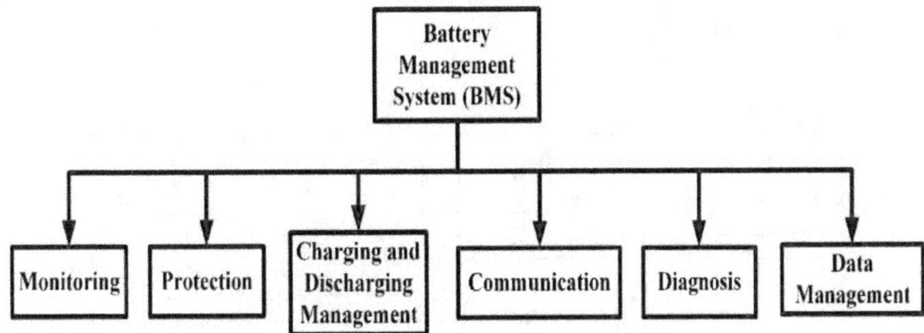

The BMS must manage the system throughout the operating cycle of the EV/HEV vehicle and ensure the following functions:

Cell Monitoring: Battery cells must be constantly monitored during charging or discharging. Out-of-specification conditions must be identified and reported along with the triggering of safety mechanisms. There are integrated circuits with cell monitoring algorithms that perform this function. There is a command chain where the cell monitoring circuit senses cell voltage and temperature and relays the data to the cell management controller.

During this phase, several algorithms are run to calculate the state of charge (SOC) and state of charge (SOH). SOC is determined so that the battery is neither overcharged nor undercharged. The SOC can also be thought of as an EV's fuel gauge, as it indicates how much charge is left in the battery. With this information, additional algorithms can be run to determine how far the electric vehicle will travel before the battery needs to be charged.

SOH is an indicator of the overall health of the battery and provides insight into the operating state of the battery. Based on this information, you can predict battery life and maintenance schedules.

Power optimization: A direct result of cell monitoring is battery performance optimization. Although the cell monitoring function determines SOC and SOH, it is the task of the EV battery management system to maintain the SOC and SOH parameters within specified values. An electric vehicle's battery management system determines the amount of current that can be allowed in each cell when the battery is being charged. During EV operation, the BMS prevents the voltage level from going too low when the EV is discharging. To ensure this, it communicates with the engine controller.

Electric Vehicle Safety: Safety is paramount when it comes to electric vehicle power and battery management systems. Undetected thermal runaways can lead to serious accidents. As mentioned earlier, BMS collects data such as voltage, temperature, and current to optimize performance. Similar records are also used to ensure security. Standards such as ISO 26262 have specific requirements that must be met to ensure that the BMS is designed as a fail-safe system. Another safety consideration is to separate the body/chassis from the battery pack to avoid electric shock to vehicle occupants.

Optimize battery charging: Battery cells degrade over time. An intelligent EV BMS takes this degradation into account, leading to changes in battery parameters such as voltage, current, etc. For example, battery cells are more susceptible to heat damage and start charging at lower voltages than other cells. The battery management system detects this error and optimizes the charging process to ensure all cells with low voltage are charged. This reduces stress on the overall battery pack and extends its life. Of course, BMS Diagnostics also saves this problem as an error code so that you can fix it later. Additionally, oxidation of battery terminals can cause voltage sag and BMS can adapt to these changes to get the best performance out of the battery.

The architecture of the Battery Management System:

A battery management system "BMS" typically consists of several functional blocks such as a cut-off field effect transmitter (FET), fuel gauge monitor, cell voltage monitor, cell voltage balance, real-time clock, temperature monitor, and state machine. The functional block groupings range from simple analog front ends like the ISL94208 which provide balancing and monitoring and require a microcontroller, to standalone integrated solutions that operate autonomously (such as the ISL94203).

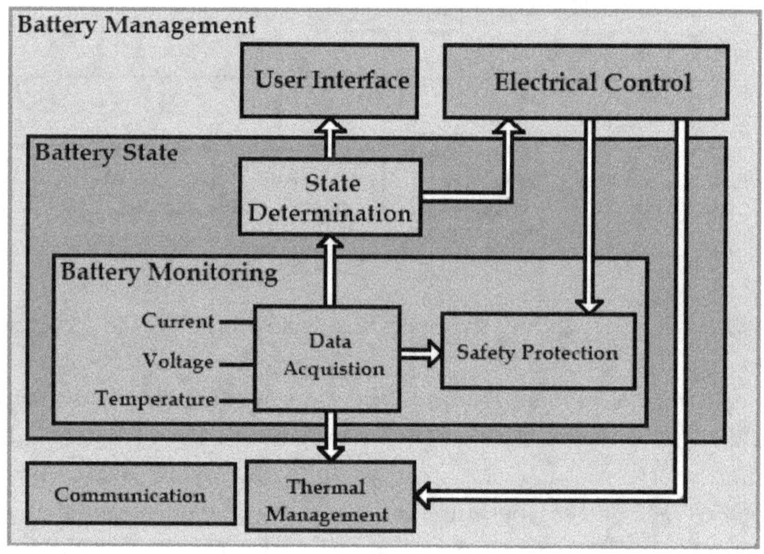

Figure 5.23: Architecture of Battery Management System

Next, let's examine the purpose and technology behind each block and the strengths and weaknesses of each technology. It has four main functional blocks:

Cut off FET

A FET driver acts as an isolation between the battery and the charger. Used to connect the high side and low side of the battery pack.

- High side - activates the NMOSFET using a charge pump driver.
- Low side - enables NMOSFET without charge pump driver

These integrated cut-off FETs reduce the overall cost of the BMS. It also eliminates the use of high voltage devices that can consume large amounts of chip area.

Fuel gauge monitor

This helps track the charge going into and out of the battery pack. The charge that flows is calculated by multiplying current by time.

Several methods are used to measure the current flow, but the most efficient and cost-effective solution is to use a 16-bit ADC with low offset and good common-mode performance to measure the voltage across the sense resistor. is to measure.

A higher ADC is beneficial for high speed and wide dynamic range.

Cell voltage sensor

Cell voltage monitoring is accessible as a standard feature of battery management systems. Helps determine battery health. All cells in a battery must operate at standard voltage levels during charge and discharge for safety reasons and extend life.

Temperature monitoring

As technology advances, batteries are designed to deliver high currents while maintaining a constant voltage. If the battery draws a large current, it will heat up quickly and may explode accidentally. It must be avoided. Therefore, the BMS continuously monitors the battery temperature and adjusts it to the nominal value. This feature is useful as it will notify you to start/stop charging or discharging when the temperature exceeds the rated value.

Other building blocks

Some other available blocks are:

- Battery Authentication - Prevents BMS electronics from connecting to 3rd party battery packs.
- Real-Time Clock (RTC) - used in black box applications
- Memory - used in black box applications
- Daisy Chain - Simplify connections between stacked devices

High-voltage battery management system (BMS) for electric vehicles:

Battery Management System "BMS" is used for batteries in high-voltage hybrid and electric vehicles. As a core component, the battery management system is integrated into the lithium-ion battery and manages all its functions. Based on collected system data, cells are individually operated and balanced under safe conditions. The BMS has a modular structure and includes a Cell Supervisory Circuit (CSC), a Battery Management Controller (BMC), and an HV sensor device.

Working on High-Voltage BMS for EVs:

- A high-voltage battery management system tracks the state of each cell in the battery pack. Determining the State of Charge (SOC) and State of Health (SOH) helps estimate the amount of current required to safely charge and discharge the battery without damaging it.
- The current limit acts as a shutdown to prevent overcharging the battery. This protects the battery pack cell voltages from high and low fluctuations so that battery life is unaffected.
- The BMS continuously tracks battery pack charge and discharge activity and monitors cell voltages. This data helps determine if the battery is discharging and keeps the passive cells in balance.
- The CAN bus (Controller Area Network) is a reliable unit for internal communication and controls most messaging protocols. IEM (Intelligent Electric Meter) estimates battery pack health parameters, total current, and battery pack voltage. Sends information to the CMU (Central Monitoring Unit) or sub-controller unit.
- The sub-controller quickly checks the temperature and voltage signals and sends the data to the CAN bus. The BCU (Battery Control Unit) receives signals from the CAN bus and responds by sending back the control signals needed to manage and model the battery pack.

Advantages of Battery Management Systems in Electric Vehicles:

1. BMS extends the life of battery cells in electric vehicles.
2. Provides stability and reliability.
3. Ensures the safety of battery packs, especially large lithium-ion batteries.
4. This is an effective system for measuring and controlling cell voltage.
5. BMS helps track down problems such as excessive heat, smoke, and fire that can destroy cells.
6. Regulates the temperature and keeps it at an ideal or optimal 45 degrees Celsius for EV batteries.
7. Optimize the performance of EV batteries.
8. Constantly monitor battery cells to avoid failures or explosions.
9. This indicates how long the battery charge lasts before it needs to be recharged.
10. The battery in the near future can predicts the functionality of the pack.

Disadvantages of Battery Management Systems in Electric Vehicles:

1. Current BMS data collection capabilities are limited.
2. This decision helped develop his SOC model for battery packs.
3. Currently, commercial BMSs lack SOC and State of Life (SOL) estimates.
4. SOC and SOL are essential characteristics for BMS to ensure the reliability of scheduled operation and battery replacement.
5. Also, each battery pack has its own BMS, making it completely impossible to develop a new BMS from existing BMS components. However, cloud BMS and digital twin technology can be potential solutions for limited data logging capabilities. Improve data storage capabilities and computing power through cloud computing.

Cell balancing

Cell balancing is a technique that extends battery life by connecting multiple cells in series to maximize battery pack capacity and make all of its energy available. A cell balancer or regulator is a function of a battery management system that performs cell balancing, commonly found in lithium-ion battery electric vehicles and ESS applications.

Individual cells within a battery pack typically have different capacities and different SOC levels. Without redistribution, the discharge would have to stop when the cell with the lowest capacity was emptied, even if the other cells were not yet emptied. This limits the energy delivery capability of the battery pack.

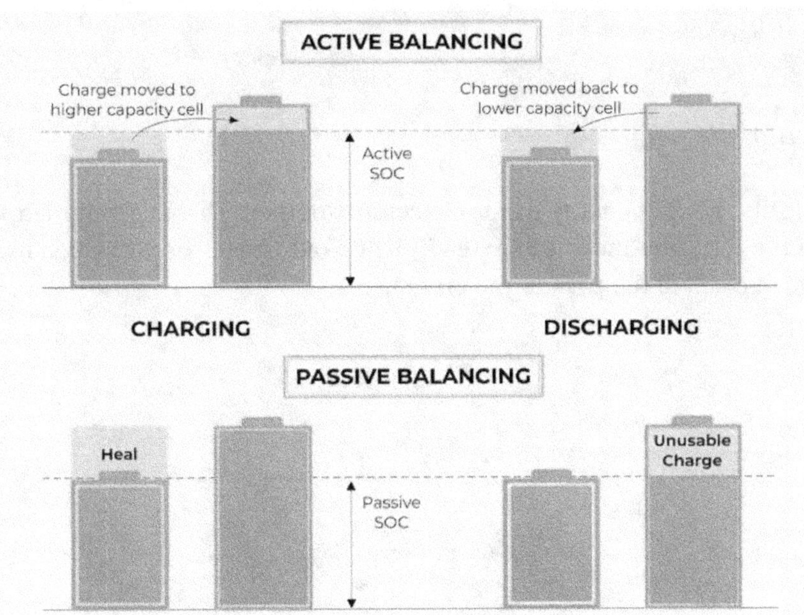

Figure 5.24: Comparison of Active and Passive balancing

During equalization, the higher-capacity cells go through a complete charge/discharge cycle. If the cells are not balanced, the cell with the slowest capacity becomes the weak point. Cell balancing is one of the core features of BMS, along with temperature monitoring, charging, and other features that help maximize battery pack life.

Reasons for the need for cell balancing:

Thermal runaway

Battery cells, especially lithium cells, are very sensitive to overcharge and over-discharge. This leads to thermal runaway when the internal heat generation rate exceeds the rate at which heat can be released. Using cell balancing, each good cell in the battery pack must be balanced to have the same relative capacity as the other good cells. Besides using cell balancing, you can keep your battery cool because heat is one of the main factors that cause thermal runaway. This minimizes heat retention inside the pack. The battery environment should be kept at room temperature.

Cell degradation

If a lithium battery is overcharged even slightly above recommended levels, the energy capacity, efficiency, and life of the battery will be reduced. Cellular deterioration is mainly caused by:

1. Mechanical deterioration of electrodes in pouch-type cells or loss of stack pressure.
2. Growth of the solid electrolyte interface (SEI) on the anode. SEI is believed to be responsible for capacity loss in most, if not all, graphite-based Li-ion cells when the charging voltage is kept below 3.92 V/cell.

3. Formation of electrolytic oxidation (EO) at the cathode. This can lead to a sudden loss of capacity.
4. Lithium plating on the anode surface with a high charge rate.

Types of Cell balancing:

1. Active cell balancing

Active cell balancers typically transfer energy from one cell to another. That is, from high voltage/high SoC to low SoC cells. The purpose of the active balancer is to extend the life of the pack or SoC when using smaller cell packs by moving more energy from one cell in the pack to the others.

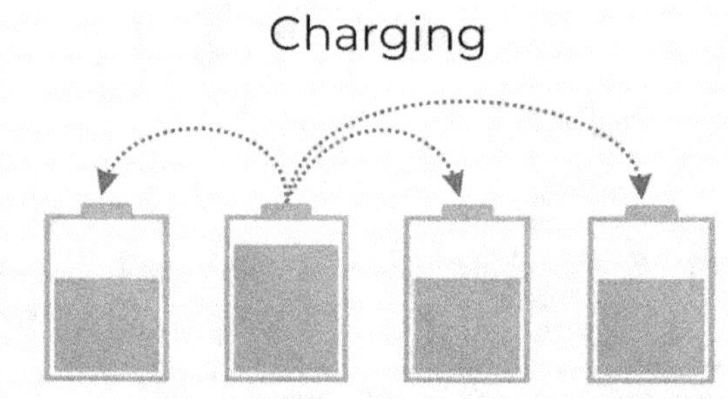

Figure 5.25: Charging of Active Cell Balancing

Rather than wasting all the energy as heat, an active cell balancer efficiently balances the cells with a small converter circuit that directs energy from the highest voltage cell to the lowest voltage cell. There are two different categories of active cell balancing processes: charge exchange and energy conversion. Charge Shuttle is used to actively transfer charge from one cell to another to achieve equal cell voltages. Energy converters use transformers and inductors to move energy between cells in a battery pack.

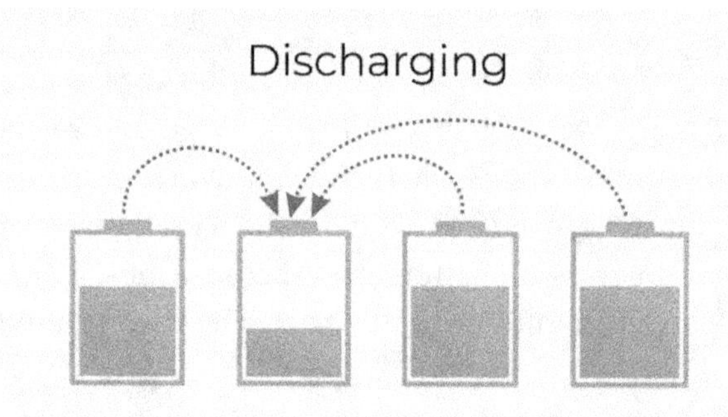

Figure 5.26: Discharging of Active Cell Balancing

Other active cells balancing circuits are usually based on capacitors, inductors or transformers, and power electronics interfaces. These include:

Based on capacitors:

Single Capacitor: This method is simple because it uses a single capacitor regardless of how many cells are connected to the battery. However, this method requires a large number of switches and intelligent control of the switches.

Multiple Capacitors: Using multiple capacitors connected to each battery, this method transfers unequal cell energy through the multiple capacitors. No voltage sensors or adjustments are required.

Based on inductor or transformer:

Single/Multiple Inductors: Single inductor cell balancing circuits have lower capacitance and cost, and multiple inductors have faster-balancing speed and better cell balancing efficiency.

Single Transformer: This method has less magnetic loss and faster-balancing speed.

Multiple Transformers: This cell balancer has a fast-balancing speed. However, expensive and complex circuitry is required to prevent the transformer from being flooded.

Based on the power electronics interface:

Flyback/Forward Converter: The energy of the high voltage cell is stored in a transformer. Highly reliable cell balancer.

Full Bridge Converter: This cell balancer features a fast balancing speed and high efficiency.

Active balancers can shift more current from one cell to another.

Advantages of Active Cell Balancing:

1. Better capacity utilization.
2. Best suited when different cell capacities are in series.
3. It increases energy efficiency.
4. It saves energy by transferring excess energy to lower energy cells instead of burning excess energy in the cells.
5. Extended lifespan.
6. Extends cell life.
7. Fast balancing.

Disadvantages of Active Cell Balancing:

1. When transferring energy from one cell to another, about 10-20% of the energy is lost.
2. The charge could only move from high cells to low cells.
3. Active cell balancers are energy efficient, but require each cell to be connected to an additional power electronics interface, which complicates the control algorithm and increases manufacturing costs.

2. Passive Cell Balancing

Passive systems may burn off excess energy from higher energy cells through resistive elements until the charge matches the lower energy cells in the pack. If you pack cells in series and find that some cells have higher energy than others with lower energy, you can simply add a resistor to the cells whose energy gives off the heat so that the energy in the upper cells can balance the burning cells. These balances the cell energies of the battery pack.

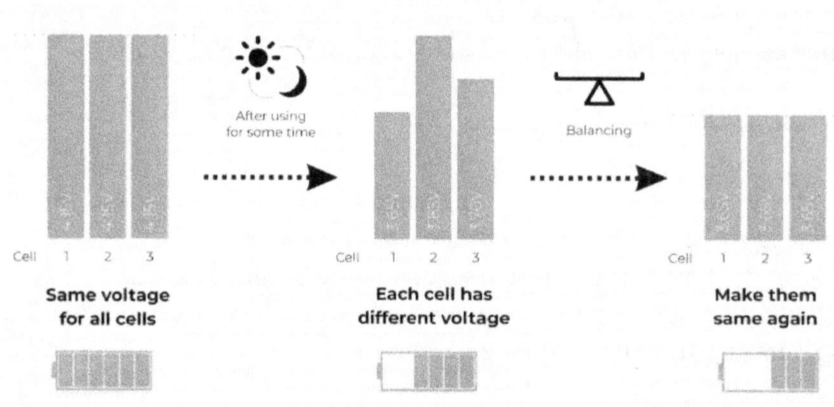

Figure 5.27: Charging/Discharging of Passive Cell Balancing

First, it burns excess energy until the cells are balanced. Passive cell balancing makes all cells appear to have the same capacity. There are two different categories of passive cell balancing methods: fixed shunt resistors and switching shunt resistors. A fixed shunt resistor circuit is usually connected to prevent the fixed shunt from being overcharged. With the help of resistors, passive balancing circuits can adjust the limits of each cell voltage without damaging the cell. The energy consumed by these resistors to balance the battery can cause heat loss in the BMS. This proves that the fixed shunt scheme is an inefficient cell balancing circuit.

Switched shunt cell balancing circuits are currently the most common cell balancing method. This method has a continuous mode and an acquisition mode, where all switches are controlled to be on or off simultaneously in the continuous mode, and a real-time voltage sensor is required for each cell in the acquisition mode. This cell balancing circuit consumes a lot of power through the balancing resistors. This cell balancing circuit is suitable for battery systems that require a small current when charging or discharging.

Advantages of Passive Cell Balancing:

1. Cells cannot waste energy they do not have. As soon as the energy bank is full, i.e. only when there is enough energy in the cell to balance it.
2. This allows all cells to have the same SoC.
3. This provides a relatively inexpensive method of cell balancing.
4. It can correct long-term self-discharge current mismatch from cell to cell.

Disadvantages of Passive Cell Balancing:

1. Poor thermal management.
2. Full SoC is not balanced. They are balanced only about 95% to the top of each cell. This is because cells with different capacities are forced to consume extra energy.
3. Its energy transfer efficiency is usually low. Electrical energy is dissipated as heat in the resistor and the circuit also considers switching losses. This means more energy loss.
4. This does not improve runtime on battery-powered systems.

Battery state estimation

Battery state estimation is required to predict battery life and diagnose aging, as well as optimize battery safety and performance. As the battery ages, the negative electrode develops a solid electrolyte interface. Cell design, battery operation, and environmental conditions are among the many factors that affect battery life. Aging reduces the usable capacity of the battery and increases internal resistance. The chart below shows the main deterioration factors that affect battery health.

Battery state estimation includes four main states: state of charge (SOC), state of health (SOH), internal temperature, and joint state estimation. These are explained in detail below:

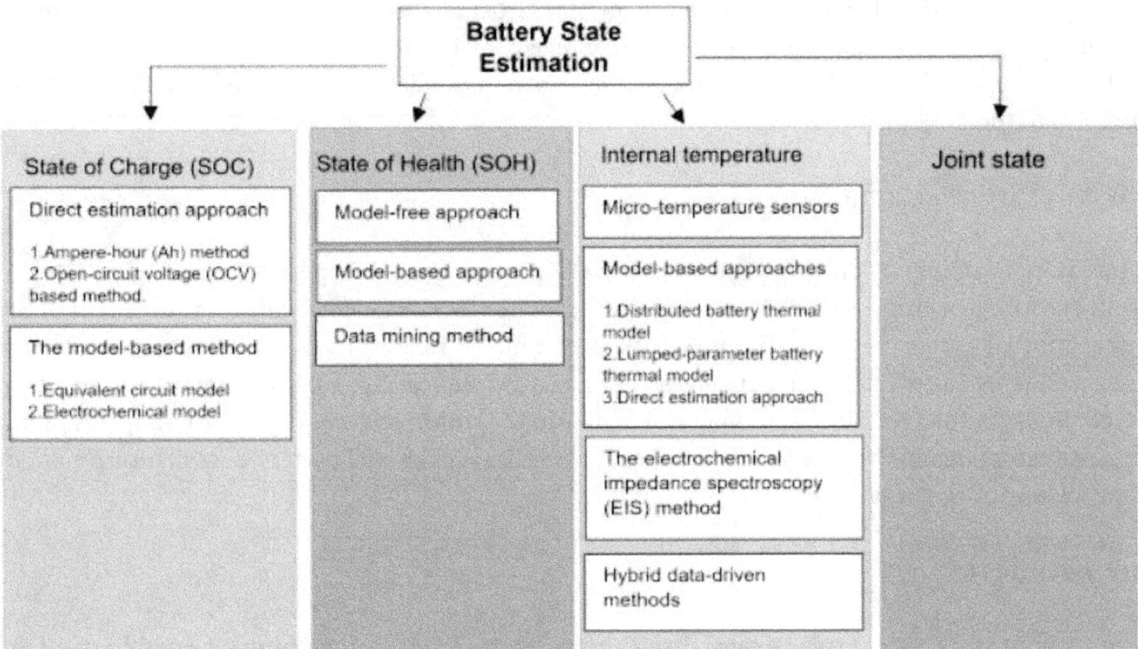

Figure 5.28: Classification of Battery State Estimation

SOC Estimation:

The SOC Battery Estimate provides information about the remaining capacity of the battery as a percentage of its total capacity. There are two commonly used approaches to SOC estimation. direct estimation and model-based estimation.

Direct Estimation Approach: This estimation approach is based on the direct measurement of battery parameters (current and voltage). The two calculation methods used are the Ampere Hour (Ah) and Open Circuit Voltage (OCV) based methods. The Ah method uses a simple measurement of charge or discharges current. Therefore, this approach is a logical choice for SOC estimation

This method is highly dependent on the measured current, and errors accumulated over time significantly affect the accuracy of the SOC estimation. Also, it is difficult to determine the exact initial SOC in a real application (for example, when the battery charges only within a limited range of 10% to 90%).

*Model-based method:*This model was developed to provide an OCV calculation that allows online SOC estimation. The most common models are the battery equivalent circuit model and the electrochemical model. The accuracy of model-based methods depends on the training of the battery model, the assumed state observer, and parameter tuning. The estimated performance of SOC is verified under limited test data and does not guarantee the estimated performance under various actual usage conditions.

SOH Estimation:

SOH indicates the battery's ability to store and deliver energy and provides information about the state of the battery compared to its optimal state. SOH is 100% with a new battery, reducing overtime. However, the initial SOH may be less than 100% if the performance of the new battery does not meet the specification.

*Model-free method:*Model-free methods use a parameter called capacity aging (C aged) or increased internal resistance (R_{inc}) to estimate battery SOH. This model is simply expressed by the following equation: where C n and R n are the nominal capacities and internal resistance of a new, unused battery:

*Direct measurement method:*Direct measurement methods use standard capacitance or pulse current tests to measure the aging capacity (C aged) and increase in internal resistance (R inc) of the battery. This method is impractical for EV applications as it requires the battery to be completely discharged, which interferes with the normal operation of the EV.

Internal temperature estimation:

Battery temperature is an important factor affecting battery performance, lifespan, efficiency, and safety. A thermal sensor is suitable for measuring the surface temperature of the battery. However, this information alone is not enough as the internal battery temperature is a critical parameter for proper battery management. High internal temperature accelerates battery aging and creates safety hazards (such as a fire). The internal battery temperature is typically much different than the surface temperature (up to 12°C for high-power applications). Designing a suitable approach for estimating the internal battery temperature prevents accelerated battery degradation and helps the BMS algorithm optimize battery energy discharge.

Joint State Estimation:

Based on the combined electrothermal model, you can get an estimate of the battery's combined state (SOC and internal temperature). These models simultaneously capture the electrical and thermal behavior of the battery. Designing a simple and accurate electrothermal battery model is the first critical step in joint state estimation. The junction state (battery SOC and internal temperature) can be estimated simultaneously from the interaction between battery resistance and internal temperature.

The safety aspect of battery management system for electric vehicles:

- Functional safety is paramount in BMS. During the charge and discharge process, it is important that the cell or module voltage, current, and temperature do not exceed defined SOA limits under monitored control.

1. Exceeding the limit for an extended period not only damages the potentially expensive battery pack but can also result in a dangerous thermal runaway condition.
2. In addition, the lower voltage limit is also strictly monitored to protect the lithium-ion cells and functional safety.
3. Ultimately, if lithium-ion batteries remain in this low-voltage state, copper dendrites can grow on the anode, leading to increased self-discharge rates and potential safety concerns.
4. The high energy density of lithium-ion powered systems comes at the cost of little room for error in battery management.

- Safety considerations for passenger car battery systems are manifold. There are important traditional electrical safety considerations to protect production workers, owners, mechanics, and vehicle breakers from high voltages and shocks. There are mechanical considerations to protect battery cells from punctures and impact damage and to contain liquids and gases that may leak or escape from the cells. Lithium-ion batteries operate safely and most efficiently within a more restricted temperature range than those found in internal combustion engine vehicles, so there are thermal safety considerations in battery pack design. There are functional safety considerations for the electrical system that keeps the battery within a safe operating range while the vehicle is in use or charging.
- Detecting and correcting malfunctions such as communication errors or battery cell and sensor connection errors to avoid dangerous events is part of functional safety.
- Functional safety is the part of overall safety related to the prevention and mitigation of potentially dangerous events caused by malfunctioning electronic systems. In the automotive industry, the International Organization for Standardization (ISO) 26262 series of road vehicle functional safety standards define the latest functional safety best practices for the development of safety-related systems for passenger vehicles, trucks, buses, and other motorcycles.
- Loss of function in some vehicle systems does not lead to danger. In the event of a malfunction within the system, the safe state of the system is for the electronics to shut down and the driver to be alerted by lights or other indicators on the dashboard. However, in some systems malfunction or loss of functionality can lead to potentially dangerous events. For systems that cannot simply be shut down, safety goals may include requirements for "safety-related availability". In this case, tolerance for some kind of failure in the system may be required for a period of time to avoid dangerous events.
- Returning to the battery monitor subsystem, the battery cell voltage and temperature sensing locations are connected to the battery monitor ASIC. The measurement information is read frequently by the control processor to calculate the current state of the battery and ensure that operation remains within safe limits. In high-voltage battery packs, the monitoring ASICs are arranged in a stack configuration, with each ASIC measuring multiple cells in parallel.

Thermal management of batteries for electric vehicles

- Battery Thermal Management System (BTMS) A device responsible for managing and dissipating the heat generated during the electrochemical processes in the cell, ensuring that the battery can operate safely and efficiently.
- The purpose of BTMS (Battery Thermal Management System) is to prevent accelerated battery aging by managing the heat generated by the components so that the battery continues to function under optimal temperature conditions.
- Existing commercial cells operate safely from -40 to 60 degrees Celsius, but the operating range recommended by manufacturers for maximum performance is actually 15 to 35 degrees Celsius. With this in mind, it is also recommended that cell-to-cell temperature differences not exceed 5 degrees Celsius within the battery pack.
- Please note that exposing the battery to extreme conditions can have fatal consequences. For example, operation at very high temperatures (>80°C) can cause a well-known thermal runaway, which can lead to fires and, in the worst case, battery explosions, affecting personal safety.
- A BTMS is a battery pack component responsible for keeping the cells operating at the optimum temperature conditions specified by the manufacturer.

Battery packs should be stored in a controlled environment where the temperature is controlled and there is no risk of thermal runaway for safety, performance (both power and capacity), and longevity reasons. A BTMS must have four key functions to ensure the correct operating state of the battery pack:

Cooling: Due to their inefficiency, battery cells generate heat as well as electricity. This heat must be dissipated from the battery pack in advance or when the battery reaches its optimum temperature. Therefore, BTMS needs a cooling function.

Heating: In cold climates, the temperature of the battery pack may drop below the minimum temperature limit. Hence such a heating function. B. A PTC heater is required to help the battery pack reach the proper temperature range in a short time.

Insulation: In extreme cold or hot weather, the temperature difference between the inside and outside of the battery pack is much greater than in moderate weather. Therefore, the temperature of the battery will drop (cold) or rise (hot) faster than the correct temperature range. To prevent this, good insulation can slow down or slow down the battery temperature, especially if the vehicle is parked outdoors.

Ventilation: Ventilation is required to exhaust harmful gases in the battery pack. In some systems such as the Air system, this function is combined with cooling and heating functions.

There is more than one choice when choosing BTMS for battery packs. The diagram below provides an overview of the major thermal management technologies that are commercially available or being researched by the scientific community:

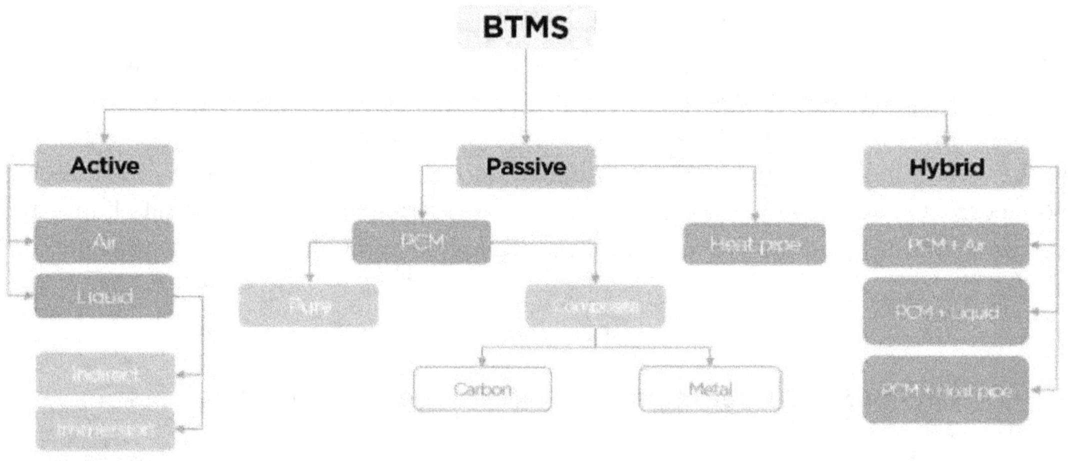

Figure 5.29: Types of Battery Thermal Management System

A. Active BTMS

Today, active BTMS based on forced air or coolant are most commonly used in electric vehicles. For example, Toyota and Lexus both use fans to circulate cool air over the battery cells. Tesla or Audi, on the other hand, use channels in direct contact with the cells through which the coolant (usually a mixture of water and ethylene glycol) circulates. Active BTMS can be categorized as:

Air System:

Air systems use air as a heat carrier. Intake air can come directly from the atmosphere or the cabin, and can also be conditioned air after a heater or air conditioning evaporator. The former is called a passive air system and the latter an active air system. Active systems can provide additional cooling or heating capacity. Passive systems can provide hundreds of watts of cooling or heating power, while active systems are limited to 1 kW of capacity.

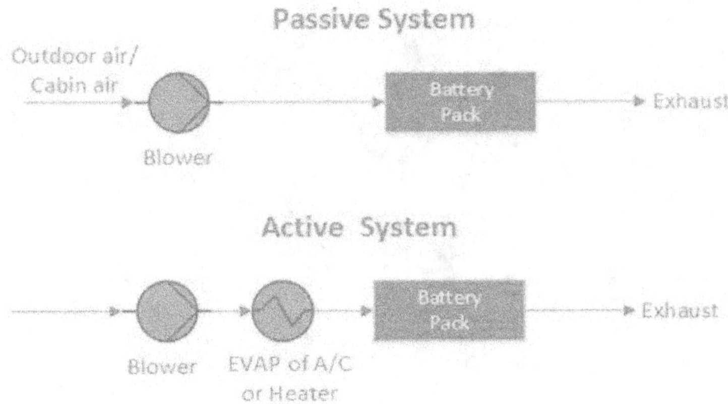

Figure 5.30: Forced Air Systems *(Passive & Active)*

A recirculation system is also mentioned, as air is supplied by a blower in both cases. The following diagram shows a schematic description of the system. A simple forced-air cooling system has the advantages of high reliability, low cost, and easy maintenance, but poor thermal management.

At high ambient temperatures such as 45°C to 50°C, the temperature inside the battery pack will exceed 55°C, higher than the operating temperature, leading to thermal runaway. The uniformity of temperature distribution is also very important due to the effects of aging and cycle life. Ignoring ambient temperature, the cell-to-cell difference is 2°C at 2C rate discharge current and 4.8°C at 6.67C rate discharge current. The uniformity of the temperature distribution is also affected by the flow rate. As the flow rate increases, the maximum temperature difference across the cell increases.

Liquid System:

Besides air, the liquid is another heat transfer medium for heat transfer. In general, he has two groups of fluids used in thermal management systems. One is a dielectric liquid (direct contact liquid), such as mineral oil, which can come into direct contact with the battery cells. The other is a conductive liquid that can only indirectly contact the battery cell (indirect contact liquid) i.e, a mixture of ethylene glycol and water. Different layouts are designed according to different liquids.

For direct liquid contact, modules are typically immersed in mineral oil. For indirect liquid contact, possible layouts are a jacket around the battery modules, separate tubes around each module, placement of the battery modules on a cooling/heating plate, or a combination of battery modules and cooling/heating fins and plates. any of the combinations. Between these two groups, indirect contact systems are preferred to improve the isolation between the battery module and the environment and improve safety performance. Liquid systems can also be divided into passive or active systems due to the different heat sinks for cooling. In passive liquid systems, the heat sink for cooling is the radiator. This system cannot be heated.

The figure shows the systematic scheme of the passive liquid system. A heat transfer fluid is circulated by a pump in a closed system. Circulating fluid absorbs heat from the battery pack and expels it through the radiator. Cooling capacity is highly dependent on the temperature between the surrounding air and the battery. A fan behind the radiator can improve cooling performance, but passive liquid systems become ineffective if the ambient air is warmer than the battery's temperature, or if the temperature difference between them is too small.

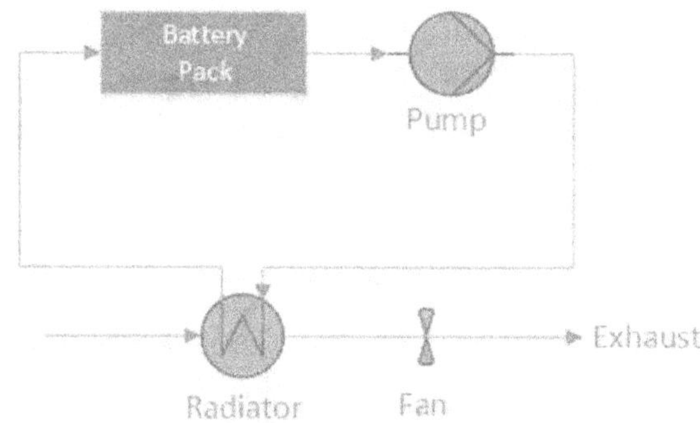

Figure 5.31: Passive Liquid Cooling System

The figure shows the systematic scheme of the active liquid system. There are 2 loops. The top loop is called the primary loop and the bottom loop is called the secondary loop. A primary loop is similar to that of a passive fluid system in which a heat transfer fluid is circulated by a pump. The secondary circuit is actually the air conditioning circuit (A/C loop). The top heat exchanger acts as a cooling operation evaporator (EVAP) rather than a cooler and connects both circuits. In heating mode, the 4-way valve switches so that the upper heat exchanger acts as a condenser (COND) and the lower heat exchanger acts as an evaporator. The heating cycle is also called the heat pump cycle.

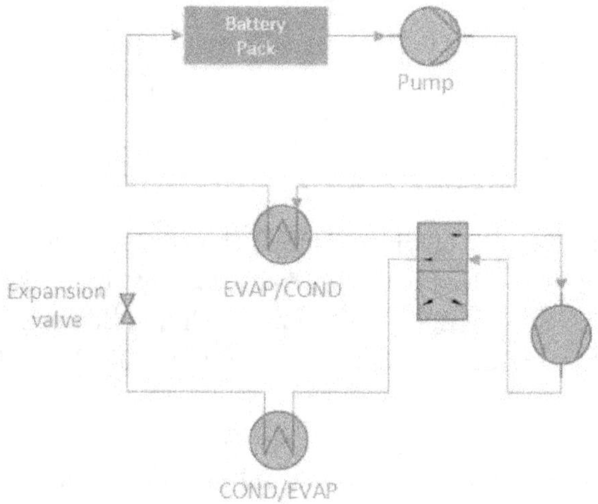

Figure 5.32: Active Liquid Cooling System

In general, the advantages and disadvantages of active BTMS can be summarized as follows:

Advantages of Active BTMS:

1. Relatively simple forced air-based construction.
2. A liquid base is more efficient at maintaining the battery pack in the desired temperature range.

Disadvantages of Active BTMS:

1. The running costs of forced ventilation systems are high due to the large airflows that must be implemented.
2. Low efficiency in achieving cell-to-cell temperature uniformity.
3. Liquid-based systems can have leakage problems. The footprint and complexity of liquid-based systems.

B. Passive BTMS

Passive systems are alternatives that overcome the shortcomings of active BTMS. Although these types of systems are currently not implemented in electric vehicles, they have become very important recently due to their operational advantages. Among the various passive solutions, the two extended families of phase change materials (PCM) and heat pipes (HP) stand out.

Phase change materials (PCM):

PCMs, especially those with solid-liquid phase transitions, have been extensively studied for their application to BTMS. The interest of these materials lies in their ability to study the high energies associated with phase changes that occur at nearly constant temperatures (typically >150 J/g). These two properties are attractive if a uniform temperature is maintained across the battery pack close to the phase change temperature of the implemented PCM.

During melting, heat is absorbed by the PCM and stored as latent heat until the maximum latent heat is reached. It keeps the temperature at the melting point for a certain period of time and delays the temperature rise.

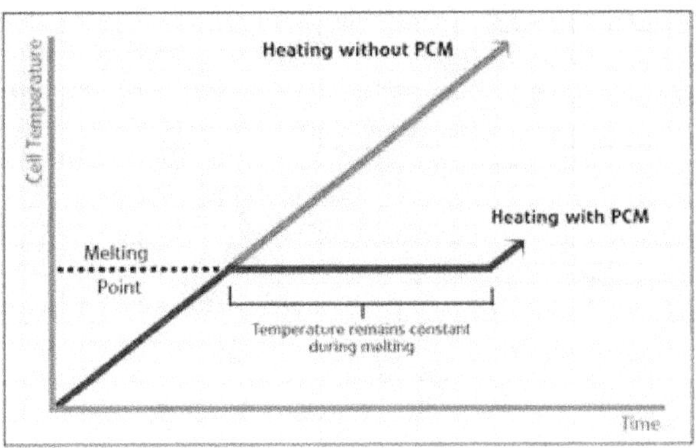

Figure 5.33: Working mechanism of PCM on Battery cells

As such, PCM is used as a conductor and buffer in battery thermal management systems. Given below figure shows the mechanism of action of PCM on battery cells. Also, the PCM is always paired with air or liquid cooling system to manage the temperature of the battery. The most studied compounds for these applications are paraffin, fatty acids, or hydrated salts. Generally, these compounds/mixtures have melting points in the range of 30-50°C, making them ideal for battery thermal management.

In general, however, the PCM family mentioned above has relatively low thermal conductivity, a feature that limits heat transfer from the cells to the PCM itself, and from the PCM to the exterior of the battery pack.

Heat pipes (HP):

In addition to thermoelectric modules, heat pipes are another way to upgrade passive air systems. The figure shows the structure of a heat pipe. The flat copper shell of the heat pipe was under partial vacuum. The capillary structure consists of sintered copper powder. Heat pipes use water as the working medium.

The water on the evaporator side absorbs heat and evaporates below 100°C due to the low internal pressure. The water in the condenser gives off heat to the surroundings and becomes liquid again. This cycle repeats all over again.

The diagram below shows a schematic description of a heat pipe cooling system. Below the heat pipe (evaporative side) is a battery as a heat source. The heat pipe (condensing side) has cooling fins as a heat sink. A heat pipe cooling system can reduce thermal resistance by 30% under natural convection compared to no heat pipe. Low wind speed convection can reduce thermal resistance by 20%.

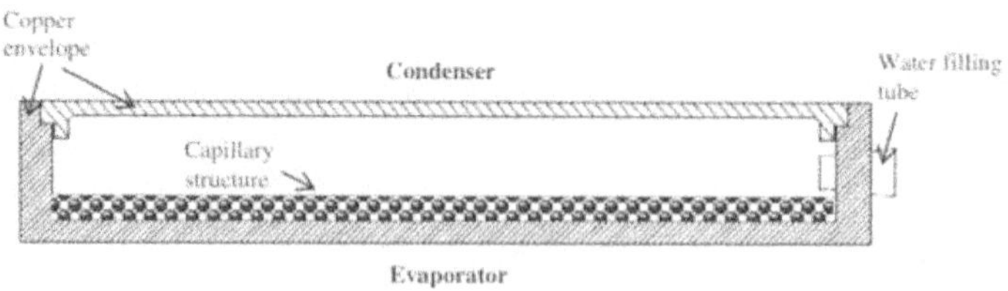

Figure 5.34: Structure of the Heat Pipe

Note that heat pipes are more reliable than thermoelectric because they have no moving parts and no power consumption. However, due to its rigid structure design, the heat pipe cannot heat the battery.

In general, the advantages and disadvantages of passive BTMS can be summarized as follows:

Advantages of Passive BTMS:

1. High efficiency
2. Easy to use and integrate
3. Uniform temperature distribution

Disadvantages of Passive BTMS:

1. Low thermal conductivity.
2. When PCM is doped, it loses its energy density.
3. Limited heat storage capacity.
4. The weight of the battery pack will increase.

C. Hybrid BTMS:

Finally, hybrid systems have emerged that combine two or more of the above alternatives to take advantage of active and passive systems. The most researched combinations include using forced air PCMs, liquid-cooled PCMs, or heat pipe PCMs. In the first case, the goal is to achieve good temperature distribution within the battery pack and dissipate the generated heat to the outside using forced air or liquid cooling.

The purpose of his PCM with heat pipes is to improve heat transfer from the PCM to the outside of the cell so that the cell can be cooled by natural convection. Although these BTMS systems work much more effectively than purely passive or active systems in thermally managing battery packs, their complexity and cost are limiting factors for their implementation in electric vehicles. increase.

• • •

CHAPTER VI

Fuel Cell Vehicles

A fuel cell electric vehicle (FCEV) or fuel cell vehicle (FCV) is an electric vehicle that uses a fuel cell in combination with a supercapacitor or small battery, to power an onboard electric motor. Automotive fuel cells typically generate electricity from atmospheric oxygen and compressed hydrogen. FCEVs use a propulsion system similar to electric vehicles, where energy stored as hydrogen is converted into electricity by a fuel cell. Unlike traditional internal combustion engine vehicles, these vehicles do not emit harmful exhaust fumes. Most fuel cell vehicles are classified as zero-emission vehicles, emitting only water and heat. Hydrogen vehicles concentrate pollutants at the hydrogen production site, where hydrogen is usually obtained from reformed natural gas, compared to internal combustion engine vehicles. Contaminants can also be produced during hydrogen transport and storage. It is more efficient than conventional internal combustion engine vehicles and produces no tailpipe emissions. It just expels water vapor and warm air. FCEVs and their fuelled hydrogen infrastructure are in the early stages of deployment. Like a conventional internal combustion engine vehicle, it can be refueled in less than four minutes and has a range of over 300 miles. FCEVs are equipped with new advanced technologies to increase efficiency i.e., a regenerative braking system that absorbs the energy lost during braking and stores it in the battery.

Operating principles of Fuel Cell:

Fuel cells are used to generate the power needed to operate various devices by converting chemical energy into electrical energy. It occurs when the fuel and oxidant undergo a series of redox reactions, forming electrons, water, carbon dioxide, and heat as by-products. Based on the type of fuel used, fuel cells can be classified into various categories which are explained in further topics.

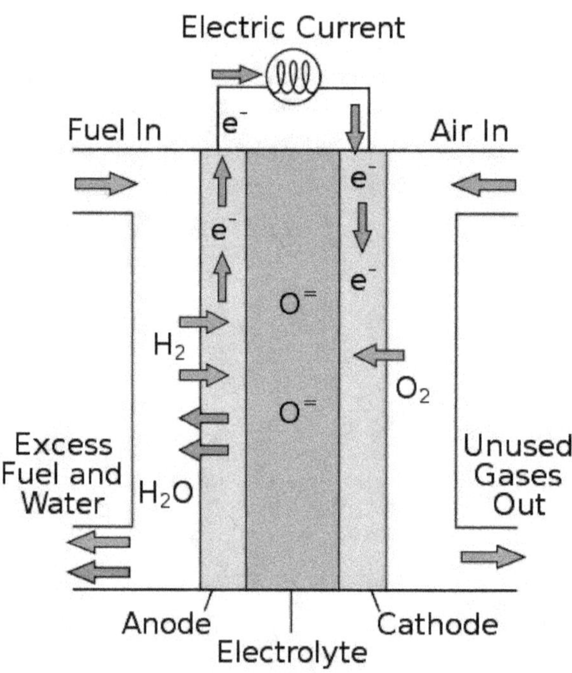

Figure 6.1: Design of Fuel Cell

Working principle of a fuel cell:

A fuel cell usually consists of two electrodes, an anode, and a cathode, separated by an electrolyte membrane. Organic fuels that can be used to generate electricity in fuel cells include hydrogen, methane, ethane, and ethanol. These fuels burn and release energy in the form of heat. Most of these reactions produce water and carbon dioxide as by-products and are the primary redox reactions. Redox reactions involve the transfer of electrons, converting chemical energy into electrical energy. There is an electrolyte material between the electrodes. Fuel is supplied separately to both electrodes. For example, in a fuel cell, assume that the anode is supplied with hydrogen and the cathode is supplied with air. Here, the catalyst present on the anode side of the cell tends to split hydrogen molecules into smaller particles. H. Protons and electrons split. Both elements try to move towards the cathode in different ways. Electrons reach the cathode from the outside and generate an electric current, and protons reach the cathode through the electrolyte membrane and combine with oxygen molecules and electrons to produce water and heat by-products.

Advantages of fuel cells:

1. The fuel cell does not require recharging. Fuel cells can regenerate energy until the fuel is supplied.
2. Fuel cells have no mechanical parts. Hence, they are noiseless.
3. Using hydrogen as input fuel, only water, heat, and electricity are observed as by-products, generating power with the highest efficiency and without toxic emissions.
4. Fuel cells do not cause air pollution.
5. Fuel cell operation does not produce smoke or smog, so fuel cells are not dangerous and pose no health hazards.
6. Fuel cells are highly efficient as they can convert chemical energy directly into electrical energy. Fuel cells are 60% more efficient than other alternatives available on the market.

Disadvantages of fuel cells:

1. Fuel cells are inherently expensive.
2. The life expectancy of fuel cells is not very long.
3. Fuel cells have relatively poor durability.
4. Fuel cells are difficult to store because the fuel that is used must be kept at constant pressure and temperature.

Application of Fuel cell:

1. *Backup power generation:* Many backup power generation systems use fuel cells in their operation. Stationary fuel cells are an integral part of uninterruptible power supplies installed in hospitals, homes, industries, offices, etc.
2. *Transportation:* Fuel cells are widely used in transportation vehicles such as buses, trucks, and passenger cars. Because fuel cells do not emit toxic gases. They are therefore a cleaner alternative to electric vehicles. Vehicles with fuel cells tend to be much more reliable. It is also used to power FCEVs.
3. *Electronic devices:* Hydrogen fuel cells offer a versatile method of powering a variety of electronic and communication devices such as mobile phones, laptops, and more.
4. *Material handling equipment:* Fuel cells are primarily used in industrial trucks to facilitate the transportation of heavy loads from one location to another.

Fuel Cell technologies:

Explaining the basic function of a fuel cell is probably not difficult. But building cheap, efficient, and reliable fuel cells is a much more complicated task. Scientists and inventors have developed different types and sizes of fuel cells in search of greater efficiency, but the technical details of each type vary. Many of the choices faced by fuel cell designers are constrained by the choice of electrolyte. For example, the electrode design and its material depend on the electrolyte. Today, the main electrolyte types are alkalis, molten carbonates, phosphoric acids, proton exchange membranes (PEMs), and solid oxides. The first three are liquid electrolytes. The last two are solid.

The fuel types also depend on the electrolyte. Some cells require pure hydrogen, so additional equipment such as a "reformer" is required to purify the fuel. Other cells can tolerate some contamination but may require higher temperatures to run efficiently. Some cells have a circulating liquid electrolyte and require pumping. The type of electrolyte also determines the operating temperature of the cell. As the name suggests, "molten" carbonate cells get hot. Each fuel cell has its pros and cons, and none is as cheap and efficient as replacing traditional methods of power generation such as coal, hydropower, or even nuclear power.

Hydrogen fuel cells use the chemical energy of hydrogen to generate electricity. This is clean energy where electricity, heat, and water are the only products and by-products. Fuel cells offer a variety of applications from transportation to backup power, and can power systems as large as power plants to systems as small as laptops.

Fuel cells offer advantages over traditional combustion-based technologies, such as higher efficiency and lower emissions. Hydrogen fuel cells only emit water, so no carbon dioxide or other pollutants are released into the atmosphere. Fuel cells are quieter in operation as they have fewer moving parts than combustion technology.

The following list describes the five main types of fuel cells:

Alkali fuel cells

Alkaline fuel cells operate on compressed hydrogen and oxygen. As electrolytes, they usually use an aqueous solution of potassium hydroxide (aka KOH). The efficiency is about 70% and the operating temperature is 150-200 °C (about 300-400 °F). Cell power ranges from 300 watts (W) to 5 kilowatts (kW). Alkaline batteries were used on the Apollo spacecraft to provide both power and drinking water. However, they require pure hydrogen fuel and platinum electrocatalysts are expensive. Also, like any container with liquid, it can leak.

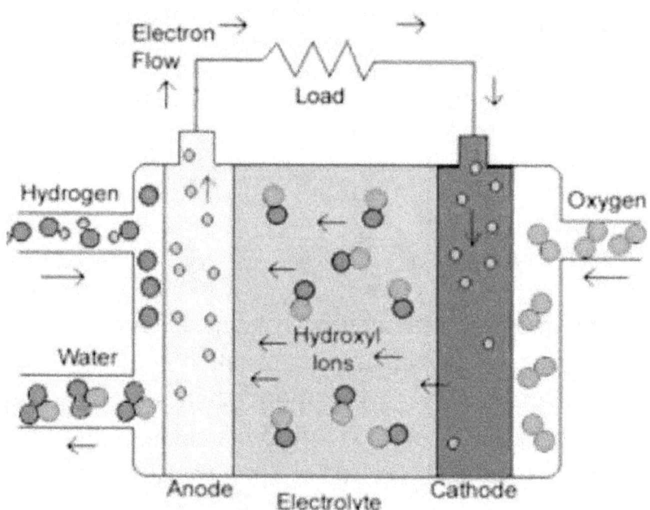

Figure 6.2: Alkali Fuel Cell

Molten carbonate fuel cells

A molten carbonate fuel cell (MCFC) uses a high-temperature compound of salt (such as sodium or magnesium) and a carbonate (chemically CO3) as the electrolyte. It has an efficiency range of 60-80% and an operating temperature of approximately 650°C (1,200°F). Units rated up to 2 megawatts (MW) have been manufactured, with designs for units up to 100 MW. The high-temperature limits damage from carbon monoxide "poisoning" of the cell, allowing waste heat to be recycled to generate additional power. The company's nickel electrocatalyst is less expensive than the platinum used in other cells. However, high temperatures also limit the materials and safe use of his MCFC. Additionally, the reaction consumes carbonate ions from the electrolyte, which must be compensated by injecting carbon dioxide.

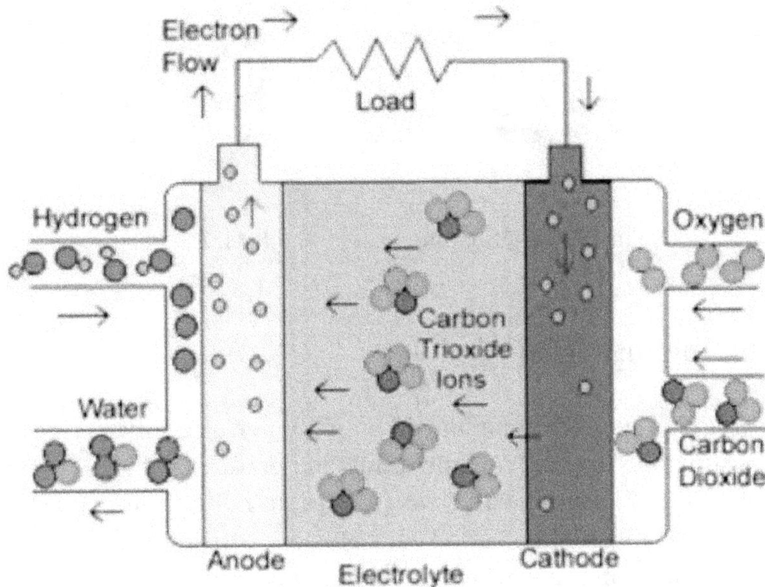

Figure 6.3: Modern Carbonate fuel cell

Phosphorous acid fuel cells

Phosphoric acid fuel cells use phosphoric acid as the electrolyte. It has an efficiency range of 40-80% and an operating temperature of 150-200°C (approximately 300-400°F). Existing phosphate cells are rated up to 200 kW, with 11 MW units being tested. PAFC can withstand carbon monoxide concentrations of approximately 1.5%, increasing the range of fuels that can be used. If gasoline is used, sulfur must be removed. A platinum electrocatalyst is required and the internal parts must withstand corrosive acids.

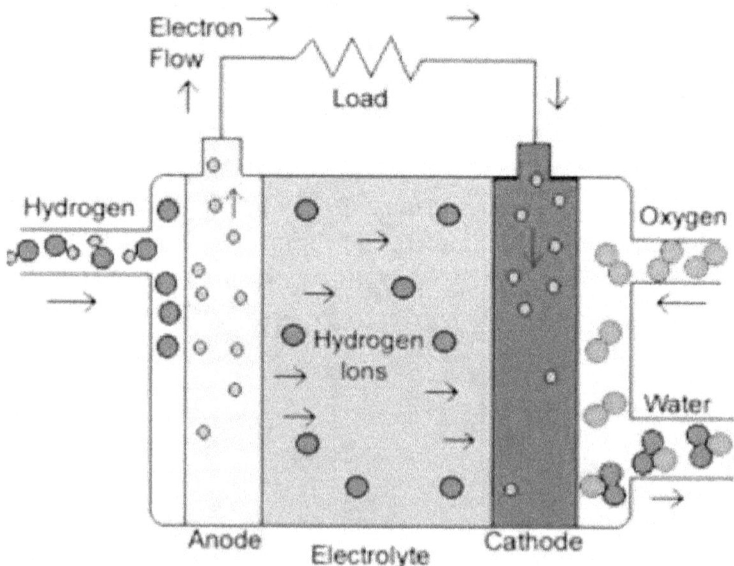

Figure 6.4: Phosphoric acid & P.E.M. Fuel Cells

Proton exchange membrane fuel cells

Proton exchange membrane (PEM) fuel cells operate with a polymer electrolyte in the form of a thin permeable membrane. The efficiency is about 40-50% and the operating temperature is about 80 degrees C (about 175 degrees F). Cell output is typically 50-250 kW. Solid, flexible electrolytes do not leak or explode, and these cells operate at temperatures cool enough to be suitable for homes and cars. However, the fuel needs to be cleaned and the platinum catalyst is used on both sides of the membrane, which increases the cost.

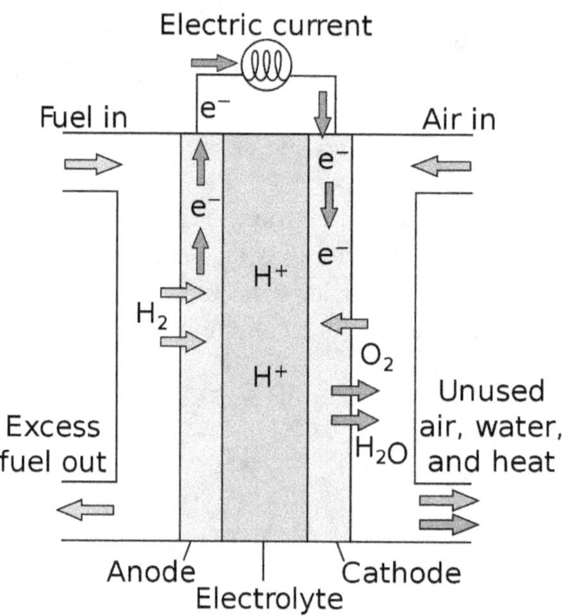

Figure 6.5: Proton exchange membrane fuel cell

Solid oxide fuel cells

Solid oxide fuel cells (SOFCs) use hard ceramic compounds (chemically O2) of metal oxides (such as calcium and zirconium) as electrolytes. The efficiency is about 60% and the operating temperature is about 1000 degrees Celsius (about 1800 degrees Fahrenheit). The cell output is up to 100 kW. At such high temperatures, no reformer is needed to extract hydrogen from the fuel, and waste heat can be reused to generate additional power. However, SOFC units have limited high-temperature applications and tend to be quite large. Solid electrolytes don't leak, but they can break.

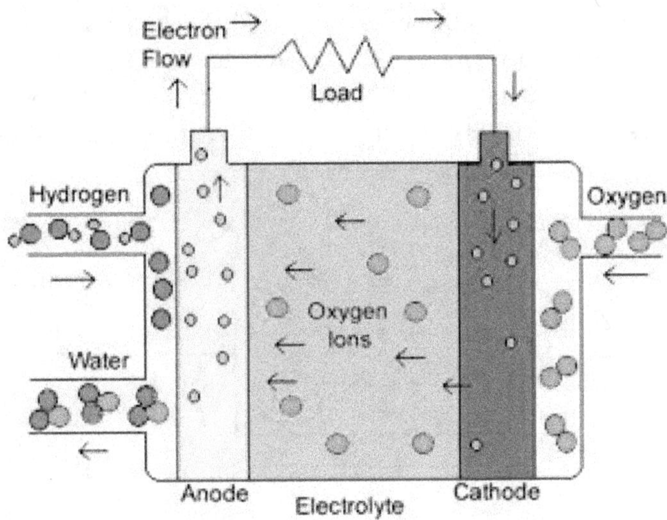

Figure 6.6: Solid oxide fuel cell

Fuel Supply

A vehicle's fuel system consists of a combination of parts such as the fuel tank, fuel lines, fuel pump, fuel filter, injectors, and carburetor (older cars). These parts work together to supply the required amount of fuel to the engine. Fuel goes through a series of stages before reaching the combustion chamber. This involves filtering and atomizing the fuel into fine particles. In order for the fuel to burn completely, it must be atomized before it enters the combustion chamber. The primary function of the fuel system is to store and supply fuel to the engine and cylinder chambers. Once there, it is mixed with air, vaporized, and then combusted to produce the energy needed to power the car. The journey initiates at the fuel feed pump. The fuel pump then draws fuel from the fuel tank through the fuel line and fuel filter and into the injectors. The fuel is then sent to the engine and injected into the combustion chamber where it burns. Once this process is complete, the engine will be running.

Therefore, the four main functions of the fuel delivery system are:

1. Required fuel storage and filtration
2. Provides enough fuel to meet engine needs under all operating conditions
3. Prevent fuel boiling by maintaining sufficient pressure in the line between the carburetor and the pump.
4. Prevents vapor lock, where the fuel temperature becomes too high and goes from a liquid to a vapor state. Fuel pumps are designed to pump liquid, not air, so any increase in pressure in the fuel line will prevent the fuel pump from moving fuel.

1. *Fuel supply system in spark ignition Engine:*

Some petrol engines have the fuel tank above the level of the carburetor. Fuel flows from the fuel tank to the carburetor by fuel pump or gravity. There are one or two filters between the fuel tank and the carburetor. A clear sediment tray is also provided to collect dust and dirt from the fuel. When the tank is below the level of the carburetor, a lift pump is provided between the tank and the carburetor to force fuel from the tank to the engine's carburetor.

In a spark ignition engine, a combustible fuel mixture is produced outside the combustion chamber. The correct air-fuel ratio is maintained with the help of the carburetor. This mixture is then introduced into the combustion chamber. The mixture depends on various conditions. As the engine requires a richer mixture when starting and a leaner mixture under normal operating conditions. Fuel is channeled from the fuel tank to the sediment bowl and to the lift pump. From there, the fuel is routed through appropriate lines to the carburetor. The fuel pump keeps the pressure constant. In the carburetor, fuel is mixed with air in the required ratio. From the carburetor, fuel travels through the engine's intake manifold to the engine cylinders.

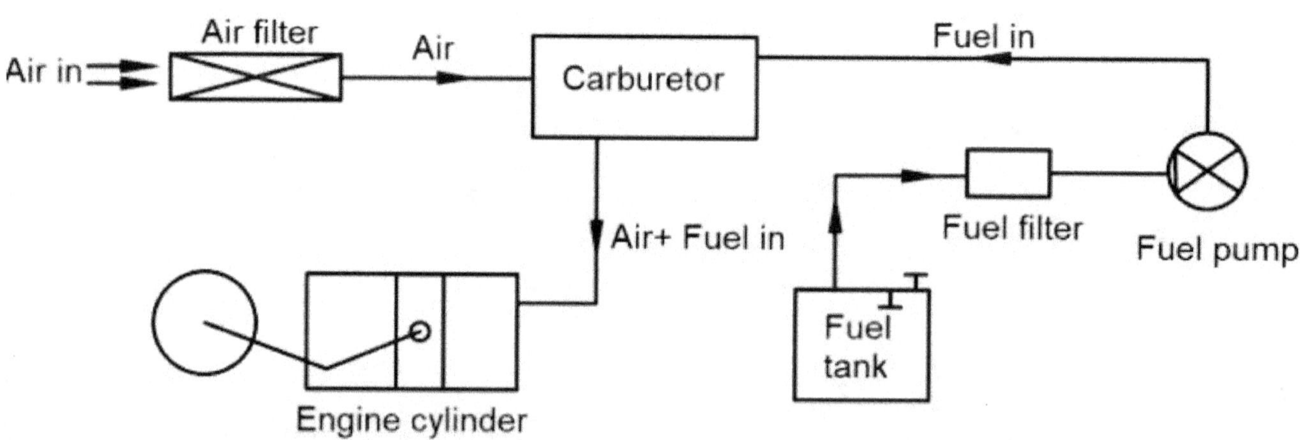

Figure 6.7: Layout of the fuel supply system in S.I. Engine

The S.I. Engine fuel supply system consists of:

Fuel tank:

The fuel tank contains fuel for the engine. It consists of a mixture of steel or aluminum or synthetic rubber and flame-retardant fiber-reinforced plastic. Also, these tanks are coated with a lead-tin alloy to protect the tank from corrosion. This tank is placed in a convenient location on the vehicle. In front-engine vehicles, the fuel tank is located in the lower rear edge of the trunk or just above the rear axle, and in rear-engine vehicles, the fuel tank is located at the front behind the compartment. When the vehicle brakes, the fuel in the vehicle rises, or when the car turns, the fuel in the tank also rises, so there are several baffles in the fuel tank, and this baffle prevents the fuel in the tank from rising. These plates divide the tank into several chambers connected by pipes.

Fuel filter:

The primary function of the fuel system is to provide clean fuel to the fuel system by removing dust, contaminants, and deposits from the fuel. A faulty fuel filter leads to a clogged fuel injection system. If the fuel filter becomes clogged with debris/dirt, it will stop functioning and the fuel pump will not be able to deliver fuel. Poor fuel filter performance leads to poor engine performance.

Performance test of fuel filter:

- Material compatibility test
- Drug test
- Filtration capacity
- Satisfaction with environmental conditions

Air purifier:

This is very important for the engine to get fresh air. Especially pistons, piston chambers, piston rings, and valves. Also, contaminated air entering the crankcase, which stores engine oil, can damage lubricating parts such as bearings. Therefore, it is necessary to install an air filter that cleans the air before it enters the engine cylinder. It also acts as a muffler for the carburetion system and as a flame arrestor in case of an engine misfire. Air filters are cleaned regularly. Lack of cleaning can increase fuel consumption and reduce engine efficiency.

The air cleaners generally used are two types:

- Heavy-duty types of an air cleaner
- Light duty types of an air cleaner

Fuel filter:

Your vehicle needs a fuel filter to clean the fuel. Very sophisticated equipment is used for this. It's a chamois that only lets gasoline through and traps water. Even fine particles cannot pass through.

Fuel gauge unit:

A fuel gauge is an instrument mounted on the dashboard of a vehicle that allows the driver to see how much fuel is in the fuel tank.

Carburetor:

The process of creating a mixture of air and fuel outside the cylinder of an engine is called carburetion, and the device in which this process occurs is called a carburetor.

Carburetor Principle:

The basic principle of all carburetor designs is that when air flows over the end of a narrow tube or nozzle containing liquid, some of the liquid is drawn into the airflow. The amount of liquid drawn into the airflow increases as the speed of the airflow across the nozzle increases, and the larger the nozzle, the greater the amount.

Carburetor Functions:

The main functions of the carburetor are:

1. adequate mixing of air and fuel;
2. atomize the fuel;
3. adjust the air/fuel ratio at different speeds and loads;
4. provide the right amount of mix at different speeds and loads;

Fuel pump:

The function of the fuel pump is to send fuel from the fuel tank to the fuel injection system.
   Fuel pump type:

1. Electric fuel pump
2. Mechanical fuel pump

Modern ECU-controlled vehicles use an electric fuel pump. Mechanical fuel pump systems are outdated technology but are still used in light commercial vehicles due to the low-cost of mechanical pump systems.

2. Fuel supply system in Diesel Engine:

SI engines use a carburetor to mix the air and fuel supply system in the desired ratio. However, in a diesel engine, only air is compressed in the cylinder. The high pressure is around 35-40 bar and the temperature of this air after compression is around 600 °C. At the end of the compression stroke, the fuel is jetted out of the fuel nozzle in a finely atomized form at a pressure higher than that of air. The diagram shows the fuel injection system of a diesel engine. It consists of a fuel tank, fuel supply pump, fuel filter, fuel injection pump, and injectors.

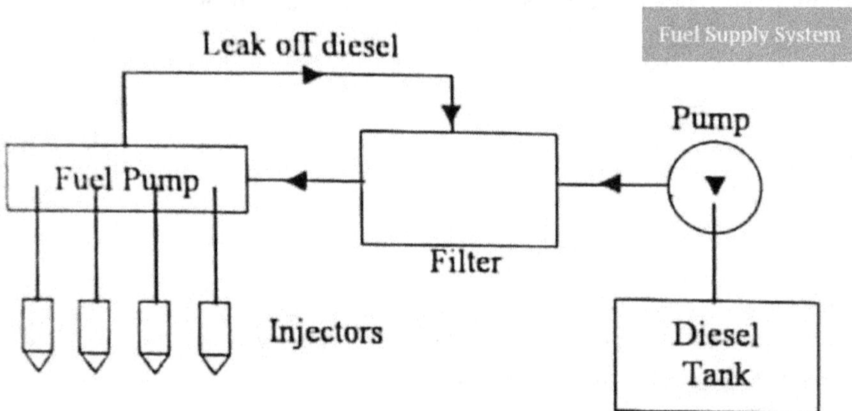

Figure 6.8: Fuel Supply system in Diesel Engine

Fuel is pumped from the fuel tank through the fuel filter to the fuel injection pump. Fuel is delivered to fuel nozzles or injectors by a fuel injection pump. These injectors inject fuel into the cylinder in the form of a fine spray.

Component of fuel supply system:

The goal of a fuel injection system is to meter, atomize, and distribute fuel throughout the air mass in the cylinder. At the same time, the required air-fuel ratio must be maintained according to engine load and speed demands. The fuel injection system consists of:

- Fuel injection pump - puts high pressure on the fuel
- High-pressure pipe - sends fuel to the injector
- Injector - Injects fuel into the cylinder
- Boost pump – pumps fuel from the fuel tank
- Fuel filter - filters the fuel

Fuel injection system requirements:

1. The beginning and end of the injection should be sharp.
2. Injects fuel at appropriate times in the cycle throughout the engine speed range.
3. Fuel injection should be done at an appropriate rate and amount as the engine load changes.
4. Atomize the fuel to the desired level.
5. Distributes fuel throughout the combustion chamber for better mixing.

The function of fuel injection:

Diesel injection systems have four main functions.

Feeding fuel:

The injection pump body incorporates pump elements such as cylinders and pistons. When the cam lifts the piston, the fuel is compressed to high pressure and sent to the fuel injectors.

Adjust fuel quantity:

In a diesel engine, the intake air volume is nearly constant regardless of engine speed or load. If the injection amount is changed by the engine speed and the injection timing is kept constant, the performance and fuel efficiency will change. Since the engine output is almost proportional to the injection amount, it is set with the accelerator pedal.

Adjust injection timing:

Ignition delay is the time from fuel injection, ignition, and combustion until maximum combustion pressure is reached. Since this time is fairly constant regardless of engine speed, a timer is used to adjust and change the injection timing for optimal combustion.

Atomizing fuel:

The fuel is pressurized by the injection pump, and when it is sprayed from the injector, it mixes well with air and improves ignitability. The result is complete combustion.

Method of fuel injection:

There are two methods of fuel injection used in C.I engines.

Air injection system

This process first uses a compressor to compress the air to very high pressure. Fuel was metered and pumped into a nozzle that was also connected to a high-pressure air source. When the nozzle opens, air blows fuel into the engine, providing a well-atomized spray. This method is no longer used due to the complexity and cost of the system.

Airless or solid injection

This method has largely replaced the air injection method. The pressurized fuel is injected directly into the combustion chamber in atomized form. A pump is required to supply fuel at high pressure (up to 300 bar abs). In addition, the following commonly used he can be categorized into two systems.

- Common rail system;
- Individual pump system.

Type of fuel injection system:

Throttle body fuel injection:

Also called single port, this was the earliest type of fuel injection to hit the market. All vehicles have an intake manifold where clean air first enters the engine. TBFI works by adding the right amount of fuel to the air before it is distributed to each cylinder. The advantage of TBFI is that it is cheap and easy to maintain. If an injector fails, simply replace the injector. Also, this injector has a fairly high flow rate, so it is less likely to clog.

The throttle valve system is technically very robust and requires little maintenance. However, throttle valve injection is rarely used today. Vehicles that still use it are old enough that maintenance becomes more of an issue than a newer, lower-mileage vehicle. Another drawback of TBFI is its imprecision. Even when the accelerator pedal is released, there is still plenty of fuel in the mixture going to the cylinders. This can cause a slight hesitation before slowing down, and in some vehicles, unburned fuel may be expelled from the exhaust. This means that TBFI systems are not as fuel efficient as modern systems.

Multi-port injection:

With the multi-port injection, the injector was moved further down into the cylinder. Clean air enters the primary manifold and is directed to each cylinder. The injector is at the end of this opening just before it is sucked through the valve and into the cylinder.

The advantage of this system is that the fuel is distributed more precisely as each cylinder gets its own fuel spray. Each injector will be smaller and more accurate for better fuel economy. The disadvantage is that while all injectors fire at the same time, cylinders fire one after the other. This means there may be fuel left during the intake period or the cylinder may be burning before the injectors deliver additional fuel. Multiport systems are best when moving at a constant speed. But when you accelerate hard or take your foot off the accelerator, this design either reduces fuel economy or performance.

Nonhydrogen fuel cells

Fuel cells are classified primarily by the type of electrolyte they use. This classification determines the type of electrochemical reactions that occur within the cell, the type of catalyst required, the temperature range in which the cell operates, the fuel required, and other factors. These properties influence the applications for which these cells are best suited. Several types of fuel cells are currently being developed, each with its own advantages, limitations, and potential applications. Some fuel cell technologies can process fuels directly other than hydrogen. Some possible pairs are listed here: ·

- Direct Methanol PEMFC
- Ammonia AFC
- Direct Hydrocarbon MCFC or SOFC Air Fuel Vapor Fuel Processing Assembly (FPA)

Similar to hydrogen-capable PEMFCs, direct-methanol PEMFCs are under active research and offer many advantages, such as no reformer, easy handling of liquid fuels, and no high temperatures in the system. I have. The main drawbacks are the need to dilute the methanol with liquid water to feed the fuel electrode and the strong carryover of methanol. This is due to the absorption in the polymer membrane, mainly due to the slow reaction rate. Ammonia AFCs13 are potential substitutes for the thermal cracking of ammonia. Ammonia gas is fed directly into the fuel cell and catalytically cracked at the anode. The ammonia fuel cell reaction has a slightly lower thermodynamic voltage and higher activation losses than the hydrogen AFC. Activation loss can be reduced by improving the catalyst layer. Interestingly, ammonia can be used directly in other fuel cell technologies if the acidic nature of the electrolyte is not destroyed by alkaline ammonia.

MCFCs and SOFCs have the ability to crack hydrocarbons directly due to their high operating temperatures. Therefore, they extract hydrogen from within rather than consuming hydrocarbons directly. Obviously, this option has all the drawbacks of high-temperature fuel cells, as discussed in the fuel cell technology section.

Fuel cell hybrid electric drive train design

Like a fully electric vehicle, a fuel cell electric vehicle (FCEV) uses electricity to power an electric motor. Unlike other electric vehicles, FCEVs use hydrogen-powered fuel cells to generate electricity rather than drawing power from batteries. During the vehicle design process, vehicle manufacturers define vehicle performance in terms of the size of the electric motor, which receives power from an appropriately sized fuel cell and battery combination. Automakers could develop FCEVs with plug-in battery charging capability, but most FCEVs today use batteries to recover braking energy and provide additional power during short accelerations, idling, or power supply. Use the off option to smooth the power delivered by the fuel cell. Fuel cells when power demand is low. The amount of energy stored on board is determined by the size of the hydrogen tanks. This differs from all-electric vehicles, where the amount of power and energy available is closely tied to the size of the battery.

Hydrogen Fuel Cell Electric Vehicle Components:

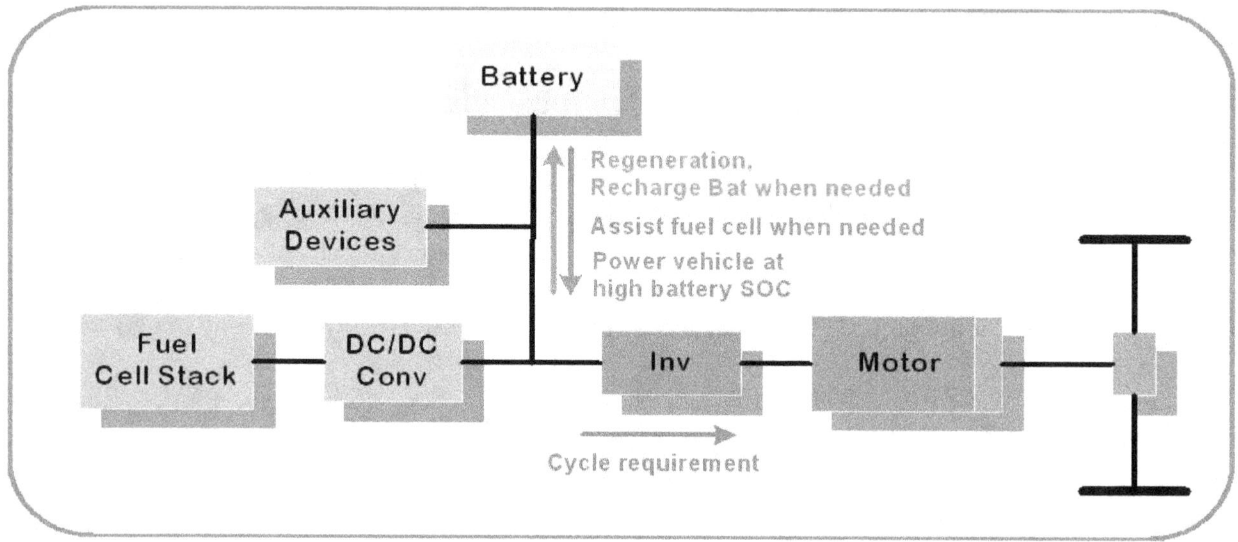

Figure 6.9: Main Components of Fuel cell hybrid electric drivetrain

Battery (Auxiliary Battery): In electric towing vehicles, a low-voltage auxiliary battery provides power to start the vehicle before the traction battery is connected. It also powers vehicle accessories.

Battery pack: This high-voltage battery stores the energy produced by regenerative braking and provides additional power to the electric traction motors.

DC/DC Converter: This device converts the high voltage DC power from the traction battery pack to the low voltage DC power required to run vehicle accessories and charge the auxiliary battery.

Electric Traction Motor (FCEV): Using power from the fuel cell and traction battery pack, this motor drives the vehicle's wheels. Some electric vehicles use motor generators that perform both regeneration and propulsion functions. Fuel cell stack: An assembly of individual membrane electrodes that uses hydrogen and oxygen to produce electricity.

Fuel Filler: A fuel pump nozzle attaches to the vehicle's receptacle to fill the tank.

Fuel Tank (Hydrogen): Stores hydrogen gas in the vehicle until needed by the fuel cell.

Power Electronics Controller (FCEV): This unit manages the flow of electrical energy provided by the fuel cell and traction battery and controls the speed and torque of the electric traction motors.

Thermal System (Cooling) - (FCEV): This system maintains proper operating temperature ranges for fuel cells, electric motors, power electronics, and other components. Transmission (electric): The transmission transfers mechanical power from the electric traction motor to drive the wheels.

Configuration:

A fuel cell hybrid powertrain is constructed as shown in the diagram, with a fuel cell system as the primary power source (PPS), an electric motor drive (motor and its controller), a vehicle controller, and an electronic system between the fuel cells. It consists of interfaces. system and his PPS. According to power or torque commands received from the accelerator or brake pedals and other actuation signals, the vehicle controller controls engine power (torque) output and energy flow between the fuel cell system, PPS, and powertrain. Both the fuel cell system and the PPS supply power to the electric motor drive when peak power is required, such as during hard acceleration. During braking, the electric motor, which acts as a generator, converts part of the braking energy into electrical energy and stores it in the PPS. The PPS can also recover power from the fuel cell system when the load power drops below the rated power of the fuel cell system. Therefore, with proper design and control strategies, the PPS does not need to be charged externally to the vehicle.

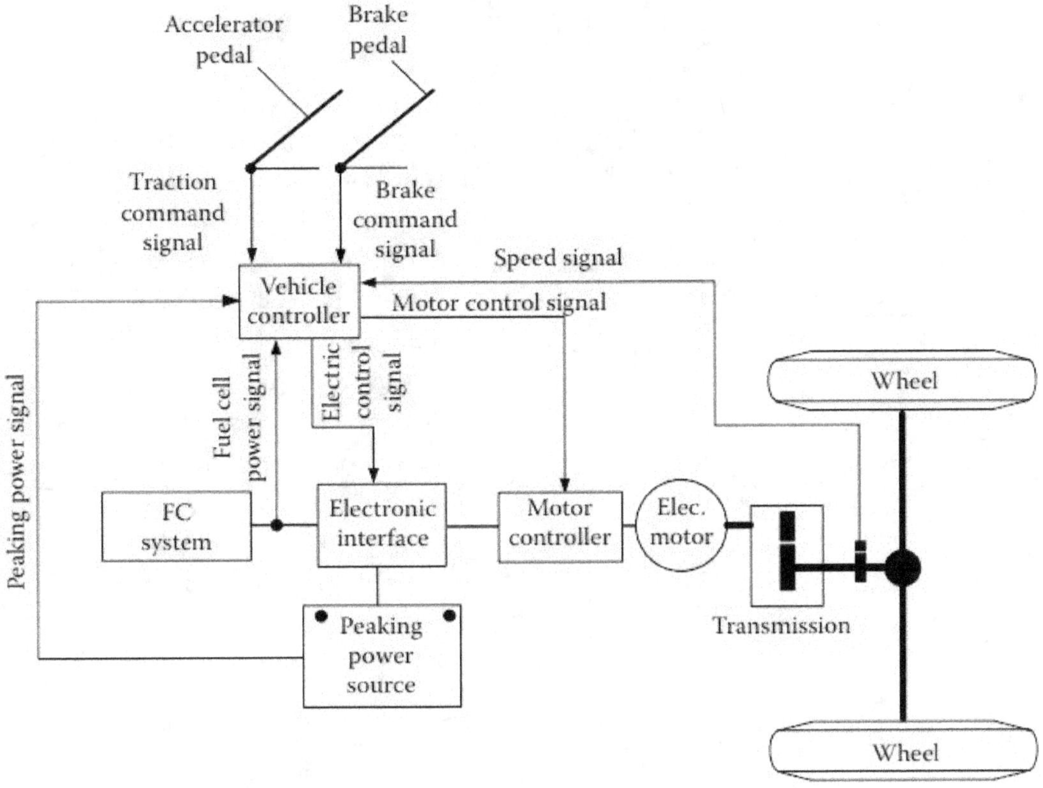

Figure 6.10: Design of Fuel cell hybrid electric drivetrain

Control Strategy:

The control strategy present in the vehicle controller is to control the power flow between the fuel cell system, PPS, and powertrain. A control strategy should ensure that:

- The electric motor output always corresponds to the power requirement.
- The energy level of PPS is always kept within the optimum range. 3. The fuel cell system is operating within its optimum operating range.

Driver issues traction or brake commands via accelerator pedal, the pedal or brake pedal is represented by the power command Pcomm, which must be generated by the engine. Therefore, in traction mode, the electrical input power of the motor drive can be expressed as

$$P_{\text{m-in}} = \frac{P_{\text{comm}}}{\eta_m}, \qquad\qquad (16.1)$$

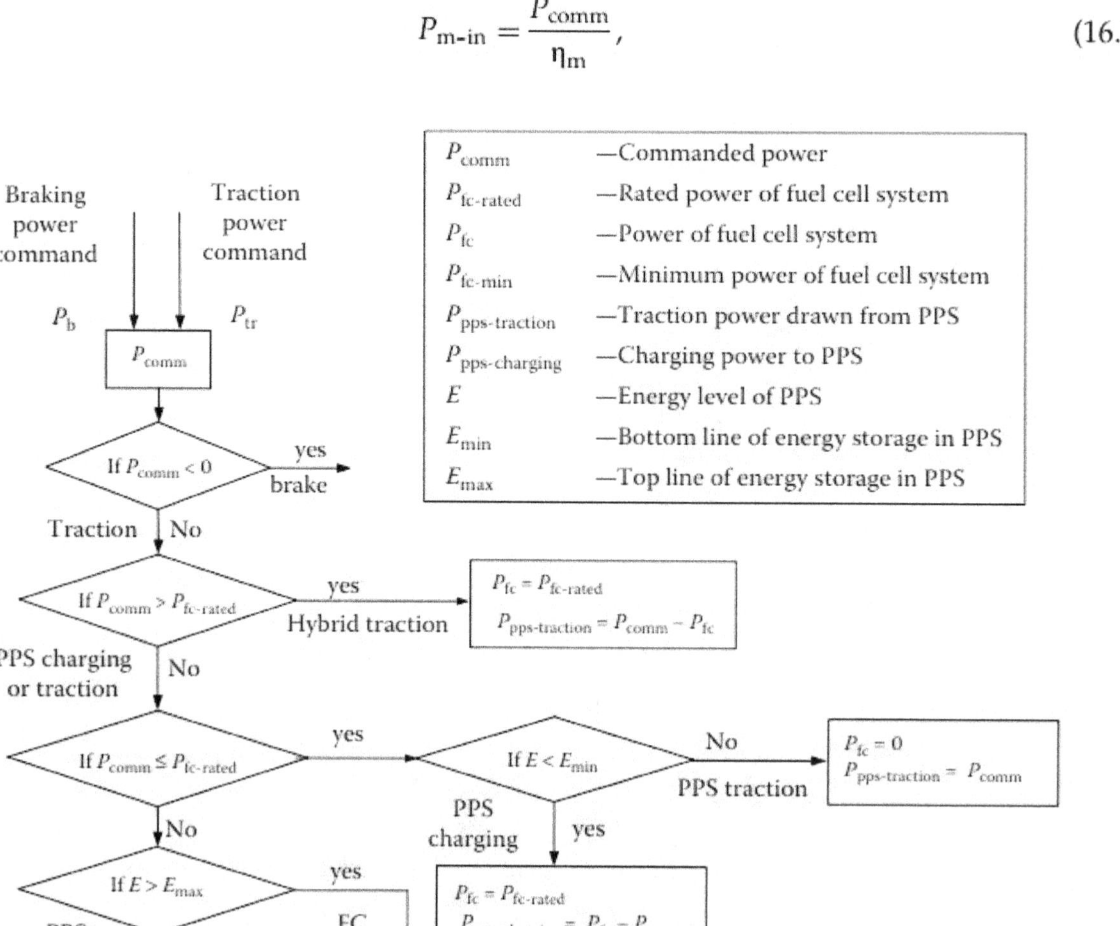

where η_m is the efficiency of the hybrid motor drive. However, when braking, the engine drive acts as a generator, and the electrical output of the engine is expressed as

$$``P_{\text{m-out}} = P_{\text{mb-comm}} \cdot \eta_m"$$

where $P_{\text{mb-comm}}$ is the braking force command to the motor and may differ from the output command P_{comm} from the brake pedal as not all of the braking force Pcomm is provided by regenerative braking. According to the engine output command and other vehicle information, depending on the energy level of the PPS and the minimum operating power of the fuel cell system (below which the fuel cell becomes significantly less efficient), the fuel cell system and PPS are controlled to produce adequate power.

Various powertrain operating modes and corresponding power control strategies are detailed.

Standstill Mode:

Neither the fuel cell system nor his PPS feeds the powertrain. The fuel cell system can be run at idle.

Braking mode:

The fuel cell system is activated when idling, and the PPS absorbs regenerative braking energy according to the operating characteristics of the braking system.

Traction mode:

1. When the commanded engine input power is greater than the fuel rating. The cell system uses a hybrid traction mode in which the fuel cell system operates. Rated power and remaining power requirements are supplied by PPS. The rated output of the fuel cell system can be set as an optimal upper limit line of the fuel cell operating range.
2. When the command motor input power is less than the set minimum power of the fuel cell system and PPS charging is required (energy level is minimum), the fuel cell system operates at nominal power - part of it goes to the powertrain and one to the PPS. Otherwise, If the PPS does not need to be charged (when the energy level is close to the maximum), among them the fuel cell system is idling and the vehicle is driven solely by the PPS. In the latter case, the peak power the PPS can produce is greater than the commanded engine input power.
3. When the load power is greater than the set minimum power and less than the minimum power. There is no need to charge the rated power of the fuel cell and PPS, the vehicle is powered by the fuel cell system alone. Otherwise, if the PPS needs to be charged, the fuel cell system operates at rated power, some of which feed the drive train that drives the vehicle while other parts are being used to charge the PPS.

Parametric Design:

Similar to engine-based hybrid powertrain design, fuel cell-driven hybrid powertrain parametric design includes traction motor performance, fuel cell system performance, PPS performance, and energy capacity design.

Motor power design:

The engine power should correspond to the acceleration power of the vehicle as explained in the previous chapter. Figure 16.4 shows the engine performance of a 1500 kg car in relation to acceleration times from 0 to 100 km/h and constant speed on a flat road and a road with a gradient of 5%. The parameters used in this example are a vehicle mass of 1500 kg, a rolling resistance coefficient of 0.01, a drag coefficient of 0.3, and a frontal area of 2 m2. Accelerating a vehicle from zero to 100 km/h in 12 seconds requires approximately 70 kW of engine power. It also shows the power requirements for driving at constant speed on a flat road and a road with a 5% gradient.

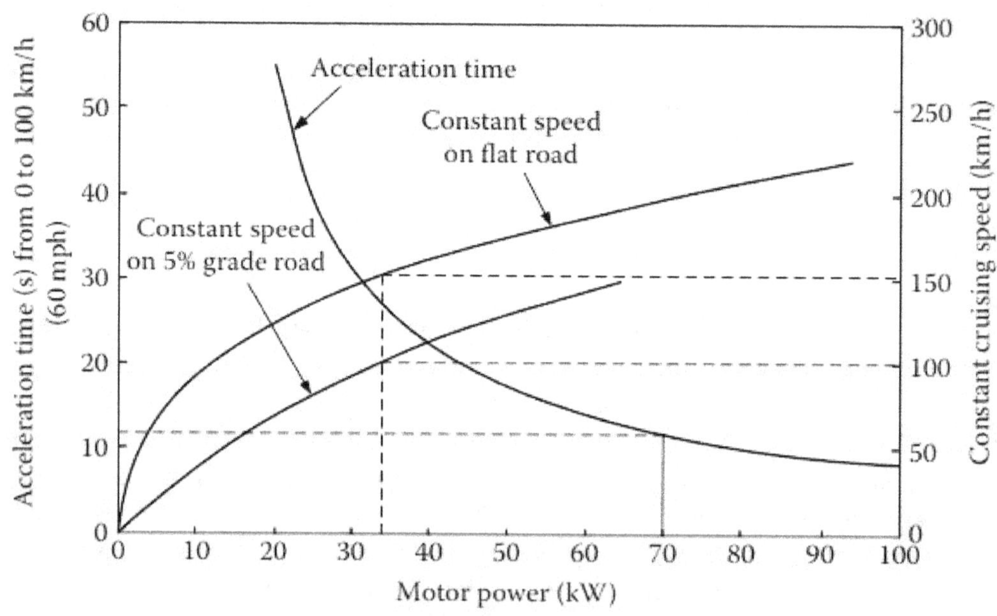

Figure 6.11: Representation of Parametric design

When driving on a flat road or a road with a gradient of 5% at 150km/h and 100km/h, it can be seen that the vehicle is supported by an engine output of 33kW. In other words, the engine power required for acceleration performance is much higher than the engine power required for constant speed cruising. Therefore, a 70 kW traction motor is a good design for this vehicle example. The figure shows the acceleration time and traveled distance during acceleration.

Power design of fuel cell system:

As explained in the previous chapter, PPS is only used to provide peak power for short periods of time and contains a limited amount of energy. Fuel cell systems, therefore, support the vehicle while traveling at a constant speed on long trips (such as intercity highway travel) and to overcome slight gradients in certain places. It must be able to provide enough power to support the vehicle. Speed up without the help of PPS. For the example, 1500 kg passenger car shown in the figure, 33 kW of engine power is required at a constant speed of about 150 km/h on flat roads and 100 km/h on roads with a 5% gradient. sufficient to cover the required power. Considering the inefficiency of the motor drive, a fuel cell system with an output of about 40 kW is required for long-distance driving (when designing a fuel cell system, the maximum output should be slightly higher than that for constant-speed driving. can be designed).

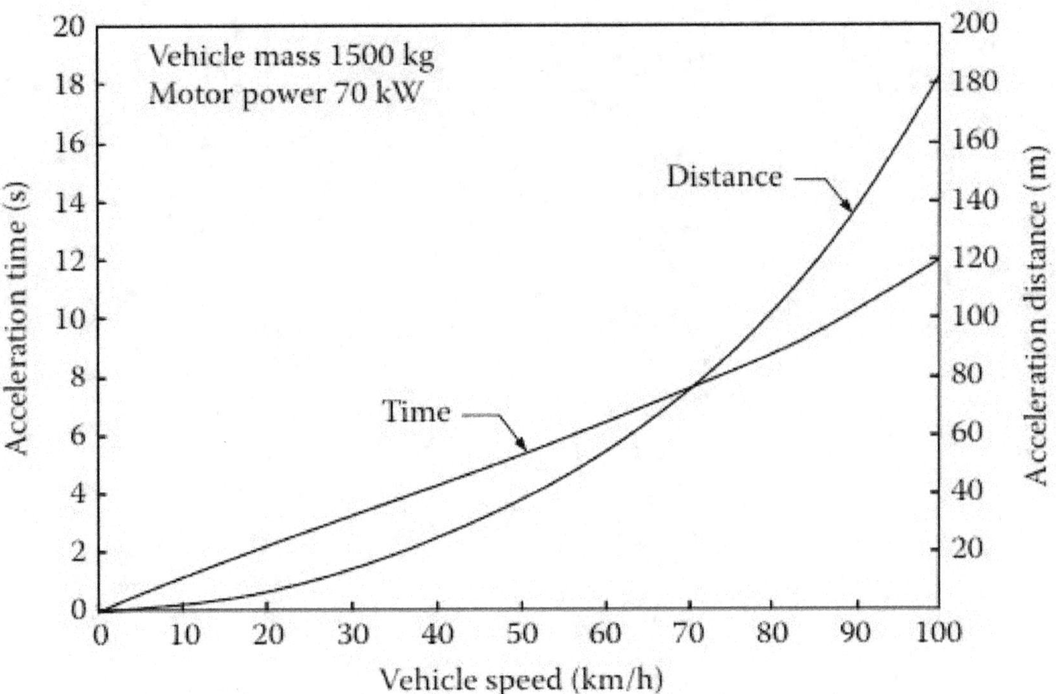

Figure 6.12: Representation of Power design in the fuel system

• • •